Studies in Natural Language Processing

Machine translation systems

Studies in Natural Language Processing

Executive Editor: Aravind K. Joshi

Sponsored by the Association for Computational Linguistics

This series publishes monographs, texts, and edited volumes within the interdisciplinary field of computational linguistics. Sponsored by the Association for Computational Linguistics, the series represents the range of topics of concern to the scholars working in this increasingly important field, whether their background is in formal linguistics, psycholinguistics, cognitive psychology or artificial intelligence.

Also in this series:

Memory and context for language interpretation by Hiyan Alshawi
Planning English sentences by Douglas E. Appelt
Computational linguistics by Ralph Grishman
Language and spatial cognition by Annette Herskovits
Semantic interpretation and the resolution of ambiguity by Graeme Hirst
Text generation by Kathleen R. McKeown
Machine translation edited by Sergei Nirenburg
Systemic text generation as problem solving by Terry Patten

Machine translation systems

Edited by
JONATHAN SLOCUM
Microelectronics and Computer Technology Corporation
Austin, Texas

The right of the University of Cambridge to print and sell all manner of books was granted by Henry VIII in 1534. The University has printed and published continuously since 1584.

CAMBRIDGE UNIVERSITY PRESS

CAMBRIDGE
NEW YORK NEW ROCHELLE
MELBOURNE SYDNEY

Published by the Press Syndicate of the University of Cambridge
The Pitt Building, Trumpington Street, Cambridge CB2 1RP
32 East 57th Street, New York, NY 10022, USA
10 Stamford Road, Oakleigh, Melbourne 3166, Australia

First published as *Computational Linguistics* vol. II (1985) nos. 1–3
(special issues on machine translation)
Reissued (with revisions) in book form by Cambridge University Press 1988

Printed in Great Britain by Redwood Burn Ltd., Trowbridge

British Library cataloguing in publication data

Machine translation systems – (Studies in natural language processing).
1. Machine translating
I. Slocum, Jonathan II. Series
418′.02 P308

Library of Congress cataloguing in publication data

Machine translation systems.
(Studies in natural language processing).
1. Machine translating. I. Slocum, Jonathan.
II. Series.
P308.M35 1987 418′.02 87–15111

ISBN 0 521 35166 9 hard covers
ISBN 0 521 35963 5 paperback

Contents

Preface

For reasons touched upon later in this volume, the subject of Machine Translation (MT) was long considered taboo in the U.S., though this was not the case elsewhere. However, a number of factors – including the technical success of the LRC MT system (METAL) being developed at the University of Texas – led to the recent awakening of interest in MT in the U.S., and in the summer of 1983 to my being asked to present the closing address at the 10th International Conference on Computational Linguistics (COLING), held at Stanford University in July, 1984. The resulting survey paper, though controversial (in the U.S.), was well received.

Out of this opportunity evolved a request for me to edit a special issue of the journal *Computational Linguistics*, to be devoted to MT and, the Editorial Board permitting, to include my COLING paper. So it was that in 1985, Issues 1-3 of Volume 11 presented a collection of papers on MT by most of the active non-commercial principals in the field. Requests for reprints have been voluminous, and at the 1986 COLING in Bonn these back-issues were in greatest demand at the ACL booth. This book is a collection of all but one of those papers – the fast-paced EUROTRA project's paper having been withdrawn because too many of its technical details were outdated. Minor revisions of the original papers from the other, more mature development projects have been sufficient to bring them up to date. The restricted MT bibliography that I compiled in early 1984, and included as a separate item in the journal, has also been updated to reflect some of the most recent literature.

I hope that this volume both illustrates and stimulates the growing interest in MT around the world, and especially in the U.S., where knowledge of the state of the art in MT (to say nothing of translation in general) is still generally lacking despite the recent trend toward increased awareness. Irrespective of academic arguments regarding the definition and feasibility of MT, the papers herein demonstrate that MT systems have succeeded in increasing translation productivity for many years, and that progress continues. MT remains one of the very few areas in the practice of Natural Language Processing where the relative successes or failures of systems have been measured in objective, even commercial, terms. Regarding NLP theory, high-quality translation is certainly one of the most challenging possible tests, and MT therefore offers a rich matrix for continued exploration and experimentation.

Jonathan Slocum

Acknowledgments

I wish to thank Yorick Wilks, Program Chairman of the 10th International Conference on Computational Linguistics, who, on behalf of the Program Committee, invited me to write the paper that eventually led to this volume. I would like to thank, as well, James F. Allen and the Editorial Board of *Computational Linguistics* for the opportunity to act as Guest Editor of the journal issues containing the papers reprinted herein.

I also wish to thank the authors who labored to proof-read their papers one last time, and in some cases composed short but significant updates. But, most of all, I wish to thank Barbara Smith, who devoted herself to the electronic transcription of a number of the papers herein, to redrawing most of the figures and tables, to formatting and producing the camera-ready version of this volume, and to proofreading it in its entirety. Without her able assistance and expertise, any results of my consequent solo efforts would not be nearly so pleasing or effective.

Jonathan Slocum
March, 1987

A Survey of Machine Translation: its History, Current Status, and Future Prospects

Jonathan Slocum
Microelectronics and Computer Technology Corporation (MCC)
Austin, Texas

Abstract

Elements of the history, state of the art, and probable future of Machine Translation (MT) are discussed. The treatment is largely tutorial, based on the assumption that the audience is, for the most part, ignorant of matters pertaining to translation in general, and MT in particular. This paper covers some of the major MT R&D groups, the general techniques they employ(ed), and the roles they play(ed) in the development of the field. The conclusions concern the seeming permanence of the translation problem, and potential re-integration of MT with mainstream Computational Linguistics.

1 Introduction

Machine Translation (MT) of natural human languages is not a subject about which most scholars feel neutral. This field has had a long, colorful career, and boasts no shortage of vociferous detractors and proponents alike. During its first decade in the 1950's, interest and support was fueled by visions of high-speed high-quality translation of arbitrary texts (especially those of interest to the military and intelligence communities, who funded MT projects quite heavily). During its second decade in the 1960's, disillusionment crept in as the number and difficulty of the linguistic problems became increasingly obvious, and as it was realized that the translation problem was not nearly so amenable to automated solution as had been thought. The climax came with the delivery of the National Academy of Sciences ALPAC report in 1966, condemning the field and, indirectly, its workers alike. The ALPAC report was criticized as narrow, biased, and short-sighted, but its recommendations were adopted (with the important exception of increased expenditures for long-term research in computational linguistics), and as a result MT projects were cancelled in the U.S. and, to a lesser extent, elsewhere around the world. By 1973, the early part of the third decade of MT, only three government-funded projects were left in the U.S., and by late 1975 there were none. Paradoxically, MT systems were still being used by various government agencies here and abroad, because there was simply no alternative means of gathering information from foreign (*i.e.*, Russian) sources so quickly. In addition, private companies were developing and selling MT systems based on the mid-60's technology so roundly castigated by ALPAC. Nevertheless the general disrepute of MT resulted in a remarkably quiet third decade.

We are now into the fourth decade of MT, and there is a resurgence of interest throughout the world – plus a growing number of MT and MAT (Machine-Aided Translation) systems in use by governments, business and industry. In 1984, approximately half a million pages of text were translated by machine. Industrial firms are also beginning to fund M(A)T R&D projects of their own; thus it can no longer be said that only government funding keeps the field alive (indeed, in the U.S. there is no government funding, though the Japanese and European governments are heavily subsidizing MT R&D). In part this interest is due to more realistic expectations of what is possible in MT, and realization that MT can be very useful though imperfect; but it is also true that the capabilities of the newer MT systems lie well beyond what was possible just one decade ago.

In light of these events, it is worth reconsidering the potential of, and prospects for, Machine Translation. After opening with an explanation of how translation is done where it is taken seriously, we will present a brief introduction to MT technology and a short historical perspective before considering the present status and state of the art, and then moving on to a discussion of the future prospects. For reasons of space and perspicuity, we shall concentrate on MT efforts in the U.S. and western Europe, though some other MT projects and less-ambitious approaches will receive attention.

2 The Human Translation Context

When evaluating the feasibility or desirability of Machine Translation, one should consider the endeavor in light of the facts of human translation for like purposes. In the U.S., it is common to conceive of translation as simply that which a human translator does. It is generally believed that a college degree (or the equivalent) in a foreign language qualifies one to be a translator for just about any material whatsoever. Native speakers of foreign languages are considered to be that much more qualified. Thus, translation is not particularly respected as a profession in the U.S., and the pay is poor.

In Canada, in Europe, and generally around the world, this myopic attitude is not held. Where translation is a fact of life rather than an oddity, it is realized that any translator's competence is sharply restricted to a few domains (this is especially true of technical areas), and that native fluency in a foreign language does not bestow on one the ability to serve as a translator. Thus, there are college-level and post-graduate schools that teach the theory (translatology) as well as the practice of translation; thus, a technical translator is trained in the few areas in which he will be doing translation.

Of special relevance to MT is the fact that essentially all translations for dissemination (export) are revised by more highly qualified translators who necessarily refer back to the original text when post-editing the translation. (This is not "pre-publication stylistic editing.") Unrevised translations are always regarded as inferior in quality, or at least suspect, and for many if not most purposes they are simply not acceptable. In the multi-national firm Siemens, even internal communications which are translated are post-edited. Such news generally comes as a surprise, if not a shock, to most people in the U.S.

It is easy to see, therefore, that the "fully-automatic high-quality Machine Translation" standard, imagined by most U.S. scholars to constitute minimum acceptability, must be radically redefined. Indeed, the most famous MT critic of all eventually recanted his strong opposition to MT, admitting that these terms could only be defined by the users, according to their own standards, for each situation [Bar-Hillel, 1971]. So an MT system does not have to print and bind the result of its translation in order to qualify as "fully automatic." "High quality" does not at all rule out post-editing, since the proscription of human revision would "prove" the infeasibility of high-quality Human Translation. Academic debates about what constitutes "high-quality" and "fully-automatic" are considered irrelevant by the users of Machine Translation (MT) and Machine-Aided Translation (MAT) systems; what matters to them are two things: whether the systems can produce output of sufficient quality for the intended use (*e.g.*, revision), and whether the operation as a whole is cost-effective or, rarely, justifiable on other grounds, like speed.

3 Machine Translation Technology

In order to appreciate the differences among translation systems (and their applications), it is necessary to understand, first, the broad categories into which they can be classified; second, the different purposes for which translations (however produced) are used; third, the intended applications of these systems; and fourth, something about the linguistic techniques which MT systems employ in attacking the translation problem.

3.1 Categories of Systems

There are three broad categories of computerized translation tools, the differences hinging on how ambitious the system is intended to be: MT, MAT, and Terminology Databanks.

MT systems are intended to perform translation without human intervention. This does not rule out pre-processing (assuming this is not for the purpose of marking phrase boundaries and resolving part-of-speech and/or other ambiguities, etc.), nor post-editing (since this is normally done for human translations anyway). However, an MT system is solely responsible for the complete translation process from input of the source text to output of the target text without human assistance, using special programs, comprehensive dictionaries, and collections of linguistic rules (to the extent they exist, varying with the MT system). MT occupies the top range of positions on the scale of computer translation ambition.

MAT systems fall into two primary subgroups: Human-Assisted Machine Translation (HAMT) and Machine-Assisted Human Translation (MAHT). These occupy successively lower ranges on the scale of computer translation ambition. HAMT refers to a system wherein the computer is responsible for producing the translation per se, but may interact with a human monitor at many stages along the way – for example, asking the human to disambiguate a word's part of speech or meaning, or to indicate where to attach a phrase, or to choose a translation for a word or phrase from among several candidates discovered in the system's dictionary. MAHT refers to a system wherein the human is responsible for producing the translation per se (on-line), but may interact with the system in certain prescribed situations – for example, requesting assistance in searching through a local dictionary/thesaurus, accessing a remote terminology databank, retrieving examples of the use of a word or phrase, or performing word processing functions like formatting. The existence of a pre-processing stage is unlikely in a MA(H)T system (the system does not need help, instead, it is making help available), but post-editing is frequently appropriate.

Terminology Databanks (TD) are the least ambitious systems because access frequently is not made during a translation task (the translator may not be working on-line), but usually is performed prior to human translation. Indeed the databank may not be accessible (to the translator) on-line at all, but may be limited to the production of printed subject-area glossaries. A TD offers access to technical terminology, but usually not to common words (the user already knows these). The chief advantage of a TD is not the fact that it is automated (even with on-line access, words can be found just as quickly in a printed dictionary), but that it is up-to-date: technical terminology is constantly changing and published dictionaries are essentially obsolete by the time they are available. It is also possible for a TD to contain more entries because it can draw on a larger group of active contributors: its users.

3.2 The Purposes of Translation

The most immediate division of translation purposes involves information acquisition *vs.* dissemination. The classic example of the former purpose is intelligence-gathering: with masses of data to sift through, there is no time, money, or incentive to carefully translate every document by normal (*i.e.*, human) means. Scientists more generally are faced with this dilemma: there is already more to read than can be read in the time available, and having to labor through texts written in foreign languages – when the probability is low that any given text is of real interest – is not worth the effort. In the past, the *lingua franca* of science has been English; this is becoming less and less true for a variety of reasons, including the rise of nationalism and the spread of technology around the world. As a result, scientists who rely on English are having greater difficulty keeping up with work in their fields. If a very rapid and inexpensive means of translation were available, then – for texts within the reader's areas of expertise – even a low-quality translation might be sufficient for information acquisition. At worst, the reader could determine whether a more careful (and more expensive) translation effort might be justified. More likely, he could understand the content of the text well enough that a more careful translation would not be necessary.

The classic example of the latter purpose of translation is technology export: an industry in one country that desires to sell its products in another country must usually provide documentation in the purchaser's chosen language. In the past, U.S. companies have escaped this responsibility by requiring that the purchasers learn English; other exporters (German, for example) have never had such luxury. In the future, with the increase of nationalism, it is less likely that English documentation will be acceptable. Translation is becoming increasingly common as more companies look to foreign markets. More to the point, texts for information dissemination (export) must be translated with a great deal of care: the translation must be "right" as well as clear. Qualified human technical translators are hard to find, expensive, and slow (translating somewhere around 4-6 pages/day, on the average). The information dissemination application is most responsible for the renewed interest in MT.

3.3 Intended Applications of M(A)T

Although literary translation is a case of information dissemination, there is little or no demand for literary translation by machine: relative to technical translation, there is no shortage of human translators capable of fulfilling this need, and in any case computers do not fare well at literary translation. By contrast, the demand for technical translation is staggering in sheer volume; moreover, the acquisition, maintenance, and consistent use of valid technical terminology is an enormous problem. Worse, in many technical fields there is a distinct shortage of qualified human translators, and it is obvious that the problem will never be alleviated by measures such as greater incentives for translators, however laudable that may be. The only hope for a solution to the technical translation problem lies with increased human productivity through computer technology: full-scale MT, less ambitious MAT, on-line terminology databanks, and word-processing all have their place. A serendipitous situation involves style: in literary translation, emphasis is placed on style, perhaps at the expense of absolute fidelity to content (especially for poetry). In technical translation, emphasis is properly placed on fidelity, even at the expense of style. M(A)T systems lack style, but excel at terminology: they are best suited for technical translation.

3.4 Linguistic Techniques

There are several perspectives from which one can view MT techniques. We will use the following: direct *vs.* indirect; interlingua *vs.* transfer; and local *vs.* global scope. (Not all eight combinations are realized in practice.) We shall characterize MT systems from these perspectives, in our discussions. In the past, *the use of semantics* was always used to distinguish MT systems; those which used semantics were labelled "good," and those which did not were labelled "bad." Now, all MT systems are claimed to make use of semantics, for obvious reasons, so this is no longer a distinguishing characteristic.

Direct translation is characteristic of a system (*e.g.*, GAT) designed from the start to translate out of one specific language and into another. Direct systems are limited to the minimum work necessary to effect that translation; for example, disambiguation is performed only to the extent necessary for translation into that one target language, irrespective of what might be required for another language. **Indirect translation**, on the other hand, is characteristic of a system (*e.g.*, EUROTRA) wherein the analysis of the source language and the synthesis of the target language are totally independent processes; for example, disambiguation is performed to the extent necessary to determine the "meaning" (however represented) of the source language input, irrespective of which target language(s) that input might be translated into.

The **interlingua approach** is characteristic of a system (*e.g.*, CETA) in which the representation of the "meaning" of the source language input is intended to be independent of any language, and this same representation is used to synthesize the target language output. The *linguistic universals* searched for and debated about by linguists and philosophers is the notion that underlies an interlingua. Thus, the representation of a given "unit of meaning" would be the same, no matter what language (or grammatical structure) that unit might be expressed in. The **transfer approach** is characteristic of a system (*e.g.*, TAUM) in which the underlying representation of the "meaning" of a grammatical unit (*e.g.*, sentence) differs depending on the language it was derived from (or into which it is to be generated). This implies the existence of a third translation stage, called Transfer, that maps one language-specific meaning representation into another. Thus, the overall transfer-style translation process is Analysis followed by Transfer and then Synthesis. The "transfer" *vs.* "interlingua" difference is not applicable to all systems; in particular, *direct* MT systems use neither the *transfer* nor the *interlingua* approach, since they do not attempt to represent "meaning."

"Local scope" *vs.* "global scope" is not so much a difference of category as degree. **Local scope** characterizes a system (*e.g.*, SYSTRAN) in which words are the essential unit driving analysis, and in which that analysis is, in effect, performed by separate procedures for each word which try to determine – based on the words to the left and/or right – the part of speech, possible idiomatic usage, and "sense" of the word keying the procedure. In such systems, for example, homographs (words which differ in part of speech and/or derivational history, thus meaning, but which are written alike) are a major problem, because a unified analysis of the sentence per se is not attempted. **Global scope** characterizes a system (*e.g.*, METAL) in which the meaning of a word is determined by its context within a unified analysis of the sentence (or, rarely, paragraph). In such systems, by contrast, homographs do not typically constitute a significant problem because the amount of context taken into account is much greater than is the case with systems of "local scope."

4 Historical Perspective

There are several comprehensive treatments of MT projects [Bruderer, 1977] and MT history [Hutchins, 1978] available in the open literature. To illustrate some continuity in the field of MT, while remaining within reasonable space limits, our brief historical overview will be restricted to defunct systems/projects which gave rise to follow-on systems/projects of current interest. These are: Georgetown's GAT, Grenoble's CETA, Texas' METAL, Montreal's TAUM, and Brigham Young University's ALP system.

4.1 GAT - Georgetown Automatic Translation

Georgetown University hosted one of the earliest MT projects. Begun in 1952, and supported by the U.S. government, Georgetown's GAT system became operational in 1964 with its delivery to the Atomic Energy Commission at Oak Ridge National Laboratory, and to Europe's corresponding research facility EURATOM in Ispra, Italy. Both systems were used for many years to translate Russian physics texts into "English." The output quality was quite poor, by comparison with human translations, but for the intended purpose of quickly scanning documents to determine their content and interest, the GAT system was nevertheless superior to the only alternatives: slow and more expensive human translation or, worse, no translation at all. GAT was not replaced at EURATOM until 1976; at ORNL [Jordan *et al.*, 1976], it seems to have been used until at least 1979.

The GAT strategy was *direct* and *local*: simple word-for-word replacement, followed by a limited amount of transposition of words to result in something vaguely resembling English. Very soon, a "word" came to be defined as a single word or a sequence of words forming an "idiom." There was no true linguistic theory underlying the GAT design; and, given the state of the art in computer science, there was no underlying computational theory either. GAT was developed by being made to work for a given text, then being modified to account for the next text, and so on. The eventual result was a monolithic system of intractable complexity: after its delivery to ORNL and EURATOM, it underwent no significant modification. The fact that it was used for so long is nothing short of remarkable – a lesson in what can be tolerated by users who desperately need translation services for which there is no viable alternative to even low-quality MT.

The Georgetown MT project was terminated in the mid-60's. Peter Toma, one of the GAT workers, incorporated LATSEC and developed the SYSTRAN system, which in 1970 replaced the IBM Mark II system at the USAF Foreign Technology Division (FTD) at Wright Patterson AFB, and in 1976 replaced GAT at EURATOM. SYSTRAN is still being used there to translate Russian into English for information-acquisition purposes. We shall return to our discussion of SYSTRAN in the next major section.

4.2 CETA - Centre d'Études pour la Traduction Automatique

In 1961 a project was started at Grenoble University in France, to translate Russian into French. Unlike GAT, Grenoble began the CETA project with a clear linguistic theory – having had a number of years in which to witness and learn from the events transpiring at Georgetown and elsewhere. In particular, it was resolved to achieve a dependency-structure analysis of every sentence (the *global* approach) rather than rely on intra-sentential heuristics to control limited word transposition (the *local* approach); with a unified analysis in hand, a reasonable synthesis effort could be mounted. The theoretical basis of CETA was *interlingua* (implying a language-independent, "neutral" meaning representation) at the grammatical level, but *transfer* (implying a mapping from one language-specific meaning representation to another) at the dictionary level. The state of the art in computer science still being primitive, Grenoble was essentially forced to adopt IBM assembly language as the software basis of CETA [Hutchins, 1978].

The CETA system was under development for ten years; during 1967-71 it was used to translate 400,000 words of Russian mathematics and physics texts into French. The major findings of this period were that the use of an interlingua erases all clues about how to express the translation; also, that it results in extremely poor or no translations of sentences for which complete analyses cannot be derived. The CETA workers learned that it is critically important in an operational system to retain surface clues about how to formulate the translation (Indo-European languages, for example, have many structural similarities, not to mention cognates, that one can take advantage of), and to have "fail-soft" measures designed into the system. An interlingua does not admit this easily, if at all, but the transfer approach does.

A change in hardware (thus software) in 1971 prompted the abandonment of the CETA system, immediately followed by the creation of a new project/system called GETA, based entirely on a fail-soft transfer design. The software included significant amounts of assembly language; this continued reliance on assembly language was soon to have deleterious effects, for reasons now obvious to anyone. We will return to our discussion of GETA below.

4.3 METAL - MEchanical Translation and Analysis of Languages

Having had the same opportunity for hindsight, the University of Texas in 1961 used U.S. government funding to establish the Linguistics Research Center, and with it the METAL project, to investigate MT – not from Russian, but from German into English. (MT research at the University actually began in 1956.) The LRC adopted Chomsky's transformational paradigm, which was quickly gaining popularity in linguistics circles, and within that framework employed a syntactic *interlingua* based on deep structures. It was soon discovered that transformational linguistics per se was not sufficiently well-developed to support an operational system, and certain compromises were made. The eventual result, in 1974, was an 80,000-line, 14-overlay FORTRAN program running on a dedicated CDC 6600. *Indirect* translation was performed in 14 steps of global analysis, transfer, and synthesis – one for each of the 14 overlays – and required prodigious amounts of CPU time and I/O from/to massive data files. U.S. government support for MT projects was winding down in any case, and the METAL project was shortly terminated.

Several years later, a small government grant resurrected the project. The FORTRAN program was rewritten in LISP to run on a DEC-10; in the process, it was pared down to just three major stages (analysis, transfer, and synthesis) comprising about 4,000 lines of code which could be accommodated in three "overlays," and its computer resource requirements were reduced by a factor of ten. Though U.S. government interest once again languished, the Sprachendienst (Language Services) department of Siemens AG in Munich had begun supporting the project, and in 1980 Siemens became the sole sponsor.

4.4 TAUM - Traduction Automatique de l'Université de Montreal

In 1965 the University of Montreal established the TAUM project with Canadian government funding. This was probably the first MT project designed strictly around the *transfer* approach. As the software basis of the project, TAUM chose the FORTRAN programming language on the CDC 6600 (later, the CYBER 173). After an initial period of more-or-less open-ended research, the Canadian government began adopting specific goals for the TAUM system. A chance remark by a bored translator in the Canadian Meteorological Center (CMC) had led to a spin-off project: TAUM-METEO. Weather forecasters already adhered to a relatively consistent style and vocabulary in their English reports. Partly as a result of this, translation into French was so monotonous a task that human translator turnover in the weather service was extraordinarily high – six months was the average tenure. TAUM was commissioned in 1975 to produce an operational English-French MT system for weather forecasts. A prototype was demonstrated in 1976, and by 1977 METEO was installed for production translation. We will discuss METEO in the next major section.

The next challenge was not long in coming: by a fixed date, TAUM had to be usable for the translation of a 90 million word set of aviation maintenance manuals from English into French (else the translation had to be started by human means, since the result was needed quickly). From this point on, TAUM concentrated on those manuals exclusively. To alleviate problems with their predominantly syntactic analysis (especially considering the many multiple-noun compounds present in such manuals), the group began in 1977 to incorporate significant semantic analysis in the TAUM-AVIATION system.

After a test in 1979, it became obvious that TAUM-AVIATION was not going to be production-ready in time for its intended use. The Canadian government organized a series of tests and evaluations to assess the status of the system. Among other things, it was discovered that the cost of writing each dictionary entry was remarkably high (3.75 man-hours, costing $35-40 Canadian), and that the system's runtime translation cost was also high (6 cents/word) considering the cost of human translation (8 cents/word), especially when the post-editing costs (10 cents/word for TAUM *vs.* 4 cents/word for human translations) were taken into account [Gervais, 1980]. TAUM-AVIATION was not yet cost-effective. Several other factors, especially the bad Canadian economic situation, combined with this to cause the cancellation of the TAUM project in 1981. There are recent signs of renewed interest in MT in Canada. State-of-the-art surveys have been commissioned [Pierre Isabelle, formerly of TAUM, personal communication], but no successor project has yet been established.

4.5 ALP - Automated Language Processing

In 1971 a project was established at Brigham Young University to translate Mormon ecclesiastical texts from English into multiple languages – starting with French, German, Portuguese and Spanish. The original aim was to produce a fully-automatic MT system based on Junction Grammar [Lytle *et al.*, 1975], but in 1973 the emphasis shifted to Machine-Aided Translation (MAT, where the system does not attempt to analyze sentences on its own, according to pre-programmed linguistic rules, but instead relies heavily on interaction with a human to effect the analysis, if one is even attempted, and complete the translation). This Interactive Translation System (ITS) performed *global* analysis of sentences (with human assistance), and then *transfer* (again, with human assistance).

The BYU project never produced an operational system (hardware costs and the amount and difficulty of human interaction prohibited cost-effectiveness), and the Mormon Church, through the University, began to dismantle the project. In 1980, a group of BYU programmers joined Weidner Communications Corporation, and helped develop the fully-automatic, direct WEIDNER MT system. At about the same time, most of the remaining BYU project members left to form Automated Language Processing Systems (ALPS) and continue development of ITS. Both of these systems are actively marketed today, and will be discussed in the next section. Some work continues at BYU, but at a very much reduced level and degree of aspiration (*e.g.*, [Melby, 1982]).

5 Current Production Systems

In this section we consider the major M(A)T systems being used and/or marketed today. Some of these originate from the "failures" described above, but other systems are essentially the result of successful (*i.e.*, continuing) MT R&D projects. The full MT systems discussed below are the following: SYSTRAN, LOGOS, METEO, WEIDNER, and SPANAM; we will also discuss the MAT systems CULT and ALPS. Most of these systems have been installed for several customers (METEO, SPANAM, and CULT are the exceptions, with only one obvious customer each). The oldest active installation dates from 1970.

A "standard installation," if it can be said to exist, includes provision for pre-processing in some cases, translation (with much human intervention in the case of MAT systems), and some amount of post-editing. To MT system users, acceptability is a function of the amount of pre- and/or post-editing that must be done (which is also the greatest determinant of cost). Van Slype [1982] reports that "acceptability to the human translator...appears negotiable when the quality of the MT system is such that the correction (*i.e.*, post-editing) ratio is lower than 20% (1 correction every 5 words) and when the human translator can be associated with the upgrading of the MT system." It is worth noting that editing time has been observed to fall with practice: Piggott [1982] reports that "...the more M.T. output a translator handles, the more proficient he becomes in making the best use of this new tool. In some cases he manages to double his output within a few months as he begins to recognize typical M.T. errors and devise more efficient ways of correcting them."

It is also important to realize that, though none of these systems produces output mistakable for human translation – at least not good human translation – their users have found sufficient reason to continue using them. Some users, indeed, are repeat customers. In short, MT and MAT systems cannot be argued not to work, for they are in fact being bought and used, and they save time and/or money for their users. Every user expresses a desire for improved quality and reduced cost, to be sure, but then the same is said about human translation. Thus, in the only valid sense of the idiom, MT and MAT have already "arrived." Future improvements in quality, and reductions in cost – both certain to take place – will serve to make M(A)T systems even more attractive.

5.1 SYSTRAN

SYSTRAN was one of the first MT systems to be marketed; the first installation replaced the IBM Mark II Russian-English system at the USAF FTD in 1970, and is still operational. NASA used SYSTRAN in 1974 to translate materials relating to the Apollo-Soyuz collaboration, and EURATOM replaced GAT with SYSTRAN in 1976. Also by

1976, FTD was augmenting SYSTRAN with word-processing equipment to increase productivity (*e.g.*, to eliminate the use of punch-cards). The system has continued to evolve, for example by the shift toward a more modular design and by the allowance of topical glossaries (essentially, dictionaries specific to the subject area of the text). The system has been argued to be ad hoc – particularly in the assignment of semantic features [Pigott, 1979]. The USAF FTD dictionaries number over a million entries; Bostad [1982] reports that dictionary updating must be severely constrained, lest a change to one entry disrupt the activities of many others. (A study by Wilks [1978] reported an improvement/degradation ratio, after dictionary updates, of 7:3, but Bostad implies a much more stable situation after the introduction of stringent quality-control measures.)

In 1975 the Commission of the European Communities purchased an English-French version of SYSTRAN for evaluation and potential use. Unlike the FTD, NASA, and EURATOM installations, where the goal was information acquisition, the intended use by CEC was for information dissemination – meaning that the output was to be carefully edited before human consumption. Van Slype [1982] reports that "the English-French standard vocabulary delivered by Prof. Toma to the Commission was found to be almost entirely useless for the Commission environment." Early evaluations were negative (*e.g.*, Van Slype [1979]), but the existing and projected overload on CEC human translators was such that investigation continued in the hope that dictionary additions would improve the system to the point of usability. Additional versions of SYSTRAN were purchased (French-English in 1977, English-Italian and French-German in 1978, and English-German in 1979). The dream of acceptable quality for post-editing purposes was eventually realized: Pigott [1982] reports that "...the enthusiasm demonstrated by [a few translators] seems to mark something of a turning point in [MT]." Currently, CEC translators in Luxembourg are using SYSTRAN on a Siemens 7740 computer for routine translation; one factor accounting for success is that the English and French dictionaries now consist of well over 100,000 entries in the very few technical areas for which SYSTRAN is being employed. Another factor is apparently the careful selection of texts to be translated: in 1982-

83 only 4,000 pages/year were translated using the French-English, English-Italian, and English-French versions (combined average), and a mid-year projection for 1984 was even lower [Nino Varile, personal communication].

In 1976, General Motors of Canada acquired SYSTRAN for translation of various manuals (for vehicle service, diesel locomotives, and highway transit coaches) from English into French on an IBM mainframe. GM's English-French dictionary had been expanded to over 130,000 terms by 1981 [Sereda, 1982]. Subsequently, GM purchased an English-Spanish version of SYSTRAN, and began to build the necessary (very large!) dictionary. Sereda [1982] reports a speed-up of 3-4 times in the productivity of his human translators (from about 1,000 words per day); he also reveals that developing SYSTRAN dictionary entries costs the company approximately $4 per term (word- or idiom-pair).

While other SYSTRAN users have applied the system to unrestricted texts (in selected subject areas), Xerox developed a restricted input language, "Multinational Customized English," after consultation with LATSEC. That is, Xerox requires its English technical writers to adhere to a specialized vocabulary and a strict manual of style. SYSTRAN is then employed to translate the resulting documents into French, Italian, Spanish, German, and Portuguese. Ruffino [1982] reports "a five-to-one gain in translation time for most texts" with the range being 2-10 times. This approach is not necessarily feasible for all organizations, but Xerox is willing to employ it and claims it also enhances source-text clarity. Xerox now uses SYSTRAN to translate approximately 90% of its technical documentation (around 55,000 pages/year).

Currently, SYSTRAN is being used in the CEC for the routine translation, followed by human post-editing, of around 1,000 pages of text per month in the couples English-French, French-English, and English-Italian [Wheeler, 1983]. Given this relative success in the CEC environment, the Commission has recently ordered an English-German version as well as a French-German version. Judging by past experience, it will be quite some time before these are ready for production use, but when ready they will probably save the CEC translation bureau valuable time, if not real money as well.

5.2 LOGOS

Development of the LOGOS system was begun in 1964. The first installation, in 1971, was used by the U.S. Air Force to translate English maintenance manuals for military equipment into Vietnamese. Due to the termination of U.S. involvement in that war, its use was ended after two years. (A report by Sinaiko and Klare [1973] disparaged LOGOS' cost-effectiveness, but this claim was argued to be seriously flawed and was formally protested [B. Scott, personal communication].) The linguistic foundations of LOGOS are not well advertised, presumably for reasons involving trade secrecy. The system developer states that "our linguistic approach...has evolved in ways analogous to case grammar/valency theory...mapping natural language into a semanto-syntactic abstraction language organized as a tree" [Scott, personal communication].

LOGOS continued to attract customers. In 1978, Siemens AG began funding the development of a LOGOS German-English system for telecommunications manuals. After three years LOGOS delivered a "production" system, but it was not found suitable for use (due in part to poor quality of the translations, and in part to the economic situation within Siemens which had resulted in a much-reduced demand for translation, hence no immediate need for an MT system). Eventually LOGOS forged an agreement with the Wang computer company which allowed the implementation of the German-English system (formerly restricted to large IBM mainframes) on Wang office computers. This system reached the commercial market, and has been purchased by several multi-national organizations (*e.g.*, Nixdorf, Triumph-Adler, Hewlett-Packard); development of other language pairs (*e.g.*, English-French, English-German) is underway [Scott, personal communication].

5.3 METEO

TAUM-METEO is the world's only example of a truly fully-automatic MT system. Developed as a spin-off of the TAUM technology, as discussed earlier, it was fully integrated into the Canadian Meteorological Center's (CMC's) nation-wide weather communications network by 1977. METEO scans the network traffic for English weather reports, translates them *directly* into French, and sends the translations back out over the communications network automatically. Rather than relying on post-editors to discover and correct errors, METEO detects its own errors and passes the offending input to human editors; output deemed "correct" by METEO is dispatched without human intervention, or even overview.

TAUM-METEO was probably also the first MT system where translators were involved in all phases of design/development/refinement; indeed, a CMC translator instigated the entire project. Since the restrictions on input to METEO were already in place before the project started (*i.e.*, METEO imposed no new restrictions on weather forecasters), METEO cannot quite be classed with the Xerox SYSTRAN system, which relies on restrictions geared to the characteristics of SYSTRAN. But METEO is not extensible – though similar systems could be built for equally restricted textual domains, if they exist.

One of the more remarkable side-effects of the METEO installation is that the translator turn-over rate within the CMC went from 6 months, prior to METEO, to several years, once the CMC translators began to trust METEO's operational decisions and not review its output [Brian Harris, personal communication]. METEO's input constitutes over 24,000 words/day, or 8.5 million words/year. Of this, it now correctly translates 90-95%, shuttling the other, "more interesting" 5-10% to the human CMC translators. Almost all of these "analysis failures" are attributable to communications noise (the CMC network garbles some traffic), misspellings (METEO does not attempt corrections), or words missing from the dictionary, though some failures are due to the inability of the system to handle certain linguistic constructions. METEO's computational requirements total about 15 CPU minutes per day on a CDC 7600 [Thouin, 1982]. By 1981, it appeared that the built-in limitations of METEO's theoretical basis had been reached, and further improvement was not likely to be cost-effective.

5.4 Weidner Communications Corporation

Weidner was established in 1977 by Bruce Weidner, who soon hired some MT programmers from the fading BYU project. Weidner delivered a production English-French system to Mitel in Canada in 1980, and a beta-test English-Spanish system to the Siemens Corporation (USA) in the same year. In 1981 Mitel took delivery on Weidner's English-Spanish and English-German systems, and Bravice (a translation service bureau in Japan) purchased the WEIDNER English-Spanish and Spanish-English systems. To date, there are 22 or more installations of the WEIDNER MT system around the world. The WEIDNER system, though "fully automatic" during translation, is marketed as a "machine aid" to translation (perhaps to avoid the stigma usually attached to MT). It is highly interactive for other purposes (the lexical pre-analysis of texts, the construction of dictionaries, etc.), and integrates word-processing software with external devices (*e.g.*, the Xerox 9700 laser printer at Mitel) for enhanced overall document production. Thus, the WEIDNER system accepts a formatted source document (actually, one containing formatting/typesetting codes) and produces a formatted translation. This is an important feature to users, since almost everyone is interested in producing formatted translations from formatted source texts.

Given the way this system is tightly integrated with modern word-processing technology, it is difficult to assess the degree to which the translation component itself enhances translator productivity, *vs.* the degree to which simple automation of formerly manual (or poorly automated) processes accounts for the productivity gains. The *direct* translation component itself is not particularly sophisticated. For example, analysis is *local*, usually confined to the noun phrase or verb phrase level (except for Japanese) – so that context available only at higher levels cannot be taken into account.

Translation is performed in four independent stages: homograph disambiguation, idiom search, structural analysis, and transfer. These stages do not interact with each other, which creates more problems; for example, homographs are resolved once and for all very early on, without any higher-level context (it is not available until later) that would make this process much more sensitive. As another example, Hundt [1982] comments that "idioms are an extremely important part of the translation procedure. ...machine assisted translation is for the most part word replacement..." Then, "It is not worthwhile discussing the various problems of the [WEIDNER] system in great depth because in the first place they are much too numerous..." Yet even though the WEIDNER translations are of low quality, users nevertheless report economic satisfaction with the results. Hundt continues "...the WEIDNER system indeed works as an aid..." and, "800 words an hour as a final figure [for translation throughput] is not unrealistic." This level of performance is very rarely observed during strictly human translation, and some users report the use of WEIDNER to be cost-effective, as well as faster, in their environments.

In 1982, Weidner delivered English-German and German-English systems to ITT in Great Britain; but there were some financial problems (a third of the employees were laid off that year) until 1983, when a controlling interest was purchased by a Japanese company: Bravice, one of Weidner's customers, owned by a group of Japanese investors. Weidner continues to market MT systems, and is presently working to develop Japanese MT systems. A commercial Japanese-English system has recently been announced by Bravice, and work continues on an English-Japanese system. In addition, Weidner has implemented its system on the IBM Personal Computer, in order to reduce its dependence on the PDP-11 in particular, and on any one machine in general. The system is written in FORTRAN, with some assembly code support, but there are plans to reimplement the software in another language to increase its flexibility.

5.5 SPANAM

Following a promising feasibility study, the Pan American Health Organization in Washington, D.C. decided in 1975 to undertake work on a machine translation system by hiring some outside consultants. The official PAHO languages are English, French, Portuguese, and Spanish; Spanish-English was chosen as the initial language pair, based on the assumption that this combination requires fewer parsing strategies in order to produce manageable output [Vasconcellos, 1985]. Actual work started in 1976, and the first prototype was running in 1978, using punched card input on an IBM mainframe. After subsequent integration into a word-processing network, limited production began in 1979.

In 1980 the source code was delivered to PAHO, and its in-house staff assumed responsibility for continued development and operation of the system. SPANAM was then made available for use on a regular production basis. In its first major application, SPANAM reduced manpower requirements by 45%, resulting in a monetary saving of 61% [Vasconcellos, 1984]. Since 1980, SPANAM has been used to translate over 2.5 million words of text, averaging about 6,500 words per day per post-editor. The post-editors have developed a "bag of tricks" for speeding the revision work, and special string functions have also been built into the word processor for handling SPANAM's English output.

Concerning the early status of SPANAM, sketchy details have implied that the grammar rules were built into the programs. The software technology was subsequently updated, the PL/I programs having been modularized later in 1980. From the reports available, SPANAM appears to adopt a *direct* translation strategy, and to settle for *local* analysis of phrases and some clauses via a sequence of independent processing stages. As of September 1985 the SPANAM dictionaries contained over 60,000 source entries. It is routinely used by PAHO translators in their work; indeed, the post-editing of SPANAM output is included as a duty in the translator job description.

A follow-on project to develop ENGSPAN (for English-Spanish), underway since 1982 and partially funded by the U.S. Agency for International Development, has also delivered a production system – this one characterized by a more advanced design (*e.g.*, an ATN parser), some features of which may find their way into SPANAM. As of September 1985 the ENGSPAN dictionaries had over 45,000 source and 47,000 target entries. As with SPANAM, PAHO translators routinely employ ENGSPAN in their work. The ENGSPAN experience is being reflected in major improvements to SPANAM. Based on the success of these two systems, development of ENGPORT (with Portuguese as the Target Language) has been initiated.

5.6 CULT - Chinese University Language Translator

CULT is one of the more successful Machine-Aided Translation systems. Development began at the Chinese University of Hong Kong around 1968. CULT translates Chinese mathematics and physics journals (published in Beijing) into English through a highly-interactive process – or, at least, with a lot of human intervention. The goal was to eliminate post-editing of the results by allowing a large amount of pre-editing of the input, and a certain degree of human intervention during translation. Although published details [Loh *et al.*, 1976, 1978, 1979] are not unambiguous, it is clear that humans intervene by marking sentence and phrase boundaries in the input, and by indicating word senses where necessary, among other things. (What is not clear is whether this is strictly a pre-editing task, or an interactive task.) CULT runs on the ICL 1904A computer.

Beginning in 1975, the CULT system was applied to the task of translating the Acta Mathematica Sinica into English; in 1976, this was joined by the Acta Physica Sinica. Originally the Chinese character transcription problem was solved by use of the standard telegraph codes invented a century ago, and the input data was punched on cards. But in 1978 the system was updated by the addition of word-processing equipment for on-line data entry and pre-/post-editing.

It is not clear how general the techniques behind CULT are – whether, for example, it could be applied to the translation of other texts – nor how cost-effective it is in operation. Other factors may justify its continued use. It is also unclear whether R&D is continuing, or whether CULT, like METEO, is unsuited to design modification beyond a certain point already reached. In the absence of answers to these questions, and perhaps despite them, CULT does appear to be an MAT success story: the amount of post-editing said to be required is trivial – limited to the re-introduction of certain untranslatable formulas, figures, etc., into the translated output. At some point, other translator intervention is required, but it seems to be limited to the manual inflection of verbs and nouns for tense and number, and perhaps the introduction of a few function words such as determiners.

5.7 ALPS - Automated Language Processing Systems

ALPS was incorporated by a group of five Brigham Young University ITS developers in 1980; this group seems to have been composed of linguists interested in producing machine aids for human translators (dictionary look-up and substitution, etc.) and later grew to include virtually all of the major figures from the ITS staff [Alan Melby and Merle Tenney, personal communication]. Thus the new ALPS system is interactive in all respects, and does not seriously pretend to perform translation; rather, ALPS provides the translator with a set of software tools to automate many of the tasks encountered in everyday translation experience. ALPS adopted the language pairs that the BYU ITS system had supported: English into French, German, Portuguese, and Spanish. Since then, other languages (*e.g.*, Arabic) have been announced, but their commercial status is unclear. In addition to selling MAT systems, ALPS now includes its own translation service bureau.

The new ALPS system is intended to work on any of three "levels" – providing capabilities from multilingual word processing and dictionary lookup, through word-for-word (actually, term-for-term) translation, to highly-automated (though human-assisted) sentence-level translation; the latter mode of operation, judging by ALPS demonstrations and the reports of users, is seldom if ever employed. The central tool provided by ALPS is thus a menu-driven word-processing system coupled to the on-line dictionary. One of the first ALPS customers seems to have been Agnew TechTran – a commercial translation bureau which acquired the ALPS system for in-house use. Other customers include Xerox, ComputerVision, Control Data (in France), IBM (in Italy) and Hewlett-Packard (in Mexico). Recently, another shake-up at Weidner Communication Corporation (the Provo R&D group was disbanded) has allowed ALPS to hire a large group of former Weidner workers: ALPS might itself be intending to enter the fully-automatic MT arena.

6 Current Research and Development

In addition to the organizations marketing or using existing M(A)T systems, there are several groups engaged in on-going R&D in this area. Operational (*i.e.*, marketed or used) systems have not yet resulted from these efforts, but deliveries are foreseen at various times in the future. We will discuss the major Japanese MT efforts briefly (as if they were unified, in a sense, though for the most part they are actually separate), and then the major U.S. and European MT systems at greater length.

6.1 MT R&D in Japan

In 1982 Japan electrified the technological world by widely publicizing its new Fifth Generation project and establishing the Institute for New Generation Computer Technology (ICOT) as its base. Its goal is to leapfrog Western technology and place Japan at the forefront of the digital electronics world in the 1990's. MITI (Japan's Ministry of International Trade and Industry) is the motivating force behind this project, and intends that the goal be achieved through the development and application of highly innovative techniques in both computer architecture and Artificial Intelligence.

Of the application areas considered as an applications candidate by the ICOT scientists and engineers, Machine Translation played a prominent role [Moto-oka, 1982]. Among the Western *Artificial Intelligentsia*, the inclusion of MT seems out of place: AI researchers have endeavored (successfully) to ignore all MT work in the two decades since the ALPAC debacle, and almost universally believe that success is impossible in the foreseeable future – in ignorance of the successful, cost-effective applications already in place. To the Japanese leadership, however, the inclusion of MT is no accident. Foreign language training aside, translation into Japanese is still one of the primary means by which Japanese researchers acquire information about what their Western competitors are doing, and how they are doing it. Translation out of Japanese is necessary before Japan can export products to its foreign markets, because the customers demand that the manuals and other documentation not be written only in

Japanese, and in general translation is seen as a way to "diffuse the Japanese scientific and technological information to the outer world" [Nagao, personal communication]. The Japanese correctly view translation as necessary to their technological survival, but have found it extremely difficult – and expensive – to accomplish by human means: the translation budgets of Japanese companies, when totalled, are estimated to exceed 1 trillion yen, and most of this involves the export trade [Philippi, 1985]. Accordingly, the Japanese government and industry have sponsored MT research for several decades. There has been no rift between AI and MT researchers in Japan, as there has been in the West – especially in the U.S.

Nomura and Shimazu [1982] number the MT R&D groups in Japan at more than eighteen. (By contrast, there might be a dozen significant MT groups in all of the U.S. and Europe, including commercial vendors.) Several of the Japanese projects are quite large. (By contrast, only one MT project in the Western world, EUROTRA, even appears as large, but most of the 80 individuals involved work on EUROTRA only a fraction of their time.) Most of the Japanese projects are engaged in research as much as development. (Most Western projects are engaged in pure development.) Japanese progress in MT has not come fast: until a few years ago, their hardware technology was inferior; so was their software competence, but this situation has been changing rapidly. Another obstacle has been the great differences between Japanese and Western languages – especially English, which is of greatest interest to them – and the relative paucity of knowledge about these differences. The Japanese are working to eliminate this ignorance: progress has been made, and production-quality systems already exist for some applications. Few of the Japanese MT systems are *direct*, and all engage in *global* analysis; most are based on a *transfer* approach, but a few groups are pursuing the *interlingua* approach.

MT research has been pursued at Kyoto University since 1964. There were once two MT projects at Kyoto (one for long-term research, one for near-term application). The former project, recently abandoned, was working on an English-Japanese translation system based on formal semantics (Cresswell's simplified version of Montague

Grammar [Nishida and Doshita, 1982, 1983]). The latter has developed a practical system for translating English titles of scientific and technical papers into Japanese [Nagao *et al.*, 1980, 1982], and is working on other applications of English-Japanese [Tsujii, 1982] as well as Japanese-English [Nagao *et al.*, 1981]. This effort, funded by the Agency of Science and Technology and headed by Prof. Nagao, "consists of more than twenty people [at Kyoto], with three other organizations involved [comprising another 20 workers]" [Nagao, personal communication]. The goal of this 4-year, $2.7 million (U.S.) project is to create a practical system for translating technical and scientific documents from Japanese into English and vice versa [Philippi, 1985]. Kyushu University has been the home of MT research since 1955, with projects by Tamachi and Shudo [Shudo, 1974]. The University of Osaka Prefecture and Fukuoka University also host MT projects.

However, most Japanese MT research (like other research) is performed in the industrial laboratories. Fujitsu [Sawai *et al.*, 1982], Hitachi, Toshiba [Amano, 1982], and NEC [Muraki and Ichiyama, 1982], among others, support large projects generally concentrating on the translation of computer manuals. Nippon Telegraph and Telephone is working on a system to translate scientific and technical articles from Japanese into English and vice versa [Nomura *et al.*, 1982], and is looking into the future as far as simultaneous machine translation of telephone conversations [Nomura, personal communication]. Recently a joint venture by Hitachi and Quick has resulted in an English-Japanese system that will be used to offer Japanese readers news from Europe and the U.S. on the economy, stock market, and commodities; eventually, this service will be offered via Quick's on-line market information service [AAT, 1984a]. In addition, Fujitsu has announced its bi-directional Atlas Japanese-English system for translating technical texts; this system is now available for lease [AAT, 1984b]. NEC and IBM Japan have also recently announced development of systems intended for near-term commercial introduction [Philippi, 1985].

Japanese industrialists are not confining their attention to work at home. Several AI groups in the U.S. (*e.g.*, SRI International) have been approached by Japanese companies desiring to fund MT R&D projects, and the Linguistics Research Center of the University of Texas is currently engaged in MT-related research funded by Hitachi. More than that, some U.S. MT vendors (SYSTRAN and Weidner, at least) have recently sold partial interests to Japanese investors, and delivered production MT systems. Various Japanese corporations (*e.g.*, NTT and Hitachi) and trade groups (*e.g.*, JEIDA [Japan Electronic Industry Development Association]) have sent teams to visit MT projects around the world and assess the state of the art. University researchers have been given sabbaticals to work at Western MT centers (Prof. Shudo at Texas, Prof. Tsujii at Grenoble). Other representatives have indicated Japan's desire to establish close working communications with the CEC's EUROTRA project [King and Nagao, personal communication]. Japan evidences a long-term, growing commitment to acquire and develop MT technology. The Japanese leadership is convinced that success in MT is vital to their future.

6.2 METAL

One of the major MT R&D groups around the world, the METAL project at the Linguistics Research Center of the University of Texas, recently delivered a commercial-grade system. The METAL German-English system passed tests in a production-style setting in late 1982, mid-83, and twice in 1984, and the system was then installed at the sponsor's site in Germany for further testing and final development of a translator interface. Renamed LITRAS, it was introduced for sale at the Hanover Fair in Germany in April, 1985. The METAL dictionaries are now being expanded for maximum possible coverage of selected technical areas, and work on other language pairs has begun in earnest.

One of the particular strengths of the METAL system is its accommodation of a variety of linguistic theories/strategies. The German analysis component is based on a context-free phrase-structure grammar, augmented by procedures with facilities for, among other things, arbitrary transformations. An experimental English analysis component, on the other hand, employs a modified Generalized Phrase-Structure Grammar (GPSG) approach, and makes no use of transformations. Analysis is completely separated from transfer, and the system is multi-lingual in that a given constituent structure analysis can be used for transfer and synthesis into multiple target languages. Translation from German into Chinese and Spanish, as well as from English into German, has transpired on an experimental basis. In 1985, Siemens established a new project at the Catholic University of Louvain, in Belgium, to produce a Dutch-French, French-Dutch system; the universities of Mons and Liège are also involved in this effort, sponsored in part by the Belgian government.

The transfer component of METAL includes two transformation packages, one used by transfer grammar rules and the other by transfer dictionary entries; these co-operate during transfer, which is effected during a top-down exploration of the highest-scoring tree produced in the analysis phase. The strategy for the top-down pass is controlled by the linguist who writes the transfer rules. These are most often paired 1-1 with the grammar rules used to perform the original analysis, so that there is no need to search through a general transfer grammar to find applicable rules (potentially allowing application of the wrong ones); however, the option of employing a more general transfer grammar is available, and is in fact used for the translation of clauses. As implied above, structural and lexical transfer are performed in the same pass, so that each may influence the operation of the other; in particular, transfer dictionary entries may specify the syntactic and/or semantic contexts in which they are valid. If no analysis is achieved for a given input, the longest phrases which together span that input are selected for independent transfer and synthesis, so that every input (a sentence, or perhaps a phrase) results in some translation.

In addition to producing a translation system per se, the Texas group has developed software packages for text processing (so as to format the output translations like the original input documents), data base management (of dictionary entries and grammar rules), rule validation (to eliminate most errors in dictionary entries and grammar rules), dictionary construction (to enhance human efficiency in coding lexical entries), etc. Aside from the word-processing front-end (developed by the project sponsor), the METAL group has developed a complete system, rather than a basic machine translation engine that leaves much drudgery for its human developers/users. Lehmann *et al.* [1981], Bennett [1982], and Slocum [1983, 1984, 1985] present more details about the METAL system.

6.3 GETA

As discussed earlier, the Groupe d'Études pour la Traduction Automatique was formed when Grenoble abandoned the CETA system. In reaction to the failures of the *interlingua* approach, GETA adopted the *transfer* approach. In addition, the former software design was largely discarded, and a new software package supporting a new style of processing was substituted. The core of the GETA translation system (ARIANE-78) is composed of three types of programs: one converts strings into trees (for, *e.g.*, word analysis), one converts trees into trees (for, *e.g.*, syntactic analysis and transfer), and the third converts trees into strings (for, *e.g.*, word synthesis). (A fourth type exists, but may be viewed as a specialized instance of one of the others.) The overall translation process is composed of a sequence of stages, wherein each stage employs one of these programs. Other modules in ARIANE-78 support editing and system maintenance functions.

One of the features of ARIANE-78 that sets it apart from other MT systems is the insistence on the part of the designers that no stage be more powerful than is minimally necessary for its proper function. Thus, rather than supplying the linguist with programming tools capable of performing any operation whatever (*e.g.*, the arbitrarily powerful Q-systems of TAUM), ARIANE-78 supplies at each stage only the minimum capability necessary to effect the desired linguistic operation, and no more. This reduces the likelihood that the linguist will become overly ambitious and create unnecessary problems, and also enables the programmers to produce software that runs more rapidly than would be possible with a more general scheme.

A "grammar" in the ROBRA subsystem is actually a network of subgrammars; that is, a grammar is a graph specifying alternative sequences of applications of the subgrammars and optional choices of which subgrammars are to be applied (at all). The top-level grammar is therefore a *control graph* over the subgrammars of rules that actually effect the linguistic operations – analysis, transfer, etc. ARIANE-78 is sufficiently general to allow implementation of any linguistic theory, or even multiple theories at once (in separate subgrammars) if such is desired. Thus, in principle, it is completely open-ended and could accommodate arbitrary semantic processing and reference to "world models" of any description.

In practice, however, the story is more complicated. In order to increase the computational flexibility, as is required to take advantage of substantially new linguistic theories, especially "world models," the underlying software would have to be changed in many various ways. Unfortunately, the underlying software is rigid (written in low-level languages), making modification extremely difficult. As a result, the GETA group has been unable to experiment with any radically new computational strategies. Back-up, for example, is a known problem [Tsujii, personal communication]: if the GETA system "pursues a wrong path" through the control graph of subgrammars, it can undo some of its work by backing up past whole graphs, discarding the results produced by entire subgrammars; but within a subgrammar, there is no possibility of backing up and reversing the effects of individual rule applications. Until GETA receives enough funding that programmers can be hired to rewrite the software in a high-level language (LISP/PROLOG is being evaluated), facilitating present and future redesign, the GETA group is "stuck" with the current software – now showing clear signs of age, to say nothing of non-transportability (to other than IBM machines).

GETA seems not to have been required to produce a full-fledged application early on, and the staff was relatively free to pursue research interests. Unless the GETA software basis can be updated, however, it may not long remain a viable system. (The GETA staff are actively seeking funding for such a project.) Meanwhile, the French government has launched a major application effort – *Projet Nationale* – to commercialize the GETA system, in which the implementation language is LISP [Peccoud, personal communication].

6.4 SUSY - Saarbrücker Übersetzungssystem

The University of the Saar at Saarbrücken, West Germany, hosts one of the larger MT projects in Europe, established in the late 1960's. After the failure of a project intended to modify GAT for Russian-German translation, a new system was designed along somewhat similar lines to translate Russian into German after *global* sentence analysis into dependency tree structures, using the *transfer* approach. Unlike most other MT projects, the Saarbrücken group was left relatively free to pursue research interests, rather than forced to produce applications, and was also funded at a level sufficient to permit significant on-going experimentation and modification. As a result, SUSY tended to track external developments in MT and AI more closely than other projects. For example, Saarbrücken helped establish the co-operative MT group LEIBNIZ (along with Grenoble and others) in 1974. Until 1975, SUSY was based on a strict transfer approach; after 1976, however, it evolved, becoming more abstract as linguistic problems mandating "deeper" analysis have forced the transfer representations to assume some of the generality of an interlingua. Also as a result of such research freedom, there was apparently no sustained attempt to develop coverage for specific end-user applications.

Developed as a multi-lingual system involving English, French, German, Russian and Esperanto, work on SUSY has tended to concentrate on translation into German from Russian and, recently, English. The strongest limiting factor in the further development of SUSY seems to be related to the initial inspiration behind the project: SUSY adopted a primitive approach in which the linguistic rules were organized into strictly independent strata and, where efficiency seemed to dictate, incorporated directly into the software [Maas, 1984]. As a consequence, the rules were virtually unreadable, and their interactions, eventually, became almost impossible to manage. In terms of application potential, therefore, SUSY seems to have failed, even though it is used (within University projects) for the translation of patent descriptions and other materials. A second-generation project, SUSY-II, begun in 1981, may fare better.

6.5 EUROTRA

EUROTRA is easily the largest MT project in the Western world. It is the first serious attempt to produce a true multi-lingual system, in this case intended for all seven European Economic Community languages. The justification for the project is simple, inescapable economics: over a third of the entire administrative budget of the EEC for 1982 was needed to pay the translation division (average individual cost: $43,000/year), which still could not keep up with the demands placed on it; technical translation costs the EEC $.20 per word for each of six translations (from the seventh original language), and doubles the cost of the technology documented; with the addition of Spain and Portugal, thus two more official languages, the translation staff would have to double for the existing demand level (unless highly productive machine aids were already in place) [Perusse, 1983]. The high cost of writing SYSTRAN dictionary entries is presently justifiable for reasons of speed in translation, but this situation is not viable in the long term. The EEC must have superior quality MT at lower cost for dictionary work. Yet human translation alone will never suffice.

EUROTRA is a true multi-national development project. There is no central laboratory where the work will take place, but instead designated University representatives of each member country will produce the analysis and synthesis modules for their native language. The transfer modules will be built by collaborating bilingual groups, and are designed to be as small as possible, consisting of little more than lexical substitution [King, 1982]. Software development will be almost entirely separated from the linguistic rule development; indeed, the production software, though formally specified by the EUROTRA members, will be written by whichever commercial software house wins the contract in bidding competition. Several co-ordinating committees are working with the various language and emphasis groups to insure co-operation.

The theoretical linguistic basis of EUROTRA is not entirely novel. The basic structures for representing "meaning" are dependency trees, marked with feature-value pairs partly at the discretion of the language groups writing the grammars (anything a group wants, it can add), and partly controlled by mutual agreement among the language groups (a certain set of feature-value combinations has been agreed to constitute minimum information; all are constrained to produce this set when analyzing sentences in their language, and all may expect it to be present when synthesizing sentences in their language) [King, 1981, 1982]. This is not to say that no new linguistic knowledge is being gained for, aside from the test of theory that EUROTRA is about to perform, there is the very substantial matter of the background contrastive linguistic investigation that has been going on since about 1978.

In one sense, the software basis of EUROTRA will not be novel either. The basic rule interpreter will be "a general re-write system with a control language over grammars/processes" [Margaret King, personal communication]. As with ARIANE-78, the linguistic rules can be bundled into packets of subgrammars, and the linguists will be provided with a means of controlling which packets of rules are applied, and when; the individual rules will be non-destructive re-write rules, so that the application of any given rule may create new structure, but will never erase any old information.

In another sense, however, the software basis of EUROTRA is quite remarkably different from other systems that have preceded it. The analysis, transfer, and synthesis strategies will not be incorporated into algorithms that the programmers implement; rather, they will be formulated by linguists and represented in a special control language (not the rule-writing language, which is algorithm-independent). This formulation of the dynamic control strategies will be compiled into a program that will then interpret the "static" rules describing the linguistic facts.

This is a bold step. There are, of course, pitfalls to any such action. Aside from the usual risk of unforeseen problems, there are two rather obvious unresolved issues. First, it remains to be seen whether linguists, trained mostly in the static, "descriptive" framework of linguistics (modern or otherwise), can accommodate themselves to the expression of dynamic algorithms – a mode of thinking that programmers (including almost all computational linguists) are far more adept at. Second, it also remains to be seen whether the system can be designed sufficiently flexibly to adjust to the wide range of experimental strategies that is sure to come when the staff is given such a large degree of freedom (remembering that the software implementation is seen as an essentially one-shot process to be performed on contract basis), while at the same time retaining sufficient speed to ensure that the computing requirements are affordable. Affordability is not merely an issue belonging to the eventual production system! On the contrary, it is critically important that a development group be able to conduct experiments that produce results in a reasonable amount of time. After too long a delay, the difference becomes one of category rather than degree, and progress is substantially – perhaps fatally – impeded.

The EUROTRA charter requires delivery of a small representative prototype system by late 1987, and a prototype covering one technical area by late 1988. The system must translate among the official languages of all member countries which sign the "contract of association"; thus, not all seven/nine EEC languages will necessarily be represented, but by law at least four languages must be represented if the project is to continue. It appears that the requisite number of member states have committed to join. It will be interesting to see whether this, the most ambitious of all MT projects, succeeds; either way, the consequences promise to be noteworthy.

7 The State of the Art

Human languages are, by nature, different. So much so, that the illusory goal of abstract perfection in translation – once and still imagined by some to be achievable – can be comfortably ruled out of the realm of possible existence, whether attempted by machine or man. Even the abstract notion of "quality" is undefinable, hence immeasurable. In its place, we must substitute the notion of evaluation of translation according to its purpose, judged by the consumer. One must therefore accept the truth that the notion of quality is inherently subjective. Certainly there will be translations hailed by most if not all as "good," and correspondingly there will be translations almost universally labelled "bad." Most translations, however, will surely fall in between these extremes, and each user must render his own judgement according to his needs.

In corporate circles, however, there is and has always been an operational definition of "good" *vs.* "bad" translation: a *good* translation is what senior translators are willing to expose to outside scrutiny (not that they are fully satisfied, for they never are); and a *bad* one is one they are not willing to release. These experienced translators – usually post-editors – impose a judgement which the corporate body is willing to accept at face value: after all, such judgement is the very purpose for having senior translators! It is arrived at subjectively, based on the purpose for which the translation is intended, but comes as close to being an objective assessment as the world is likely to see. In a post-editing context, a *good* original translation is one worth revising – *i.e.*, one that the editor will endeavor to change, rather than reject or replace with his own original translation.

Therefore, any rational position on the state of the art in MT and MAT must respect the operational decisions about the quality of MT and MAT as made by the present users. These systems are all, of course, based on old technology ("ancient," by the standards of AI researchers); but by the time systems employing today's AI technology hit the market, they too will be "antiquated" by the research laboratory standards of their time. Such is the nature of technology. We will therefore distinguish, in our assessment, between what is available and/or used now ("old," yet operationally current, technology), and what is around the next corner (techniques working in research labs today), and what is farther down the road (experimental approaches).

7.1 Production Systems

Production M(A)T systems are based on old technology; some, for example, still (or until very recently did) employ punch-cards and print(ed) out translations in all upper-case. Few if any attempt a comprehensive global analysis at the sentence level (trade secrets make this hard to discern), and none go beyond that to the paragraph level. None use a significant amount of semantic information (though all claim to use some). Most if not all perform as *idiots savants*, making use of enormous amounts of very unsophisticated pragmatic information and brute-force computation to determine the proper word-for-word or idiom-for-idiom translation, followed by local rearrangement of word order – leaving the translation chaotic, even if understandable.

But they work! Some of them do, anyway – well enough that their customers find reason to invest enormous amounts of time and capital developing the necessary massive dictionaries specialized to their applications. Translation time is certainly reduced. Translator frustration is increased or decreased, as the case may be (it seems that personality differences, among other things, have a large bearing on this). Some translators resist their introduction – there are those who still resist the introduction of typewriters, to say nothing of word processors – with varying degrees of success. But most are thinking about accepting the place of computers in translation, and a few actually look forward to relief from much of the drudgery they now face. Current MT systems seem to take some getting used to, and further productivity increases are realized as time goes by; they are usually accepted, eventually, as a boon to the bored translator. New products embodying old technology are constantly introduced; most are found not viable, and quickly disappear from the market. But those which have been around for years must be economically justifiable to their users – else, presumably, they would no longer exist.

7.2 Development Systems

Systems being developed for near-term introduction employ Computational Linguistics (CL) techniques of the late 1970's, if not the 80's. Essentially all are full MT, not MAT, systems. As Hutchins [1982] notes, "...there is now considerable agreement on the basic strategy, *i.e.*, a 'transfer' system with some semantic analysis and some interlingual features in order to simplify transfer components." These systems employ one of a variety of sophisticated parsing/transducing techniques, typically based on charts, whether the grammar is expressed via phrase-structure rules (*e.g.*, METAL) or [strings of] trees (*e.g.*, GETA, EUROTRA); they operate at the sentence level, or higher, and make significant use of semantic features. Proper linguistic theories, whether elegant or not quite, and heuristic software strategies take the place of simple word substitution and brute-force programming. If the analysis attempt succeeds, the translation stands a fair chance of being acceptable to the revisor; if analysis fails, then fail-soft measures are likely to produce something equivalent to the output of a current production MT system.

These systems work well enough in experimental settings to give their sponsors and waiting customers (to say nothing of their implementors) reason to hope for near-term success in application. Their technology is based on some of the latest techniques which appear to be workable in immediate large-scale application. Most "pure AI" techniques do not fall in this category; thus, serious AI researchers look down on these development systems (to say nothing of production systems) as old, uninteresting – and probably useless. Some likely are. But others, though "old," will soon find an application niche, and will begin displacing any of the current production systems which try to compete. (Since the present crop of development systems all seem to be aimed at the "information dissemination" application, the current production systems that are aimed at the "information acquisition" market may survive for some time.) The major hurdle is time: time to write and debug the grammars (a very hard task), and time to develop lexicons with roughly ten thousand general vocabulary items, and the few tens of thousands of technical terms required per subject area. Some development projects have invested the necessary time, and stand ready to deliver commercial applications (*e.g.*, GETA) or have just recently done so (*e.g.*, METAL, under the market name LITRAS).

7.3 Research Systems

The biggest problem associated with MT research systems is their scarcity (nonexistence, in the U.S.). If current CL and AI researchers were seriously interested in foreign languages – even if not for translation per se – this would not necessarily be a bad situation. But in the U.S. very few are so interested, and in Europe, CL and AI research has not yet reached the level achieved in the U.S. Western business and industry are more concerned with near-term payoff, and some track development systems; very few support MT development directly, and none yet support pure MT research at a significant level. (The Dutch firm Philips may, indeed, have the only long-term research project in the West.) Some European governments fund significant R&D projects (*e.g.*, Germany and France), but Japan is making by far the world's largest investment in MT research. The U.S. government, which otherwise supports the best overall AI and (English) CL research in the world, is not involved.

Where pure MT research projects do exist, they tend to concentrate on the problems of deep meaning representations – striving to pursue the goal of a true AI system, which would presumably include language-independent meaning representations of great depth and complexity. Translation here is seen as just one application of such a system: the system "understands" natural language input, then "generates" natural language output; if the languages happen to be different, then translation has been performed via paraphrase. Translation could thus be viewed as one of the ultimate tests of an Artificial Intelligence: if a system "translates correctly," then to some extent it can be argued to have "understood correctly," and in any case will tell us much about what translation is all about. In this role, MT research holds out its greatest promise as a once-again scientifically respectable discipline. The first requirement, however, is the existence of research groups interested in, and funded for, the study of multiple languages and translation among them within the framework of AI research. At the present time only Japan, and to a somewhat lesser extent western Europe, can boast such groups.

8 Future Prospects

The world has changed in the two decades since ALPAC. The need and demand for technical translation has increased dramatically, and the supply of qualified human technical translators has not kept pace. (Indeed, it is debatable whether there existed a sufficient supply of qualified technical translators even in 1966, contrary to ALPAC's claims.) The classic "law of supply and demand" has not worked in this instance, for whatever reasons: the shortage is real, all over the world; nothing is yet serving to stem this worsening situation; and nothing seems capable of doing so outside of dramatic productivity increases via computer automation. In the EEC, for example, the already overwhelming load of technical translation is projected to rise sixfold within five years.

The future promises greater acceptance by translators of the role of machine aids – running the gamut from word processing systems and on-line term banks to MT systems – in technical translation. Correspondingly, M(A)T systems will experience greater success in the marketplace. As these systems continue to drive down the cost of translation, the demand and capacity for translation will grow even more than it would otherwise: many "new" needs for translation, not presently economically justifiable, will surface. If MT systems are to continue to improve so as to further reduce the burden on human translators, there will be a greater need and demand for continuing MT R&D efforts.

9 Conclusions

The translation problem will not go away, and human solutions (short of full automation) do not now, and never will, suffice. MT systems have already scored successes among the user community, and the trend can hardly fail to continue as users demand further improvements and greater speed, and MT system vendors respond. The half-million pages of text translated by machine in 1984 is but a drop in the bucket of translation demand. Of course, the need for research is great, but some current and future applications will continue to succeed on economic grounds alone – and to the user community, this is virtually the only measure of success or failure.

It is important to note that translation systems are not going to "fall out" of AI efforts which are not seriously contending with multiple languages from the start. There are two reasons for this. First, English is not a representative language. Relatively speaking, it is not even a very hard language from the standpoint of Computational

Linguistics: Japanese, Chinese, Russian, and even German, for example, seem more difficult to deal with using existing CL techniques – surely in part due to the nearly total concentration of CL workers on English, and their consequent development of tools specifically for English (and, accidentally, for English-like languages). Developing translation ability will require similar concentration by CL workers on other languages; nothing less will suffice.

Second, it would seem that translation is not by any means a simple matter of understanding the source text, then reproducing it in the target language – even though many translators (and virtually every layman) will say this is so. On the one hand, there is the serious question of whether, in for example the case of an article on front-line research in semiconductor switching theory, or particle physics, a translator really does "fully comprehend" the content of the article he is translating. One would suspect not. (Johnson [1983] makes a point of claiming that he has produced translations, judged good by informed peers, in technical areas where his expertise is deficient, and his understanding incomplete.) On the other hand, it is also true that translation schools expend considerable effort teaching techniques for low-level lexical and syntactic manipulation – a curious fact to contrast with the usual "full comprehension" claim. In any event, every qualified translator will agree that there is much more to translation than simple analysis/synthesis (an almost *prima facie* proof of the necessity for Transfer).

What this means is that the development of MT as an application of Computational Linguistics will require substantial research in its own right in addition to the work necessary in order to provide the basic multi-lingual analysis and synthesis tools. Translators must be consulted, for they are the experts in translation. None of this will happen by accident; it must result from design.

References

AAT. Hitachi develops English-to-Japanese Translating Machine. AAT Report 66, Advanced American Technology, Inc., Los Angeles, 1 October 1984(a), p. 8.

AAT. Fujitsu has 2-way Translator System. AAT Report 66, Advanced American Technology, Inc., Los Angeles, 1 October 1984(b), p. 8.

Amano, S. Machine Translation Project at Toshiba Corporation. Technical note, Toshiba Corporation, R&D Center, Information Systems Laboratory, Kawasaki, Japan, November 1982.

Bar-Hillel, Y., "Some Reflections on the Present Outlook for High-Quality Machine Translation," in W. P. Lehmann and R. Stachowitz (eds.), *Feasibility Study on Fully Automatic High Quality Translation.* Final technical report RADC-TR-71-295. Linguistics Research Center, University of Texas at Austin, December 1971.

Bennett, W. S., The Linguistic Component of METAL. Working paper LRC-82-2, Linguistics Research Center, University of Texas at Austin, July 1982.

Bostad, D. A., "Quality Control Procedures in Modification of the Air Force Russian-English MT System," in V. Lawson (ed.), *Practical Experience of Machine Translation.* North-Holland, Amsterdam, 1982, pp. 129-133.

Bruderer, H. E., "The Present State of Machine and Machine-Assisted Translation," in Commission of the European Communities, *Overcoming the Language Barrier: Proceedings of the Third European Congress on Information Systems and Networks, Luxembourg, 3-6 May 1977*, vol. 1. Verlag Dokumentation, Munich, 1977, pp. 529-556.

Gervais A. Evaluation of the TAUM-AVIATION Machine Translation Pilot System. Translation Bureau, Secretary of State, Ottawa,

Ontario, Canada, June 1980.

Hundt, M. G., "Working with the WEIDNER Machine-Aided Translation System," in V. Lawson (ed.), *Practical Experience of Machine Translation.* North-Holland, Amsterdam, 1982, pp. 45-51.

Hutchins, W. J., "Progress in Documentation: Machine Translation and Machine-Aided Translation," *Journal of Documentation* 34, 2, June 1978, pp. 119-159.

Hutchins, W. J., "The Evolution of Machine Translation Systems," in V. Lawson (ed.), *Practical Experience of Machine Translation.* North-Holland, Amsterdam, 1982, pp. 21-37.

Johnson, R. L., "Parsing - an MT Perspective," in K. S. Jones and Y. Wilks (eds.), *Automatic Natural Language Parsing.* Ellis Horwood, Ltd., Chichester, Great Britain, 1983.

Jordan, S. R., A. F. R. Brown, and F. C. Hutton, "Computerized Russian Translation at ORNL," in *Proceedings of the ASIS Annual Meeting*, San Francisco, 1976, p. 163; also in *ASIS Journal* 28, 1, 1977, pp. 26-33.

King, M., "Design Characteristics of a Machine Translation System," *Proceedings of the Seventh IJCAI*, Vancouver, B.C., Canada, Aug. 1981, vol. 1, pp. 43-46.

King, M., "EUROTRA: An Attempt to Achieve Multilingual MT," in V. Lawson (ed.), *Practical Experience of Machine Translation.* North-Holland, Amsterdam, 1982, pp. 139-147.

Lehmann, W. P., W. S. Bennett, J. Slocum, H. Smith, S. M. V. Pfluger, and S. A. Eveland. The METAL System. Final technical report RADC-TR-80-374, Linguistics Research Center, University of Texas at Austin, January 1981. NTIS report AO-97896.

Loh, S.-C., "Machine Translation: Past, Present, and Future," *ALLC Bulletin* 4, 2, March 1976, pp. 105-114.

Loh, S.-C., and L. Kong, "An Interactive On-Line Machine Translation System (Chinese into English)," in B. M. Snell (ed.), *Translating and the Computer.* North-Holland, Amsterdam, 1979, pp. 135-148.

Loh, S.-C., L. Kong, and H.-S. Hung, "Machine Translation of Chinese Mathematical Articles," *ALLC Bulletin* 6, 2, 1978, pp. 111-120.

Lytle, E. G., D. Packard, D. Gibb, A. K. Melby, and F. H. Billings, "Junction Grammar as a Base for Natural Language Processing," *AJCL* 12, 3, 1975, microfiche 26, pp. 1-77.

Maas, H.-D., "The MT system SUSY," presented at the ISSCO Tutorial on Machine Translation, Lugano, Switzerland, 2-6 April 1984.

Melby, A. K. "Multi-level Translation Aids in a Distributed System," *Proceedings of the 9th ICCL* [COLING 82], Prague, Czechoslovakia, July 1982, pp. 215-220.

Moto-oka, T., "Challenge for Knowledge Information Processing Systems (Preliminary Report on Fifth Generation Computer Systems)," in T. Moto-oka (ed.), *Fifth Generation Computer Systems [Proceedings of the International Conference on Fifth-Generation Computer Systems*, Tokyo, 19-22 October 1981]. North Holland, Amsterdam, 1982.

Muraki, K., and S. Ichiyama. An Overview of Machine Translation Project at NEC Corporation. Technical note. NEC Corporation, C & C Systems Research Laboratories, 1982.

Nagao, M., J. Tsujii, K. Mitamura, H. Hirakawa, and M. Kume, "A Machine Translation System from Japanese into English: Another Perspective of MT Systems," *Proceedings of the 8th ICCL* [COLING 80], Tokyo, 1980, pp. 414-423.

Nagao, M., *et al.* On English Generation for a Japanese-English Translation System. Technical Report on Natural Language

Processing 25. Information Processing of Japan, 1981.

Nagao, M., J. Tsujii, K. Yada, and T. Kakimoto, "An English Japanese Machine Translation System of the Titles of Scientific and Engineering Papers," *Proceedings of the 9th ICCL* [COLING 82], Prague, 5-10 July 1982, pp. 245-252.

Nishida, F., and S. Takamatsu, "Japanese-English Translation Through Internal Expressions," *Proceedings of the 9th ICCL* [COLING 82], Prague, 5-10 July 1982, pp. 271-276.

Nishida, T., and S. Doshita, "An English-Japanese Machine Translation System Based on Formal Semantics of Natural Language," *Proceedings of the 9th ICCL* [COLING 82], Prague, 5-10 July 1982, pp. 277-282.

Nishida, T., and S. Doshita. An Application of Montague Grammar to English-Japanese Machine Translation. *Proceedings of the ACL-NRL Conference on Applied Natural Language Processing*, Santa Monica, California, February 1983, pp. 156-165.

Nomura, H., and A. Shimazu. Machine Translation in Japan. Technical note. Nippon Telegraph and Telephone Public Corporation, Musashino Electrical Communication Laboratory, Tokyo, November 1982.

Nomura, H., A. Shimazu, H. Iida, Y. Katagiri, Y. Saito, S. Naito, K. Ogura, A. Yokoo, and M. Mikami. Introduction to LUTE (Language Understander, Translator & Editor). Technical note, Musashino Electrical Communication Laboratory, Research Division, Nippon Telegraph and Telephone Public Corporation, Tokyo, November 1982.

Perusse, D., "Machine Translation," *ATA Chronicle* 12, 8, 1983, pp. 6-8.

Philippi, D. L., "Machine Translation in Japan – a Survey," *Japan Intelligence* 1, 4, (April) 1985.

Pigott, I. M., "Theoretical Options and Practical Limitations of Using Semantics to Solve Problems of Natural Language Analysis and Machine Translation," in M. MacCafferty and K. Gray (eds.), *The Analysis of Meaning: Informatics 5.* Aslib, London, 1979, pp. 239-268.

Pigott, I. M., "The Importance of Feedback from Translators in the Development of High-Quality Machine Translation," in V. Lawson (ed.), *Practical Experience of Machine Translation.* North-Holland, Amsterdam, 1982, pp. 61-73.

Ruffino, J. R., "Coping with Machine Translation," in V. Lawson (ed.), *Practical Experience of Machine Translation.* North-Holland, Amsterdam, 1982, pp. 57-60.

Sawai, S., H. Fukushima, M. Sugimoto, and N. Ukai, "Knowledge Representation and Machine Translation," *Proceedings of the 9th ICCL* [COLING 82], Prague, 5-10 July 1982, pp. 351-356.

Sereda, S. P., "Practical Experience of Machine Translation," in V. Lawson (ed.), *Practical Experience of Machine Translation.* North-Holland, Amsterdam, 1982, pp. 119-123.

Shudo, K., "On Machine Translation from Japanese into English for a Technical Field," *Information Processing in Japan* 14, 1974, pp. 44-50.

Sinaiko, H. W., and G. R. Klare, "Further Experiments in Language Translation: A Second Evaluation of the Readability of Computer Translations," *ITL* 19, 1973, pp. 29-52.

Slocum, J. "A Status Report on the LRC Machine Translation System," *Proceedings of the ACL-NRL Conference on Applied Natural Language Processing*, Santa Monica, California, 1-3 February 1983, pp. 166-173.

Slocum, J., "METAL: The LRC Machine Translation System," presented at the ISSCO Tutorial on Machine Translation, Lugano, Switzerland, 2-6 April 1984.

Slocum, J., W. S. Bennett, L. Whiffin, and E. Norcross, "An Evaluation of METAL: the LRC Machine Translation System," presented at the Second Annual Conference of the European Chapter of the Association for Computational Linguistics, University of Geneva, Switzerland, 28-29 March 1985.

Thouin, B., "The METEO System," in V. Lawson (ed.), *Practical Experience of Machine Translation.* North-Holland, Amsterdam, 1982, pp. 39-44.

Tsujii, J., "The Transfer Phase in an English-Japanese Translation System," *Proceedings of the 9th ICCL* [COLING 82], Prague, 5-10 July 1982, pp. 383-390.

van Slype, G., "Évaluation du système de traduction automatique SYSTRAN anglais-français, version 1978, de la Commission des Communautés Européennes," *Babel* 25, 3, 1979, pp. 157-162.

van Slype, G., "Economic Aspects of Machine Translation," in V. Lawson (ed.), *Practical Experience of Machine Translation.* North-Holland, Amsterdam, 1982, pp. 79-93.

Vasconcellos, M., "Machine Translation at the Pan American Health Organization: A Review of Highlights and Insights," in *BCS Natural Language Translation Specialist Group Newsletter* 14, 1984, pp. 17-34.

Vasconcellos, M., "Management of the Machine Translation Environment," in V. Lawson (ed.), *Tools for the Trade.* Aslib, London, 1985, pp. 115-129.

Wheeler, P. J., "The Errant Avocado (Approaches to Ambiguity in SYSTRAN Translation)," *BCS Natural Language Translation Specialist Group Newsletter* 13, February 1983.

Wilks, Y., and LATSEC, Inc. Comparative Translation Quality Analysis. Final report on contract F-33657-77-C-0695. 1978.

ASCOF: a Modular Multilevel System for French-German Translation

Axel Biewer, Christian Féneyrol, Johannes Ritzke, Erwin Stegentritt
Universität des Saarlandes
D-6600 Saarbrücken
West Germany

Abstract

This paper is an overview of ASCOF, a modular multilevel system for French-German Translation. In ASCOF, the classical divisions of the translation process (analysis, transfer, synthesis) have been adopted. Analysis is realized by three phases: (1) morphological analysis, (2) identification of non-complex syntactic phrases and the macrostructure of the sentence, and (3) determination of the structure of complex syntactic phrases and the syntactic functions, in which syntactic and semantic criteria are used. Semantic criteria are stored in a semantic network. The syntax-oriented parts of the system interact with this semantic network during the identification of the syntactic functions. Lexical transfer operates on the standardized output tree of the analysis. Structural transfer and syntactic synthesis are achieved by transformational grammars; morphological synthesis, finally, generates the word form of the target language (German).

1 Project History and Status

ASCOF (Analysis and Synthesis of French by means of COMSKEE) is a computer system for the processing of natural language with the purpose of translating written French texts into German texts. This system has been under development since 1981 at the University of the Saarland at Saarbrücken, West Germany (Project C of SFB 100). At present (1984-1985), the research team, which has drawn upon the experience and findings of previous studies, consists of six members.

SFB 100 is a research group in which different linguistic and computer science-oriented projects cooperate. The SFB 100 was founded in 1973 and is financed by the DFG (German Research Foundation). Other projects of the SFB 100 have been developing the programming language COMSKEE and the systems SUSY and SUSY II. ASCOF is an independent system especially conceived for French and German. General descriptions of ASCOF are given in [Féneyrol, Ritzke, and Stegentritt, 1984] and [Stegentritt, 1983]. Detailed descriptions of the various problems and their solutions are discussed in [Féneyrol and Stegentritt, 1982] and in [Ritzke, 1982].

2 Application Environment

The system is programmed in COMSKEE (Computing and String Keeping Language; cf. [Mueller-von Brochowski *et al.*, 1981], [Messerschmidt, 1984]). For the computer scientist, COMSKEE is a procedural (imperative) format-free, block-oriented programming language such as ALGOL and PASCAL, yet comprising some of the qualities of functional languages (such as LISP or PROLOG).

For the linguist, COMSKEE is a powerful device especially due to its dynamic data types – dictionary, set, sentence, and string – and its dynamic operations – such as positional and contextual substring access and assignment.

The system runs on a SIEMENS 7561 under the system BS 2000. ASCOF has been conceived as a completely automatic translation system. As yet, we have been less concerned with end-user applications than with fundamental research. For this reason, we have focused primarily upon linguistic and computer science problems, rather than upon processing speed and the like.

3 General Translation Approach

3.1

In ASCOF the "classical" divisions (cf. [Vauquois, 1975]) have been adopted: analysis, transfer, and synthesis. The result of the sentence analysis is represented as a standardized tree structure, which then serves as input for transfer and synthesis of the target language.

3.2

The ASCOF analysis takes place in three steps based on different grammar and algorithm types. The morphological analysis PHASE I is carried out by an algorithm that realizes actually a mere pattern matching; in PHASE II context-free grammars identify non-complex syntactic phrases and the macrostructure of the sentence. A reduction in the homographies of word classes is simultaneously achieved for the complete sentence. PHASE III determines the syntactic functions within the sentence, using syntactic and semantic criteria, and carries out the semantic disambiguation of lexemes. This phase of analysis is performed by algorithms similar to ATN, representing an interactive system. (The term **interactive system** might be problematic in this context as this term often denotes components interacting with the user. Here we are concerned with the process communication between different components.) Consequently, the ASCOF analysis does not constitute a one-pass parser but a system of parsers (cf. Figure 1a). The strategy applied resembles that of cascaded ATNs [Woods, 1980] and was chosen for the following reason: the complexity and length of the sentences to be analyzed require – for reasons of efficiency – parsing strategies appropriate to the different problems, that is, context-free grammars for PHASE II, which works exclusively with syntactic information, and formalisms similar to ATN for PHASE III, where syntactic and semantic information is combined. A similar combination of syntax and semantics often occurs in modern parsers of various orientations, *e.g.*, in the deterministic parser put forward by Marcus [1980].

This approach not only allows a step-by-step realization of the test phases required for the development but also provides the user with alternative options for the output owing to the different depths of analysis in PHASE II and PHASE III.

3.3

Beyond the phase of analysis, ASCOF includes a phase of transfer and synthesis, where the words of the source language are exchanged for those of the target language and where simultaneously structures are altered in the tree structure if necessary. The changes of structure are carried out by a transformational grammar. The grammar operates on trees; grammar and algorithm are separate from each other and the algorithm interprets the externally stored rules of the grammar. (The documentation of the transformational component is put forward by Reding [1985]; for the discussion of transformational grammars in machine translation, cf. [Vauquois, 1975], [Boitet, Guillaume and Quézel-Ambrunaz, 1982], and [Huckert, 1979].)

On the leaves of the output tree, produced by the syntactic synthesis, a further algorithm operates, which interprets a set of morphological rules in order to generate the correct word forms of the target language. The transfer and synthesis components of ASCOF are shown in Figure 1b.

The separation of grammar and algorithms allows the application of the above-mentioned components in other languages as well, provided that the grammar is replaced.

4 Linguistic Techniques and Computational Realization

The most sophisticated phase within ASCOF concerns analysis (French); the synthesizing phase (German) has not yet been developed to such an elaborate extent.

This paper consequently concentrates on the description of the analyzing phase. Much space is devoted to segment analysis, the interaction of the complement analysis and the analysis of complex noun phrases, which is discussed in detail and illustrated by examples.

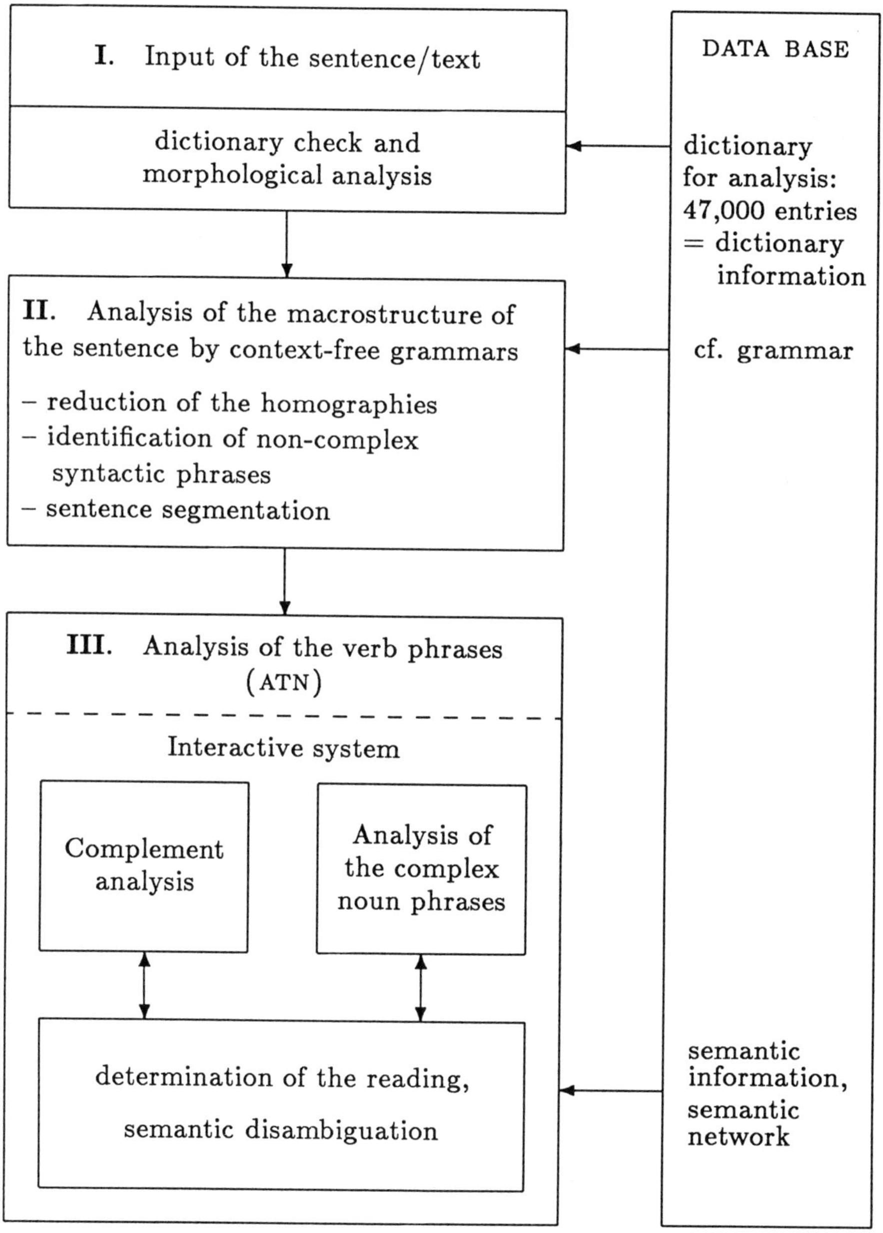

Figure 1a. Analysis components in ASCOF.

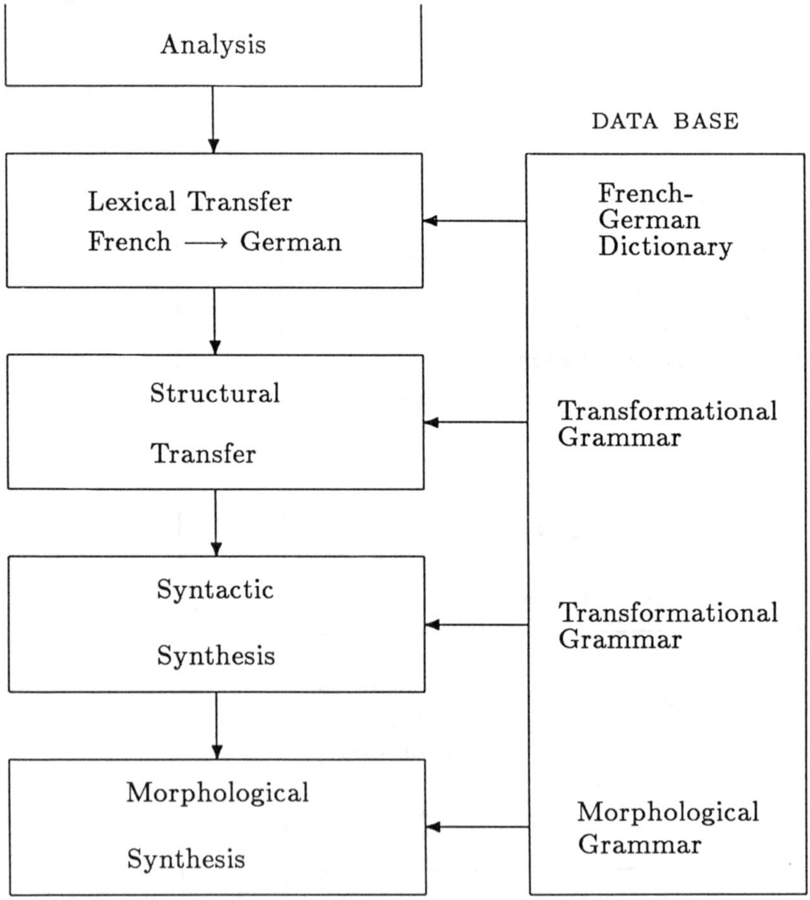

Figure 1b. Transfer and synthesis in ASCOF.

PHASE I of the analysis consists of the sentence/text input and the morphological analysis. Each word form is assigned the set of possible categories as well as the morpho-syntactic information. A full form and a stem dictionary (both approximately 47,000 entries) as well as a suffix dictionary (inflectional suffixes) are available. Unknown word forms undergo a derivational analysis (based on [Stegentritt, 1978]).

The second phase of ASCOF operates upon a chain of word classes or, given word class ambiguities, upon several word class chains, as they arise from the dictionary check and inflectional analysis. The range of functions of PHASE II comprises three sections:

a) disambiguation of the word class homographies
b) identification of non-complex syntactic groups
c) segmentation of the entire sentence into parts

These three steps are not carried out successively, in a particular sequence, but simultaneously, by applying a context-free grammar which operates upon chains of word classes; since the grammar represents a restricted syntactic (macrostructural) sentence analysis, it can be used to resolve word class homographies by the formation of simple syntactic groups and to disambiguate ambiguous syntactic groups when the overall sentence context is taken into consideration.

Here an example may help to illustrate. Let us take the sentence:

(1) Pour une détection des pathologies du larynx, l'analyse démontre l'importance des caractéristiques de la prononciation.

After PHASE I has been completed, there remains a series of word class ambiguities which lead to ambiguous syntactic groups; by means of the overall sentence analysis, the context-free grammar can be used to reject, for example, the reading "nominal group" for the groups *des caractéristiques* and *de la prononciation* in the sequence of the unambiguous nominal group *l'importance.* The same holds true for the reading "verbal group" of *l'analyse*, perfectly conceivable after a comma, which is neglected owing to the lack of an appropriate left-hand context (for example, an already available verbal group or a suitable nominal completion). As a result of the restricted grammar (owing to the functions of 'a' to 'c'), the output for sentence (1) is the chain of simple syntactic groups:

(2) pg pg pg , nog fiv nog pg pg .

For a more complex example:

(3) la directive du Conseil du 20 juillet, qui, à l'article 4, prévoit une augmentation du prix du maïs de 3%, touche les régions du sud et les pays africains qui dépendent de ce produit d'importation.

This allows us to demonstrate important operating steps in the further course of the analysis, with the aid of the above-mentioned CFG, we thus obtain a tree structure in Figure 2, which serves as input for PHASE III.

Table 1: List of Abbreviations

TXS	Text Sentence
CS	Complex Sentence
S	Sentence
PREV	Preverbal Field
VG	Verbal Group
POST	Postverbal Field
CNG	Complex Noun Group
RELC	Relative Clause
nog	Nominal Group
pg	Prepositional Group
fiv	Finite Verb Form
rel	Relative Word
coord	Coordinating Word
adjg	Adjective Group
eos	End of Sentence

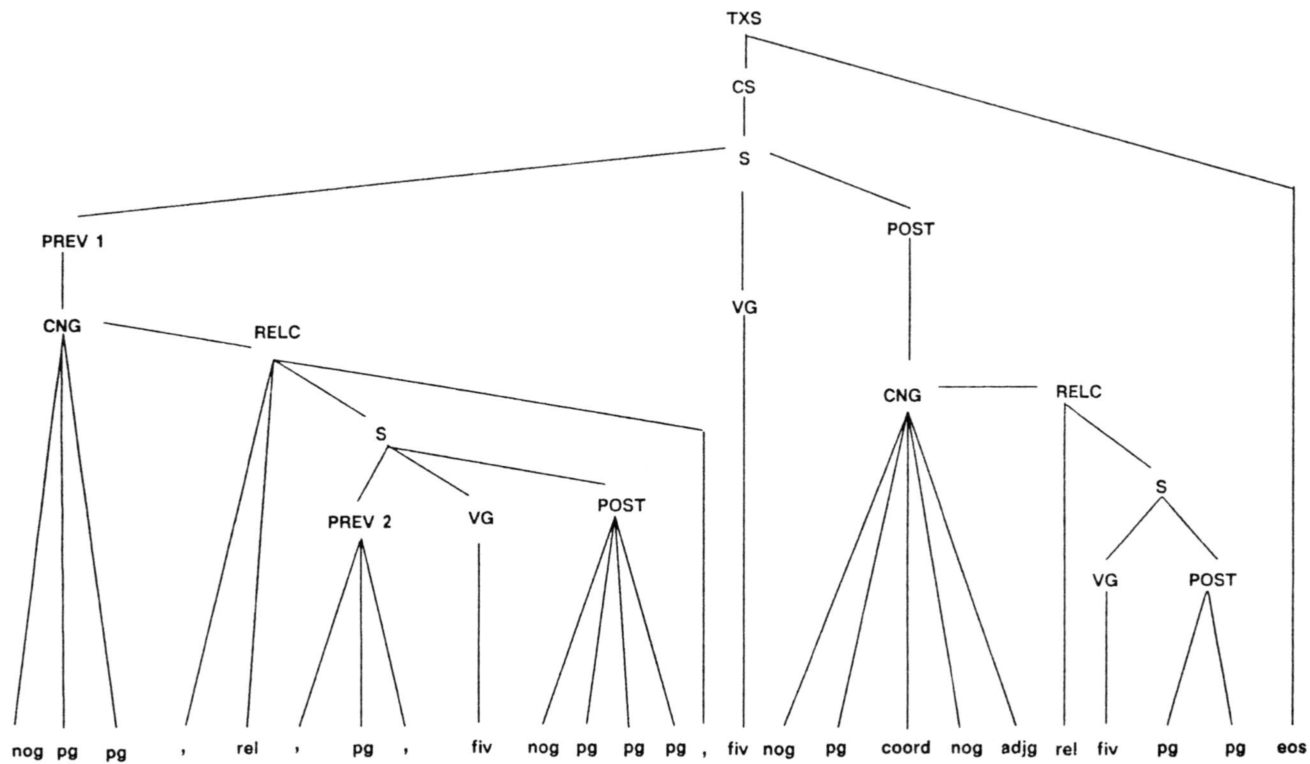

Figure 2.
Tree structure of the segmented sentence at the end of PHASE II.

It can be easily demonstrated that some other derivation attempts will not succeed; thus, for instance, if we try a coordination of main clauses through the conjunction *et*, the second presumed main clause will not be completable since a verb phrase is missing (in contrast to a sequence such as ... *et les pays africains* (relative clause) *souffriront de la famine*). Another case of an ineffectual attempt, which would initiate a coordinate sequence of subordinate clauses, would lead to a missing verb phrase belonging to the first CNG of the sentence.

Each correct result – such as the one in Figure 2 – forms the basis upon which the subsequent PHASE III of ASCOF will then operate clause by clause.

4.1

The task of analyzing verb sequences, the first step of PHASE III (cf. Figure 1a), is to group together isolated verb elements (finite verbs, participle I, participle II, infinitive) within a segment to assign a structural description to these phrases (*e.g.*, to determine VOICE and TENSE) and – ultimately – to interpret those phrases as nodes of a tree stucture.

The grammar of the verbal analysis is conceived as a two-step ATN (cf. [Biewer, 1985]).

The transitions between the different states of the ATN are guided primarily by a subclassification of verb elements (*e.g.*, participle II of *avoir*). The conception of the ATN enables the processing of an unlimited number of infinitive phrases; the integration of these infinitive phrases into the tree structure is governed by categorical information – recorded in dictionaries – as well as by tests concerning the syntactic context. Nevertheless, the interpretation of non-complex infinitive phrases as nodes of a dependency tree does not exclude ambiguities that cannot be resolved at this stage of the verbal analysis. Accordingly, it is a set of hypothetical structures gained by purely syntactic and surface-related data, that forms the output of the verbal analysis.

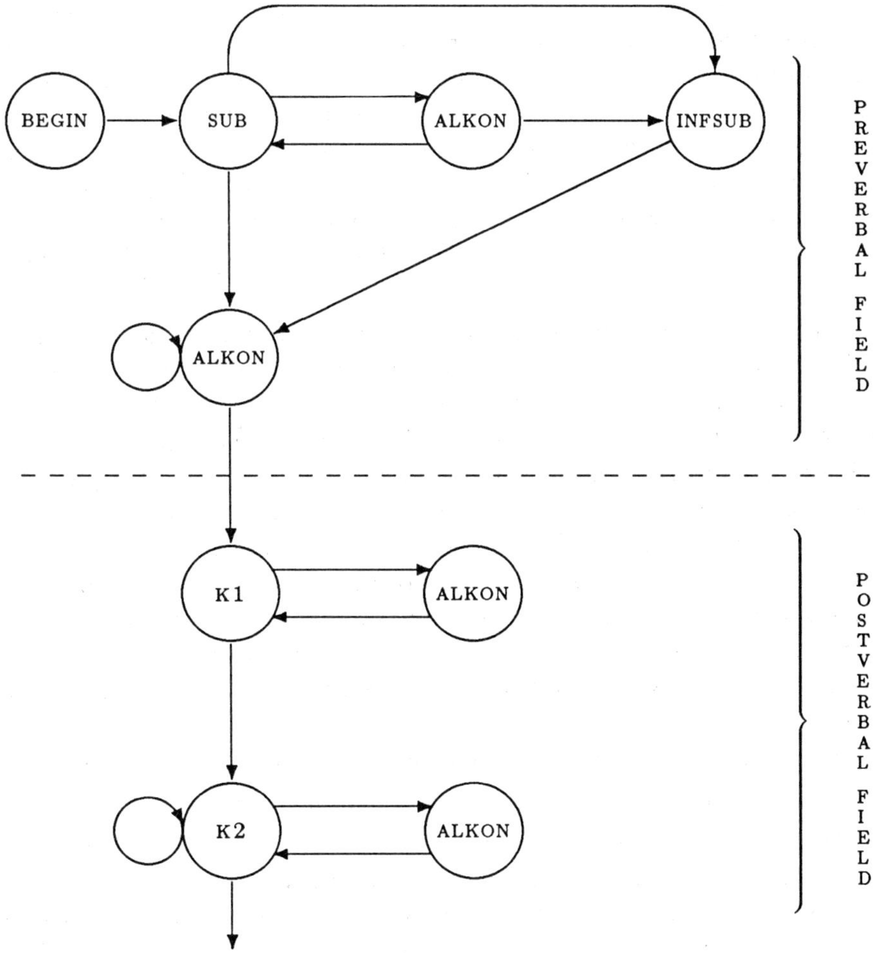

Figure 3. Interaction of different components in Phase III.

4.2

When the analysis of verb phrases is completed, the sentence is structured in such a way that parts of main and subordinate clauses and their interrelations are identified. Furthermore, non-complex syntactic (mono-nuclear) noun and prepositional phrases as well as verb sequences are determined. An interactive component operates on this input performing (1) complement analysis, (2) the analysis of complex (multinuclear) noun and prepositional phrases, and (3) the disambiguation of lexical items, all according to syntactic and semantic criteria.

In contrast to many other systems of machine translation or linguistic data processing, semantics and syntax are here equally treated, neither having priority over the other. Another characteristic feature is the interaction between each step of analysis: the complement analysis determines the head of a complement (SUB, K1, K2 in Figure 3), and the internal structure of the complement itself (hypotactic and paratactic relations) is determined by the complex nominal analysis (ALKON), the findings of which are then returned to complement analysis (cf. Figure 3). This interactive procedure is guided by the syntactic-semantic features of the dominating verb. The required syntactic features have already been calculated in the previous analysis; in contrast, the semantic information is memorized in the data base of the semantic network and must be taken from there (cf. 4.4).

ASCOF analysis offers, as output, syntactic-functional structure trees representing a synthesis of constituents and dependencies.

In the complement analysis, the dictionary entries of the verb – the verb being the central node of the sentence – determine those noun or prepositional phrases that belong to the verbal frame. The remaining phrases are parts of complex noun or prepositional phrases or of adverbials. For the preverbal and postverbal fields, complement analysis operates separately, reflecting the dissimilar structure of both fields. The component SUB, operating in the preverbal field, defines subjects of nondominated verbs as well as possibly occurring pronominal complements; dominated verbs (*e.g.*, causative constructions) are analyzed by another component, not described in this paper (INFSUB, cf. [Stegentritt, 1982, 1984]). In the postverbal field, the components K1 and K2 are activated for the complement analysis. In every case, only the first constituent of the complement is determined. Then the component ALKON (cf. 4.3) is called and investigates the structure of the identified complement.

The component determining the subject (SUB) is bipartite; in addition to the preverbal pronominal complements, the first part also defines the subject, provided that it is a pronominal subject. If there is no pronominal subject, part two defines a nominal subject. In the first part, the analysis progresses from right to left, starting at the finite verb/auxiliary. All preverbial elements are processed subsequently, until a pronominal subject is found.

Figure 4 represents the first phase of SUB as an ATN. The different paths correspond to the possible distributions of syntactic phrases in the preverbal field of the French language. If the verb is directly preceded by a comma, it is highly probable that this comma indicates the end of an insertion, such as in sentence (4). In this case, the analysis is continued up to the next comma, with no consideration of the insertion. The edges and states of the ATN that had been activated are listed in (4a).

(4) ... qui, à l'article 4, prévoit ...
(4a) 1 – COMMA –2– (not COMMA)*4 – 2 –COMMA –1

In the first phase, combinations of clitics as noted in (5-7) may be identified.

(5) il ne le lui propose pas
(5a) 1 – JUMP – 9 – LUI – 10 – PRN(acc) – 12 – JUMP – 5 – NEG – 6 – PRN-Subject – 8 – STOP

(6) il me le donne
(6a) 1 – JUMP – 9 – JUMP – 10 PRN(acc) – 11 – PRN(dat) – 12 – JUMP – 5 JUMP – 6 PRN-Subject – 8 – STOP

(7) il m'en parle
(7a) 1 – EN – 3 – JUMP – PRN(dat) – 5 – JUMP – 6 – PRN-Subject – 8 – STOP

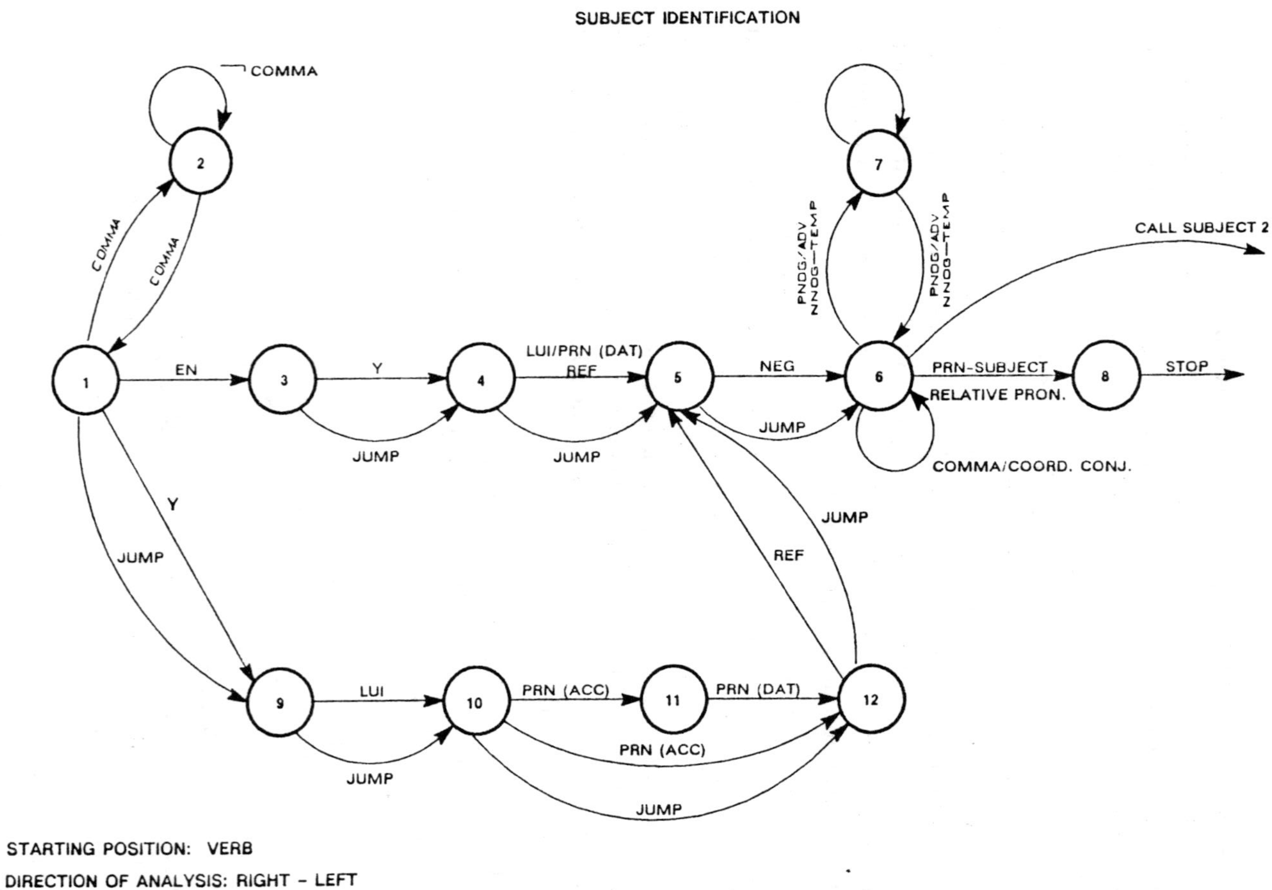

Figure 4. ATN grammar of the preverbal field.

If the network comes to the end of a clause or meets a configuration not covered by the rules, PHASE II of analysis – starting at the beginning of the clause in the reverse direction of analysis – is called to search for the first nominal phrase (*i.e.*, the leftmost). This is, however, a mere candidate for subject function, the form of a syntactic phrase (NNOG) not yet indicating the actual function of this phrase. As an illustration, compare (8).

(8) Aprés les changements de cours pour le froment,
l'avoine et la seigle, la directive (...)
touche (...)

As the set of rules in this second phase supplies the first noun phrase (NNOG, = *l'avoine* in (8)) as a subject, the phrase in question must be checked as to whether or not it is part of a coordination of prepositional phrases in which the preposition can be deleted. This subject-control mechanism presupposes that the coordinating conjunctions *et* or *ou* always indicate the end of a coordination. It follows that the subject candidate cannot be the subject if the following structure is given:

(9) CANDIDATE-COORD-NNOG-COMMA-NNOG-VERB

In this structure, however, the final preverbal NNOG (in (8), *la directive*) is the correct subject. In structure (10):

(10) CANDIDATE-COORD-NNOG-VERB

the subject candidate is confirmed. The head of the subject having been identified, phase ALKON is called to examine a possible complex internal structure of the subject and further potentially complex nominal sentence elements in the preverbal field – as, for example, the adverbial insertion *à l'article 4* in sentence (4) (cf. 4.3).

The complement analysis in the postverbal field is carried out by another pair of components (K1 and K2), also cooperating with ALKON. K1 is the less sophisticated complex, identifying nothing but direct complements – which it recognizes merely by form – and prepositional complements obligatorily demanded by the verb. Yet because of the various functions prepositional phrases may assume, prepositional complements at this stage are to be identified only if no more than one PG within the segment is a potential candidate. Applied to example sentence (3), the results are:

for *prévoir*: *une augmentation* is a direct object
for *toucher*: *les régions* is a direct object.

Again, the determination of the coordinative relationship between *régions* and *pays* is given within ALKON (cf. 4.3).

Yet, whenever the prepositional complement is optional or when more than one candidate for an obligatory prepositional complement is available, semantic criteria must be observed *in addition* to formal and syntactic criteria in order to correctly determine the complements.

The semantic restrictions that must be respected when a certain phrase is attributed the function of a complement are denoted in the verb entry in the dictionary. According to these (semantic) restrictions, the algorithm searches for the required criteria, namely among the nuclear lexemes of the potential complement phrase under consideration. The semantic information for these lexemes, however, is not stored with their dictionary entries (*e.g.*, nouns) themselves, but is represented by a semantic network (cf. 4.4).

The strategy used by ASCOF in K2 will be illustrated by the three verbs in sentence (3).

Prévoir does not demand the attribution of a further complement, the verbal frame being saturated as soon as *une augmentation* is identified as a direct complement. The verb *toucher* raises other problems; *toucher* may occur

a) without any complement: *le tireur d'élite a touché.*
b) with a direct complement: *il touche ma main.*
c) with an *à*-complement: *le chercheur touche au but.*
d) with a direct complement and an optional *de*-complement: *il m'a touché du doigt.*

As to sentence (3), the direct complement *les régions* having been located, it must still be examined whether one of the following *de*-phrases is a complement; that is, whether verbal frame (b) or (d) is valid. A *de*-phrase, however, can for instance be the complement of *toucher* if the noun of this phrase is semantically labeled as "part of the body." Consequently, the semantic value of the nuclear lexemes of the *de*-phrase following *les régions* must be examined in this respect. The results obtained through consultation of the semantic network show that the nuclear lexeme (*sud*) of this phrase does not satisfy the required condition. It follows that verbal frame (b) is actualized in this sentence. Simultaneously, this analysis defines the reading of the verb.

As to the last verb of sentence (3), *dépendre*, no direct complement can be found. Thus the reading "to be dependent on" versus the reading "to take down" is immediately determined. This reading of *dépendre* demands an obligatory *de*-valency. Yet no restrictions can be formulated for the semantic quality of the nuclear lexeme of the *de*-phrase. This implies that only formal and syntactic criteria can be considered. In the case of the first phrase, *de ce produit*, the formal and syntactic criteria hold true (a preposition introducing a phrase, an article) and thus allow this phrase to be identified as a complement and handed over as a head-phrase to the analysis of the complex noun phrases. A second run of K2 checks the following phrase, *d'importation*, which is rejected by those criteria identifying this phrase as a compound in ALKON. The criteria are: no proper noun, number = singular, no article, no attribute. One single attribution is performed accordingly.

An interesting variant of sentence (3) is:

(11) ... dépendent de l'effet de l'importation.

where both phrases may function as a complement. If the second phrase *(de l'importation)* is identified as a complement, the first post-verbal phrase can only be attributed to the function of an adverbial. In a concluding control phase for those phrases scheduled as adverbials, the structure variant of *de l'effet* as an adverbial and *de l'importation* as a complement can be erased, *effet* not being apt to assume the function of an adverbial in this phrase, in contrast to prepositional phrases, such as *de cette manière* or *de cette façon*.

4.3

The task of the analysis of complex noun phrases (multinuclear noun and prepositional phrases) is to identify their boundaries and to describe their internal structures, *i.e.*, to determine the syntactic-functional relations between the various parts of the complex. (For more details, cf. [Ritzke, 1985, 1986].)

The following syntactic-functional relations are defined for the analysis:

- head-function of the central phrase of a complex (*la maison du père*)
- paratactic relations of phrases depending on the head:
  coordination (CO): the coordinated phrase has the same syntactic function as the phrase with which it is coordinated (*l'étude de la détermination et de la classification*).
  apposition (AP): a paratactic relation on the level of syntactic analysis (*du froment tendre, plante comestible qui...*)
- hypotactic relations of phrases depending on the head:
  prepositional complement/object (PO): signals a very close relation between two phrases; the preposition of the second phrase is mostly synsemantic; the PO and the inflectional case of the two languages (French, German) frequently correspond to each other (*la voix de son maître – die Stimme seines Herrn*). (For more details concerning the function of prepositions and their analysis, cf. [Ritzke, 1981].)
  prepositional complement/part of a compound (PC): implies an even closer unity of the two phrases; PC and the governing phrase, in contrast to other structural units, represent primary units often functioning as a mono-nuclear phrase; this is of great importance to the language pair French and German, the complex phrase in French being equivalent to a German one-word compound (*e.g., la notation de base – Basisnotation*).
  prepositional attribute (PA): signals a relatively free relation to position and introductory preposition, which is always

autosemantic; for this reason, the PA may assume many different semantic values (*e.g.*, temporal or local attribute): *un groupe simple à l'intérieur du syntagme.*

Basic elements for the analysis of complex noun phrases are syntactic phrases having only one nucleus. They may occur in the form of noun phrases, prepositional phrases, or pronouns functioning as nouns.

Every mono-nuclear noun – or prepositional – phrase of these basic elements is directly relevant to the analysis of complex noun phrases as a potential element of a complex phrase. Every non-nominal phrase (*e.g.*, verb phrase) is indirectly relevant as an indicator of the boundary of the complex.

As for French, the identification of the left boundary of a complex noun phrase presents no problem since the phrase farthest left in a complex is its central phrase (its head) in the majority of cases. The head represents the syntactic function of the whole complex on the sentence level and at the same time marks the boundary of the left side. Further phrases are located on the right side of the head, the analysis being directed from left to right.

The head of a complex noun phrase is identified and determined in syntax and function by means of the analysis of verb complements. The complement analysis forms an interacting system with the analysis of nominal complexes – as explained above. The potential head of a potential complex noun phrase, identified by complement analysis, is a signal for the call of the complex nominal analysis.

The search for further phrases on the right side of the head begins at the head. Here, two phrases are checked to identify a boundary. These phrases consist of the head on the left and a dependent phrase on the right which is connected with this head. The syntactic function is simultaneously identified. Thereupon, complement analysis is called again to determine further complements or non-complements, respectively.

Non-complements (adverbials) may also have a complex internal structure. Accordingly, after the analysis of complex-structured complements, non-complements are analyzed as to their possibly complex structure. The preverbal field is investigated first. If, for example, the complex structure of a subject has been identified there, a further complex nominal analysis is undertaken for the first phrase of the sentence – provided that this phrase is identified as adverbial and that other phrases follow in the field between its position and the head of the subject. This is done in order to clarify whether this phrase is a central phrase of an adverbial complex.

A similar approach is applied for the postverbal field: first the complements, then the non-complements, are analyzed as to their possibly complex internal structures.

In principle every phrase can be related to another phrase in its direct neighborhood. This phrase again may dominate a subsequent phrase, etc., so that highly recursive structures may appear within a nominal complex (right-branching cascades).

At the same time two related phrases may be separated by other phrases when several phrases of different syntactical relations are dependent upon the same phrases. In addition to the potentially recursive structures, discontinuous relations must be detected as well.

The algorithm ALKON has been conceived especially for the solution of those recursions and discontinuities within the complex nominal syntax (cf. Figure 5).

ALKON is a procedural (sub)system similar to an ATN. Each syntactic function has its own procedure. The procedures are called successively by the main program whenever a pair of phrases – the head and the actual phrase – is examined. The identification of the relation that is – or is not – established between both phrases is governed by rules containing conditions for the head and the actual phrase. Each procedure is provided by a proper set of rules; the monitoring of the rule conditions is carried out by test operations on edges.

If the testing of a rule attains a positive result – that is, if the conditions in this rule for head and actual phrase hold true – the phrases are unified and their relation interpreted according to the procedure where the rule was found. Valid conditions in the procedure PO, for example, have the effect that the relation between the phrases is identified as a prepositional complement/object. The approach is analogous for the remaining procedures.

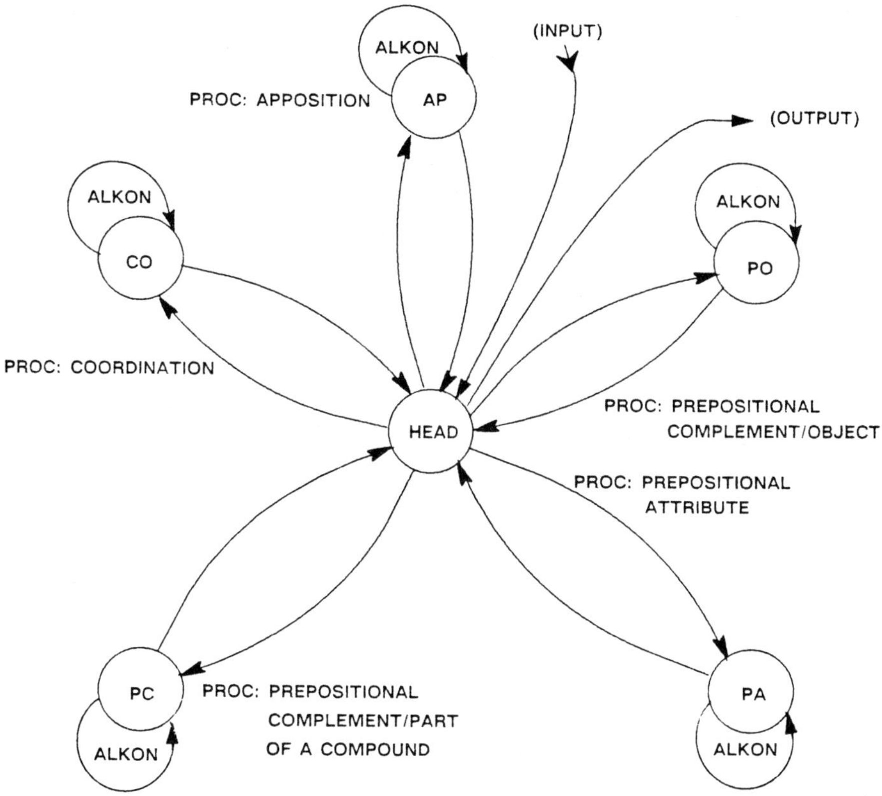

Figure 5. The subsystem NOMAL.

The actual phrase having thus been attributed a function, it becomes the head itself in the next run; the actual phrase will then be the subsequent phrase. Analogously, further positive results gradually move the actual phrase to the head of the next run; the head is deferred to the right, thus allowing the correct analysis of recursive cascades.

If none of the procedures attains a positive result, the new run is begun with another head, that is, with the phrase to the left of the head last tested. If there is still no positive result, the head keeps moving analogously to the left, until all the possibilities have been tried. The actual phrase is identical for all runs, thus allowing the analysis of relations between two discontinuous phrases.

In every case, a boundary is reached when none of the runs offers a positive result. The former actual phrase then no longer belongs to the complex but rather indicates its boundary.

The conditions denoted in the rules consist of morpho-syntactic and semantic information. Morpho-syntactic information (*e.g.*, an article, the form of an introductory preposition) can be read directly, the previous step of the analysis having made it available. In contrast, the semantic information must be deduced from the semantic network, which serves as a data base for the syntactic-functional analysis (c.f. 4.4).

The importance that evaluating rule conditions holds for the analysis will be demonstrated in the following by the complex noun phrases in example (3).

The nominal complex *les régions du sud et les pays africains*:

> Formal indicators can be checked at this point for the determination of the paratactic relation – in our example, the coordinating conjunction *et*. Commas and the sequences of comma and conjunction may be evaluated as well. Yet the mere checking of such indicators is generally not sufficient for determining the proper parts of coordination.
>
> In order to determine the correct parts, the semantics of the nouns must also be checked, that is, the closeness of the semantic relation between the candidates in question must be

checked in the example. This is accomplished by retrieving operations within the semantic network using the nominal lexemes of the different phrases. The common generic term (geographic place), which is reached by *région* and *pays*, satisfy the two conditions: coordination indicator *et* and greatest semantic closeness. They are parts of the coordination, the phrase *du sud* is recognized to be a prepositional complement/object of the first phrase by the procedure PO. The result is the following structure:

((les régions (du sud)(PO))(les pays africains)(CO))

The nominal complex *la directive du Conseil du 20 juillet*:

For hypotactic relations, too, the examination of semantic criteria is necessary over and above that of the syntactic conditions. The search for a certain preposition at the beginning of a clause – in our example, *de* as an indicator of object references – must be performed by examining the semantic closeness of the nuclei (nouns) of the phrases. In the given example, the direct time indication, which suggests an attributive relation, is thus identified. In the network, a temporal attribution is closer to the information of 'act of legislation' (connected with the lexeme *directive*) than to 'institution' (connected with the actual reading of the lexeme *Conseil*). Accordingly, valid conditions exist for the relation of prepositional complement/object between *la directive* and *du Conseil* and for the relation prepositional attribute between *la directive* and *du 20 juillet*. The last relation is discontinuous. The result of the analysis is the following structure:

((la directive(du Conseil)(PO))(du 20 juillet)(PA))

The nominal complex *une augmentation du prix du maïs de 3%*:

The last non-complex phrase, *de 3%*, of this complex phrase holds a (likewise discontinuous) relation to the first phrase,

> *une augmentation*, whereas the remaining *de*-phrases form a cascade and each depends upon its preceding phrase (the relation of prepositional complement/object).
>
> The phrase *de 3%*, an indication of quantity, is more closely related to the action, *augmentation* (action/state of affairs: increase), by the corresponding edge configuration in the network than to *prix* (notion of a measure) or to *maïs* (plant, agricultural product). Accordingly, a relation is established between *de 3%* and *une augmentation*, disregarding the interposed phrases. The result is the following structure:
>
> ((une augmentation((du prix (du maïs)(PO))(PO))(de 3%)(PA)))

The nominal complex *de ce produit d'importation*:

> In order to determine the relation between the two phrases, formal criteria may be more readily applied than in the previous cases. The second phrase is characterized by the fact that neither a determinative nor an attributive element is contained or follows. Moreover, the nominal nucleus neither is in the plural nor is it a proper name. The phrase is introduced by the preposition *de*. All the characteristics are rule conditions for an actual phrase in the procedure prepositional complement/part of a compound. These conditions being fulfilled and no other candidate being present, the relation between the phrases may be determined in this particular case without semantic examinations. The result is the bracketing:
>
> (de ce produit (d'importation)(PC))

As it is difficult in many cases, mainly in the postverbal field, to determine a function with certainty after a single run of the analysis of complex noun phrases, decisions are made only if there is no doubt (*e.g.*, if there is only one potential candidate or if candidates can be excluded because of semantic incompatibility, etc.). Otherwise a solution must be sought through repeated interaction with its complement analysis, which must then be given priority. Yet, given the basic alternative of the PP-attachment (complement, adverbial, part of a complex noun phrase), a reliable solution cannot always be found and several solutions may be admitted in such doubtful cases.

4.4

Conceding that structural descriptions within machine translation – functioning as the input for a transfer component and thus defining a sort of "interlingua" – cannot be established without semantic information, the appropriate form for representing this information as well as its integration into the analysis process appears to be controversial.

With regard to the various ways of integrating semantic information, and above all to the proper moment of its integration, there are two extremely different points of view. On the one hand, syntax may be accorded absolute priority, in such a way that all syntactic and structural descriptions of a given input sentence are generated and only then semantically interpreted and filtered according to the semantic information. On the other hand, the analyzing algorithm can be guided by semantic information, the "level" of syntactic relations only being consulted as a secondary control mechanism.

Most machine translation systems favor the first point of view, partly owing to the history of this science. Yet then, of course, the problem with highly complex sentences is how to deal with syntactic ambiguities. If, for example, an input sentence is attributed a number of tree structures by the syntax-driven analysis, some of the syntactic relations will necessarily be represented redundantly; if, on the other hand, the input sentence is attributed a chart or chart-like structural description by the syntactic analysis, much more time must be sacrificed to the semantic component – as a consequence of the more complex input structure.

Semantically driven parsers, whose equivalents can mainly be found in language-oriented AI research, guarantee a highly efficient parsing, but are extremely dependent upon their discourse area, due to their considerably limited "expectancy," and generally operate on non-complex sentences, linguistically speaking.

In order to isolate correct structural descriptions as soon as possible, cross-connections between syntax and semantics are established by the ASCOF system (cf. 4.2). This is to say that semantic information is made available for the identification of syntactic-functional relations and that, *vice versa*, syntactic and functional relations can be used for semantic interpretation (disambiguation).

The flow of information between syntax and semantics in ASCOF analysis is therefore not based on a phase model (*e.g.*, the sequential operations of separate modules). The semantic information in the ASCOF system is stored in a semantic network. (For different conceptions of semantic networks, cf., above all, [Findler, 1979].)

The implementation of the network structure is based on the COMSKEE data-structure dictionary, which is a string-indexed array (of variable length) over strings (of variable length) that can be held externally. "Of variable length" means that a string can be of any size so that its length is only limited by the memory space of the machine.

ARRAY	STRING	indentifier	[STRING]	extern
	↑		↑	↑
	the entry can also be a composed data type (a record)		the index (keyword) can take an arbitrary value of the data type string	the (optional) EXTERN-marking means that the dictionary is stored in an external mass storage

Figure 6. Declaration of the COMSKEE data-structure dictionary.

A module that interprets this structure as a network operates on the dictionary, as shown in Figure 7a. A part of the entry can be the index (keyword) of another entry. Thus it is not necessary to store explicitly the information that a person has a head; rather this information can be deduced on demand by following an ISA path, which means, in our implementation, interpreting an array element defining a word (such as A in Figure 7b) as a pointer to another word (B) labelled by ISA, as in Figure 7c.

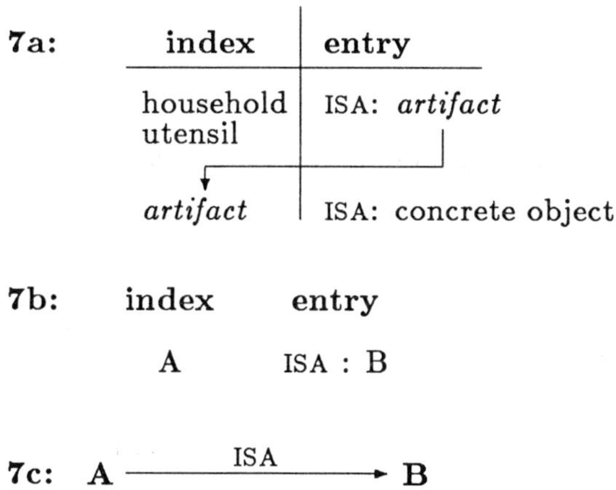

Figures 7a-c. Structures of the dictionary entry.

All directly addressable nodes in the network represent basic forms that point to semantically unambiguous readings following denoting edges. Consequently, they represent the FORM-CONTENT relation. For example, the basic lexical form *cuisinière* points in the semantic readings of "female cook" and "oven," following the denoting edges, as Figure 8 shows.

As also shown in Figure 8, several basic lexical forms may refer to the same semantic reading when following the denoting edges. The relation defined by denoting edges thus takes into account the linguistic phenomena of synonymy and polysemy.

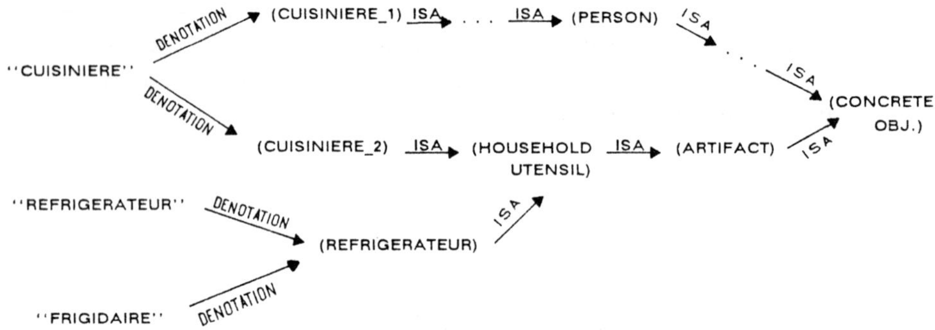

Figure 8. Example of the network structure.

Figure 9a-b. Possible phrase-structures of (12).

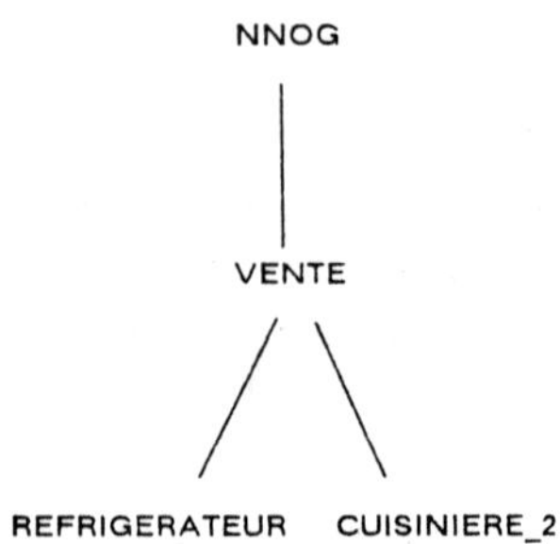

Figure 9c. Correct interpretation of (12).

ISA edges, which define a special implicit relation, are important for two reasons. First, they allow the defining of a sort of semantic distance between linguistic units, and second, they economically administer information deducible by inheritance paths.

Semantic distance in the linguistic sense may be of importance for the correct identification of coordinative structures. The complex noun phrase in

(12) La vente des réfrigérateurs et des cuisinières

may – on a purely syntactic level – be attributed two structures (*des* can be interpreted as a preposition as well as an indefinite article), cf. Figures 9a and 9b.

Based on the information as illustrated in Figure 8, it is now possible to carry out a lexical disambiguation of *cuisinière* (namely, as CUISINIÈRE/2) as well as to give structure 9a priority over structure 9b, since CUISINIÈRE/2 is semantically more closely related to RÉFRIGÉRATEUR than CUISINIÈRE/1 and, furthermore, since CUISINIÈRE/1 and CUISINIÈRE/2 are more closely related to the node RÉFRIGÉRATEUR than to VENTE. Because of the relations expressed in Figure 8, structure 9c can be assigned to sentence (12).

As made clear by this example, syntactic-functional and semantic decisions are made almost simultaneously in ASCOF. A system admitting a two-phase model for the informational flow between syntax and semantics would not only have to organize the ambiguity of structures in sentence (12) but – in order to undertake a lexical disambiguation of *cuisinière* – would also have to construct exactly those syntactic relations directly available in an interactive system like ASCOF.

For lexical disambiguation as well as the identification of syntactic-functional relations, linguistic units that may function as predicates are of major importance. These are primarily adjectives and verbs. Each "verbal node" following denoting edges refers to a set of verbal frames whose complement slots are described by syntactic and semantic conditions.

In detail, each complement slot has the following information:

- A complex of conditions that must be fulfilled by a syntactic phrase in order to function as the corresponding complement:

- syntactic conditions
- semantic conditions (to be fulfilled by the head of the phrase in question)

  e.g., for *toucher* in 4.2, the formal-syntactic condition for the prepositional object is: preposition = *de*; the semantic condition for the relevant head is: ISA part-of-the-body.
- the necessary occurrence of the argument
- the possibility of rejecting competitive verbal frames

In the following, the procedure and the efficiency of the semantic network within the syntactic-functional analysis will be explained with the aid of a representative example.

The French verb *fumer*, for instance, is assigned three frames; they correspond to the readings of "to smoke a cigarette, to give off smoke, to smoke a trout" (cf. Figure 10).

As in Figure 10, a network relation between entity nodes and predicate nodes is established according to semantic conditions defining the restrictions for the different complement slots. In Figure 10, this allows the interpretation of *fumer* as "to give off smoke" and the rejection of the other interpretations (cf. the action commands within verbal frames). This is to say that once *cheminée* is identified as a subject, there is no need to look for a direct object. Furthermore, Figure 10 demonstrates that "semantic markers" alone do *not* guarantee correct semantic interpretations. It is by no means sufficient to know that *poisson* is a concrete object in order to interpret *fumer* in

(13) La cuisinière fume du poisson

in the sense of "to smoke-dry," because the selection of FUMER/3 "to smoke-dry" *vs.* FUMER/2 "to smoke" – as in (14) – is not decidable by the semantic marker /concrete/.

(14) La cuisinière fume une cigarette

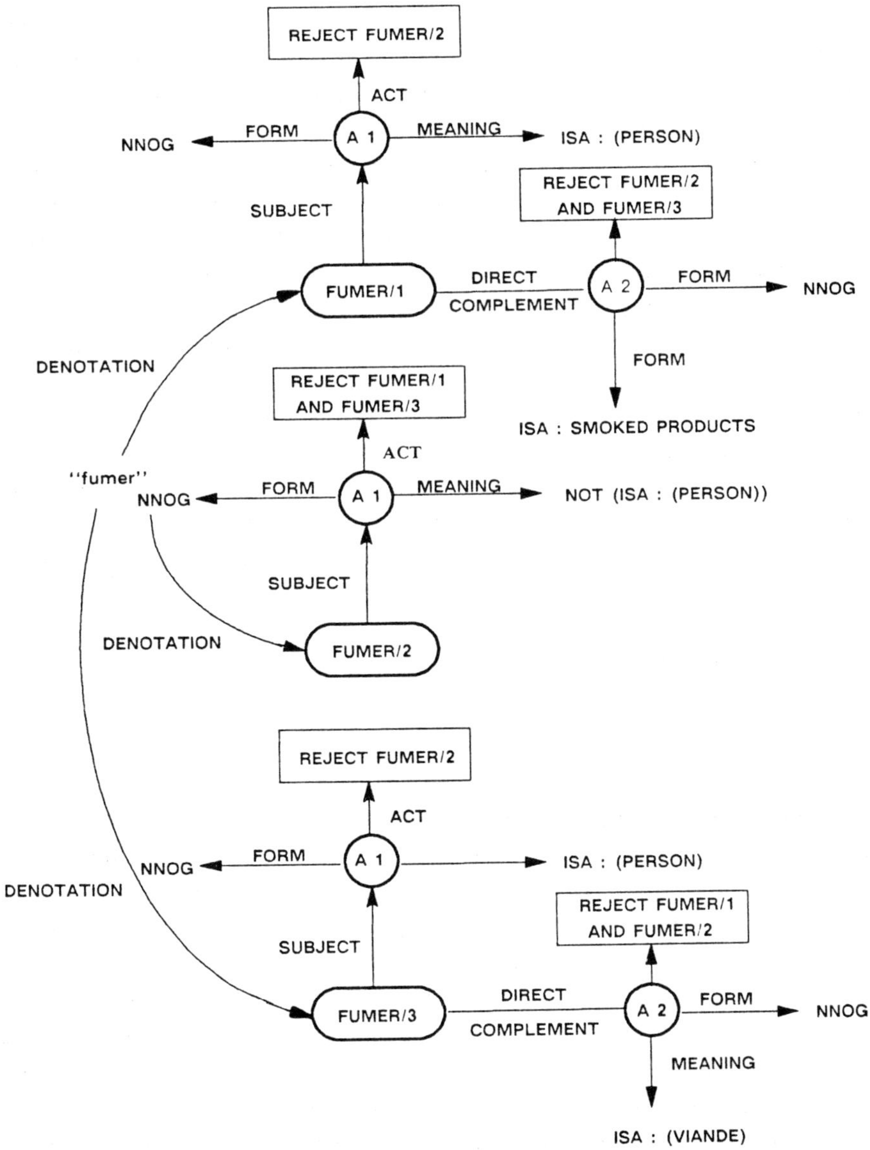

Figure 10. Verbal frame of the verb *fumer*.

In a componential model, every animal would have to be marked /can be smoked (dried)/, whereas in the network model this information may be deduced by following a FUNCTION arc from "animal" to "viande." Moreover, with the complement identification, semantic conditions attributed to the different complement slots may be considered for lexical disambiguation. For example, the reading "oven" for the noun *cuisinière* in (13) and (14) can be rejected on grounds of the semantic conditions attributed to the subject slots.

At the end of this part of the analysis, the syntactic-functional structure of the sentence is produced (*i.e.*, main and sub-/co-ordinate clauses, the verb predicate and its complements, adverbials, as well as the internal structure of noun and prepositional phrases are identified). The analysis yields no interlingual structures but rather structures more closely related to the source language. These are represented by canonical trees. At the same time, due to the interaction between syntax and semantics, many of the lexical ambiguities are resolved. Before starting ASCOF's final two phases of transfer and synthesis, any remaining ambiguities must be cleared up, largely by means of further semantic information.

4.5

The phases of the system subsequent to analysis include a transformation component (transfer and syntactic synthesis) and a morphological synthesis. In the transfer phase, the source language lemmata are first replaced by their target language equivalents. Here it is not sufficient to merely exchange lexemes since target language differences of a lexical nature arising from syntax and/or semantics need to be borne in mind. Instead, the replacement process must take into consideration the information contained in the analysis tree, for example, the syntactic and semantic verb frame actualization. Subsequent to the lexical transfer, the analysis structures are transferred to the structures appropriate to the target language (syntactic synthesis). This transfer component is implemented as a **tree transformation algorithm** that interprets externally stored rules (transformation instructions). Linguistic data and algorithm are thus strictly separated from one another so that the software may also be used for other language pairs. The transformation algorithm runs through the analysis tree in preorder, tests for each node whether a package of rules exists for the given node label and – provided that the conditions of a rule are fulfilled – carries out the instructions that refer to some few elementary operations. The conditions and the transformation instructions can refer to both subtrees and the attribute-value pairs associated with the node (for example, the inheritance of the gender of the target language head of a NOG by the attribute and determiner complex).

The input for morphological synthesis is the labelled tree taken from the syntactic synthesis. In contrast to syntactic synthesis, morphological synthesis operates only locally, in other words, the preterminal nodes are examined and processed in isolation from each other. Tree transformations are thus no longer carried out. The basic forms of the lexemes and the morpho-syntactic information from the preterminal nodes serve as keys that call the appropriate rule of the morphological generative grammar. Grammar and algorithm are separate. The grammar for the morphological synthesis of German is able to generate German word forms, provided that the necessary information supplied from all of the preceding phases is complete and accurate.

5 Future Prospects

The ASCOF system has been implemented in the sections described in the present paper and has in part already been tested. Here we have a version that covers syntactic structures and vocabulary based on texts (EC bulletins) taken from the agricultural sphere. The vocabulary of this sphere is completely covered on the morpho-syntactic level. As yet, owing to the complexity of the semantics, the semantic data base (semantic network) has been developed only as a prototype. The improvement of the quality of the translations performed by ASCOF is basically dependent upon the development and elaboration of the semantic networks.

References

Bates, Madeleine (1978), The Theory and Practice of Augmented Transition Network Grammars, in Bolc, Leonard (ed.), *Natural Language Communication with Computers*, Springer, Berlin, Heidelberg, New York, W. Germany/USA, 191-259.

Biewer, Axel (1985), Ein ATN zur Verbalgruppenanalyse des Französischen, in Figge, Udo L., 1985, 13-26.

Boitet, Christian, Guillaume, P., and Quézel-Ambrunaz, Maurice (1982), Implementation and Conversational Environment of ARIANE 78-4. An Integrated System for Automated Translation and Human Revision, in Fix *et al.*, 1985, 225-236.

Féneyrol, Christian (1982), La forme en (-ant): un problème de l'analyse automatique du français, in Fix *et al.*, 1985, 237-262.

Féneyrol, Christian (1983), La segmentation automatique de la phrase dans le cadre de l'analyse du français, in *Actes du Colloque International Informatique et Sciences Humaines, 1981, LASLA, Université de Liège*, Liège, Belgium, 353-368.

Féneyrol, Christian, Ritzke, Johannes, and Stegentritt, Erwin (1984), Esquisse d'une analyse fonctionnelle du français (ASCOF), in *Actes de la XIe Conférence Internationale de l'ALLC*, Louvain-la-Neuve, Champion/Slatkine, Paris/Genève, 53-72.

Féneyrol, Christian, and Stegentritt, Erwin (1982), Komplementanalyse in komplexen Sätzen des Französischen, in Stegentritt, Erwin (ed.), *Maschinelle Sprachverarbeitung 1981, Vorträge auf der 12. Jahrestagung der GAL, Mainz 1981. Sektion Maschinelle Sprachverarbeitung. Sprachwissenschaft - Computerlinguistik 8*, AQ, Dudweiler, W. Germany, 55-68.

Figge, Udo L., ed. (1985), *Romanistik und Datenverarbeitung 1983. Akten des Deutschen Romanistentages, Berlin 1983. Sektion Romanistik und Datenverarbeitung. Sprachwissenschaft -*

Computerlinguistik 11, AQ, Dudweiler, W. Germany.

Findler, Nicholas (1979), *Associative Networks, Representation and Use of Knowledge by Computers.* Academic Press, New York, San Francisco, London.

Fix, Hans, Rothkegel, Annely, and Stegentritt, Erwin (eds.) (1985), *Sprachen und Computer, Festschrift zum 75. Geburtstag von Hans Eggers. Sprachwissenschaft - Computerlinguistik* 9, AQ, Dudweiler, W. Germany.

Huckert, Edgar (1979), *Automatische Synthese des Französischen aus einer logischen Basis. Sprachwissenschaft - Computerlinguistik* 2, AQ, Dudweiler, W. Germany.

Marcus, Mitchell P. (1980), *A Theory of Syntactic Recognition for Natural Language.* MIT Press, Cambridge, USA/London, England.

Messerschmidt, Jan (1984), *Linguistische Datenverarbeitung mit COMSKEE.* Teubner, Stuttgart, W. Germany.

Mueller-von Brochowski *et al.* (1981), *The Programming Language COMSKEE, 2nd Revised Report. Linguistische Arbeiten, Neue Folge* 4, SFB 100, Saarbrücken, W. Germany.

Reding, Helene (1985), *Transformationskomponente für Baumstrukturen. Linguistische Arbeiten, Neue Folge* 11, SFB 100, Saarbrücken, W. Germany.

Ritzke, Johannes (1981), Problèmes de l'analyse automatique des prépositions du français, in Schwarze, Christoph (ed.), *Analyse des prépositions. IIIe Colloque franco-allemand de linguistique théorique du 2 au 4 février 1981 à Constance.* Niemeyer, Tübingen, W. Germany, 139-157.

Ritzke, Johannes (1982), Zur automatischen Analyse adverbialer Relationen, in Fix *et al.*, 1985, 287-307.

Ritzke, Johannes (1985), Automatische Analyse des Französischen: Komplexe Nominalstrukturen, in Figge, Udo L., 1985, 37-54.

Ritzke, Johannes (1986), Die französische Präpositionalphrase und ihre automatische analyse. *Sprachwissenschaft-Computerlinguistik 13*, AQ, Dudweiler, W. Germany.

Stegentritt, Erwin (1978), *MORPHO II B. Automatische derivationelle Analyse des Französischen. Sprachwissenschaft - Computerlinguistik 1*, AQ, Dudweiler, W. Germany.

Stegentritt, Erwin (1982), LAISSER + Infinitiv – Konstruktionen in der automatischen Analyse des Französischen, in Fix *et al.*, 1985, 309-327.

Stegentritt, Erwin (1983), Aperçu d'une analyse automatique du français, in Cignoni, Laura and Peters, Carol (eds.), *Linguistica Computazionale, Vol. III. Supplement Actes due VIIe Congrès de l'ALLC, Pisa, 1982*, 243-250.

Stegentritt, Erwin (1984), Automatische Subjektidentifizierung in französischen Infinitivsätzen des Typs FAIRE + Infinitiv, in Figge, Udo L. (ed.), *Romanistik und Datenverarbeitung 1981. Akten der 10. Sektion des Deutschen Romanistentages, Regensburg 1981. Sprachwissenschaft - Computerlinguistik 7.* AQ, Dudweiler, W. Germany, 22-38.

Vauquois, Bernard (1975), *La traduction automatique à Grenoble.* Dunod, Paris, France.

Woods, William A. (1980), Cascaded ATN Grammars, *AJCL* 6, 1, 1-12.

Automated Translation at Grenoble University

Bernard Vauquois and Christian Boitet
Groupe d'Études pour la Traduction Automatique
Boite Postale 68
Université de Grenoble
38402 Saint-Martin-d'Hères, France

1 Project History

1.1 Dates and Funding Sources

Founded in 1972, GETA is one of the laboratories of the Computer Science Department at Grenoble University. From its inception it was supported by CNRS, the French National Center for Research, by means of association contracts renewed every four years, and by the University, having the status of "University Research Team associated with CNRS." Also, several projects have been partially supported by contracts from the Ministries of Defense, Telecommunications, and Industry.

Before that, in 1961, CNRS had created CETA (Centre d'Études pour la Traduction Automatique) as a "laboratoire propre," that is, a laboratory supported by CNRS funds and various contracts but not by the University.

From 1961 to 1971, CETA elaborated some basic software tools for MT, and experimented with it mainly on translation from Russian to French. Some investigations were also carried out into the analysis of German and Japanese. In 1971, a corpus including about 400,000 running words had been translated from Russian into French, after several years of development of the various grammars and dictionaries (the "lingware," so to speak).

The system was typically second generation: finite-state morphological analysis, augmented context-free syntactic analysis, direct mapping into a dependency analysis, procedural semantic analysis (using a specialized low-level programming language to transform tree structures) into an interlingua (the famous *langage pivot*, or "pivot language"), lexical transfer, syntactic generation (using the same low-level tree-transformation language), and morphological generation (beginning with a recursive top-down procedure applied to the tree to get the correct order of the leaves to be transformed into words).

Since 1972, another approach has been followed that relies more on the use of SLLPs (Specialized Languages for Linguistic Programming), that is, on procedural techniques like controlled production systems and heuristic programming. Also, a main goal has been to design the basic software and the various lingwares with a view to multilingual translation.

A completely integrated programming environment (ARIANE-78) has been developed and used to build a variety of linguistic models, in order to test the general multilingual design and the various facilities for lingware preparation, debugging, and actual use, as well as for human pre- and post-editing.

1.2 Languages Translated: Project and System Sizes

The first three subsections below describe the kinds of experiments performed at GETA.

1.2.1 Writing of Very Reduced Scale Models

The writing of very reduced scale models is mainly oriented to training researchers in the methodology of MT and the use of the various SLLPs available under ARIANE-78.

As an example, Feng Zhi Wei (ISTIC, Beijing) has written a small multilingual translation system from Chinese into Japanese, French, English, German, and Russian, that (of course) uses the same analysis modules for all language pairs.

A transfer from English (using a bigger model of English analysis) to Chinese and a generation of Chinese has been produced by

Yang Ping (ISTIC). In a similar way, using the same analysis of English, Professor Jun-Ichi Tsujii (of Kyoto University) conducted an experiment into English-Japanese translation.

1.2.2 Construction of Small Scale Models

The construction of small scale models – that is, with small dictionaries but medium size grammars – has been done for feasibility studies and training.

A French-English system was constructed by J. Ph. Guilbaud and M. Dymetman in the framework of a feasibility study for the Ministry of Telecommunications during 1981. This system has recently been reused to implement a rough "self grading" technique to be used in connection with a translator work station (A. Melby, BYU).

Another example is the development of a German-French system, using the same generation as the Russian-French system (see below). This work was started around 1979, with J. Ph. Guilbaud of GETA in charge of morphological analysis and transfer, and Professor Stahl (Paris) in charge of structural analysis.

In cooperation with IFCI (Institut de Formation et de Conseil en Informatique, Grenoble), another system, BEX-FEX, has been developed for teaching purposes (B. Roudaud, S. Chappuy, and E. Guilbaud). The analysis is a simplified version of the IN1 analysis (see below), and the dictionaries are purposely very small (500 lexical units for each language).

In order to give an idea of the complexity of such a system, rather than measure the number of grammatical rules, because they can be very simple or very complex, we measured the number of source lines of the grammars written in the SLLPs ATEF, ROBRA or SYGMOR. BEX-FEX contains

420	lines for the morphological	analysis
2500	lines for the structural	analysis
300	lines for the structural	transfer
1000	lines for the syntactic	generation
100	lines for the morphological	generation

Also in connection with IFCI, a feasibility study for an English-Arabic system was started in 1984 and has led to a working prototype (W. Moneimne).

1.2.3 Building of Large Scale Systems

Large scale systems have been built at the level of laboratory prototypes.

The largest system with regard to the vocabulary, and the most experimented with, is the Russian-French system RUB-FRB. According to an estimate made in June 1984, the dictionaries contained 7000 Russian lexical units (about 17000 words) and 5600 French lexical units (about 16000 words).

By "word," we mean here **lemma**, that is, a normal form of occurrence, usually used to identify an item in a "natural" dictionary. The various grammars contained

1350	lines for the morphological	analysis
3100	lines for the structural	analysis
380	lines for the structural	transfer
930	lines for the syntactic	generation
120	lines for the morphological	generation

Since 1983 this system has been used to test an experimental "translation unit" using a production-oriented subset of ARIANE-78, PROTRA. Photocopies of technical abstracts from the *Referativnyij Zhurnal* are regularly received by the unit, manually inputted, checked for typing errors (by using the morphological analyzer), machine translated, manually revised (using a multiwindow editor), and sent back. The revision effort includes a search for the source of errors encountered.

As it is, and taking into account that manual input represents the major bottleneck, around 50 to 60 abstracts per month (5000 to 7500 running words) were processed in 1983. Fields covered include space sciences and metallurgy. A direct use by end-users is planned in 1986.

Next comes the English-Malay system (IN1-BM1). In 1979, a co-operative project with USM (Universiti Sains Malaysia, Penang) was launched. The aim of this project is to produce an English-Malay system for the translation of teaching material in technical fields. The level of laboratory prototype was attained by the end of 1984. In 1984-85, the domain was changed to computer science. A working system is planned by 1988.

The analysis part has been jointly developed by GETA and USM. It is the same that was mentioned earlier: having initially been started for this project, it has been reused for experiments of translation into other languages. As far as size is concerned, the dictionaries contained (in 1984) 1800 English lexical units (about 3000 words) and 1800 Malay lexical units (about 2700 words). The various grammars contained

420	lines for the morphological	analysis
5000	lines for the structural	analysis
600	lines for the structural	transfer
1500	lines for the syntactic	generation
670	lines for the morphological	generation

More recently, a similar project was started with several Universities of Thailand (Chulalongkorn and Rakhamhaeng in Bangkok, Prince of Songkla in Had-Yai) for translation into Thai.

Last but not least, ARIANE-78 and the related linguistic techniques have been selected as the basis for an industrial development, in the framework of the French National Project. After a preparation phase in 1982-83 (ESOPE project), this project was formally launched in late 1983, with a group of private companies around SG2 as industrial partners.

1.2.4 Project Size

As far as the number of people "engaged in the project" is concerned, no easy answer may be given, because of the multiplicity of the experiments. GETA itself has a core of about ten people engaged in software or lingware, plus a varying number of students not working directly on MT, and some visitors. The core includes two professors and eight research engineers and linguists (supported by the CNRS), four of them constituting the Russian-French team.

For the National Project, about nine or ten people from GETA or IFCI are working part or full time, while about the same number, coming from the industrial partners, are working full time (as of mid-1984).

2 Application Environment

2.1 Pre-/Post-Editing

Pre-editing is optional. In our terminology, pre-editing means that some conventional marks are inserted in the input text, which is not otherwise modified by replacing words with "synonyms" or by rewriting parts to change the syntactical structure. When pre-editing is used, the inserted marks refer to some lexical ambiguity (for example, ambiguity between noun and verb), or indicate the scope of a coordination, the antecedent of a relative pronoun, etc.

The structural analysis grammars are then organized in such a way that these marks, if any, are used first by the disambiguation modules. Until now, this technique has only been employed in the analysis of Portuguese (POR), by P. Daun-Fraga.

Post-editing is necessary in all cases where high quality of output must be attained, as opposed to situations where information gathering is the main purpose. ARIANE-78 contains a subenvironment for post-editing (REVISION), under which the reviser may simply use the multiwindow editor, or call the THAM subsystem, under which special tools are offered for manipulating and accessing a terminology file.

2.2 Human Interaction

During translation, there is normally no human interaction, with the possible exception of morphological analysis, where the operator may correct spelling errors, or insert items in dynamic dictionaries. We don't normally operate this way.

Of course, for debugging purposes, the system may operate in a step-by-step way.

2.3 Integration of the System

ARIANE-78 is a complete integrated environment for linguistic programming, debugging and actual operation.

3 General Translation Approach

The method followed in all current systems written in ARIANE-78 is based on a combination of transfer and interlingua techniques. The process of translation is divided into three phases: analysis, transfer, and generation. The word "synthesis" might be more appropriate, but "generation," as in "code generation," for compilers, is used.

3.1 Analysis

This phase is performed by a sequence of two separate sub-phases: morphological analysis and structural analysis.

3.1.1 Morphological Analysis

The input is the source text, in ARIANE-78's internal transcription, with optional pre-editing marks, SCRIPT formatting commands, and special occurrences to stand for the *hors-texte* (figures, charts, equations, and other untranslatable material).

The output is a "decorated" (annotated) AND/OR tree structure. The root identifies the text, and its decoration contains ULTXT as value of the UL (lexical unit) "variable" (property, in other terminologies).

The nodes directly under the root correspond to the sentences, and contain the lexical unit ULFRA (FRA for *phrase* – "sentence").

The nodes at level 2, under the sentence nodes, correspond to the occurrences (running words), and contain the lexical unit ULOCC.

Nodes at level 3 correspond to the result(s) of the morphological analysis. If a given result is "simple," the node contains the corresponding lexical unit, and all grammatical properties, as computed by the grammar. If, on the other hand, a result corresponds to the analysis of the occurrence as a compound word, the node at level 3 contains the lexical unit ULMCP, and dominates a sequence of nodes containing the result of the morphological analysis of the elements of the compound.

The information contained in a solution node (always a leaf) is of the following types:

- the lexical reference, or **lexical unit** – a string;
- grammatical information computed by the grammar from the information on the segments (affixes, root), coming from the dictionaries, such as derivation status, negation status, syntactic category and subcategory, number, tense, person, etc.;
- the syntactic properties of the lexical unit (*e.g.*, the syntactic valencies of a verb or an adjective), which come from the dictionaries;
- the semantic properties of the lexical unit (semantic features and valencies), which also come from the dictionaries.

3.1.2 Structural Analysis

The goal of the structural analysis phase is to reach a level of interpretation that is far enough removed from the morphological and syntactic peculiarities of expression in the considered natural language to represent in the same way various expressions having the same "meaning." Furthermore, the interface structure (the result of the structural analysis) keeps a trace of various more "superficial" levels.

To be more concrete, the interface structure of a text is again a decorated tree structure, with the ULTXT and ULFRA nodes at levels 0 and 1. In a subtree corresponding to a sentence,

- the geometry of the tree structure represents only a bracketing of the sentence in terms of syntagmatic classes (non-terminal categories) such as **verbal clause, noun phrase, adjectival phrase,** etc.
- the relations between words or groups of words are expressed by linguistic attributes (called variables in ARIANE-78's terminology), such as syntactic function (SF), logical relation (RL), or semantic relation (RS).

The syntactic functions may be "subject of a verb," "attribute of the subject," "attribute of the object," "modifier of a clause," etc. The logical relation variable expresses the relations between a predicate (predicative lexical unit such as a verb or certain type of adjective) and its arguments. For example, in the following utterances, the lexical units COMPOUND and CARBON are, respectively, argument 0 and 1 of the predicative lexical unit INCLUDE.

The COMPOUND INCLUDES CARBON...
CARBON is INCLUDED in the COMPOUND
The INCLUSION of CARBON in the COMPOUND

Arguments of predicates are sometimes elsewhere called **inner cases.** When a word or a group of words is related to a predicative unit, without being one of its arguments, we express this relation by some value of the semantic relation property. This is the situation for circumstantial complements (sometimes known as **outer cases**). Possible values of RS include cause, condition, consequence, manner, quantification, etc.

Many other properties are contained in the nodes of the structure. Some are only "traces," that is, surface variables such as number or gender. Others are of higher level, for example the determination or actualization properties.

As the units of translation are not restricted to be sentences, but may well include several sentences or paragraphs, it is possible to use the available context to solve anaphora, in case no suitable candidate is found in the sentence. The solution is expressed by copying some of the information relative to the referred element onto the node representing the anaphoric element. This node has the "reference" property set to the adequate value, as well as the "representative" syntactic category.

3.2 Transfer

Transfer is also performed in two sequential subphases: lexical transfer and structural transfer.

3.2.1 Lexical Transfer

During this step, target language lexical units are substituted for the source language lexical units. Several cases must be considered.

- simple-to-simple substitution
- simple-to-complex substitution (a single source unit is translated by several target units, *e.g.*, *avec* → *by means of*)
- complex-to-simple or complex-to-complex substitution (*e.g.*, *computer science* → *informatique*, *let ... know* → *informer*).

Moreover, the selection of an appropriate substitution for a given lexical unit may be conditional. The condition may be local, that is, it bears on the properties of the node under consideration (and perhaps some immediate neighbors), or global, in which case a wider context must be examined.

Let us give two examples:

- syntactic valency: the English verb *look* has at least four values for the **object valency** (for argument 1), namely, *at, for, like, after*. According to the syntactic structure that has been built, only one possibility remains after analysis (on the node containing *look*). We may then express the conditional substitution by an item in a TRANSF dictionary of the following (simplified) form:

LOOK	: if	VAL1=AT	then	'REGARDER'
	elseif	VAL1=FOR	then	'CHERCHER'
	elseif	VAL1=LIKE	then	'RESSEMBLER'
	else			'S/OCCUPER'

- presence or absence of an argument: the usual translation of *give* is *donner* in French; however, if there is no first argument explicit in the sentence (*e.g.*, *John was given a book*), the translation of *give* may be *recevoir*, with the indication that the third argument of *give* becomes the first argument of *recevoir* (*e.g.*, *Jean a reçu un livre*).

Basically, the TRANSF SLLP provides the means to write bilingual multi-choice dictionaries. Each node of the input tree is replaced by a subtree in the output tree. This subtree may be selected from several possibilities, according to the evaluation of a predicate on the attributes of the input node and its immediate neighbors.

In simple cases, the selected subtree is reduced to one node. In more complex cases, the selected subtree may:

- give several possible equivalents, for further testing in subsequent phases, or production of a multiple equivalent in the final translation (*e.g.*, *process* → *processus* or *procédé* from English into French).

- express the prediction that the considered element may be part of a complex expression in the source language (*e.g.*, *let ... know*). In this case, the subtree will contain nodes describing the type of complex predicted, the other elements of the complex, and the translation of the complex (which may again be simple or complex). It will then be one of the tasks of the structural transfer to confirm or refute this prediction, by using the whole available context, and to take appropriate action; use the translation of the complex if "yes," leave the simple translation if "no."

This organization has been consciously designed in order to limit the cost of indexing in dictionaries: the lexicographers don't have to write complex tree-transformation rules. Instead, they write (static) subtrees of well-defined (sort of AND/OR) forms, in which some of the information is later used as an indirect call to transformational procedures written by specialized computational linguists in the structural transfer grammar.

3.2.2 Structural Transfer

We have already begun to explain the role of structural transfer.

- It must finish a part of the lexical transfer, by using the appropriate context to choose between several remaining equivalents (*e.g.*, on the basis of the semantic features of other elements in the clause), and to handle the translation of complex expressions as explained above.

- If there is no satisfactory universal representation of some phenomenon, the corresponding attributes of the target language are computed in a contrastive way . This is now the case for aspect, tense, and modality of verbs, as well as for determination of noun phrases.

- Finally, it may be necessary to perform true structural transfer operations, although this seldom occurs. In practice, we use this as a "safety net," in cases where the higher levels of interpretation have not been computed by the analysis on some part of the text, so that a mapping between low-level structures is better than nothing.

3.3 Generation

Generation too is composed of two phases: syntactic followed by morphological generation.

3.3.1 Syntactic Generation

Normally, the purpose of syntactic generation is to compute a surface syntactic structure from the interface structures. Starting with the semantic and logical relations, the syntactic functions have to be determined first, and then the syntagmatic classes are computed, in a top-down recursive manner.

The choice between various syntactic structures may be guided by the values of the low-level attributes, as transferred or transformed by the transfer phase. For instance, we may give priority to a passive construction over an active construction, if the (target) interface structure contains the indication of passive. But this passive mark may well have been computed by the transfer (*e.g.*, for an impersonal construction in French preferably translated by a passive in English).

Syntactic transfer will also be used to compute the correct order of the elements in the final translation, as well as all low-level information necessary for morphological generation, such as number, person, tense, gender, etc.

3.3.2 Morphological Generation

The left-to-right sequence of the leaves of the tree resulting from syntactic generation is the input to morphological generation (written in SYGMOR).

The grammar directs the construction of the output occurrence(s) by testing the values of the attributes of the current node (and some other bounded context) and referring to dictionaries of strings, accessed by the UL or other variables, to get the various morphs to be combined (root, prefix, affixes, suffix, ...).

Also, purely morphological variations are handled by using string-transformation functions (*e.g.*, elision in French, or generation of upper/lower case codes).

4 Linguistic Techniques

Basically, every linguistic phase is constructed by successively writing two different sets of descriptions.

The first is the analog of the set of specifications for a conventional program. We call it the static description of the desired correspondence, which is usually many-to-many.

B. Vauquois and S. Chappuy have developed a formalism called SCSG (Structural Correspondence Static Grammar), or **static grammars** for short (Chappuy 1983), not unlike M. Kay's unification grammar formalism, but suitable for the kind of structures we customarily manipulate.

A static grammar describes the correspondence between the strings of a natural language and their interface structures. Such a description is neutral with respect to analysis and generation, and does not express any particular strategy for computing the correspondence.

We have yet to devise a similar formalism to describe the correspondence between interface structures of two given natural languages.

The second part of the work consists in writing and debugging the **dynamic (procedural) grammars** in the appropriate SLLPs (ATEF and ROBRA for analysis, ROBRA and SYGMOR for generation). In the most recent applications, the analysis and generation structural grammars are, in effect, (manually) generated from the static grammar of the considered language. Moreover, it is possible to construct several dynamic grammars referring to the same static grammar, in order to experiment with different strategies, trying to make the best of the various possibilities of heuristic programming available in the SLLPs.

4.1 Low Level

Morphological ambiguities are detected by the morphological analysis phase and handed over to the structural analysis phase. If the analysis is successful, these ambiguities are resolved in the process (*e.g.*, noun/verb, etc.). Some polysemic words may be handled as well, if the semantic features associated to the different meanings are distinct enough to be separated by the agreement conditions incorporated in the grammar rules.

4.2 High Level

Although the units of translation may be broader than sentences, the bulk of analysis and generation operates essentially at the sentence level. In current applications, there is no discourse analysis leading to some representation of the "hypersyntax" or "hypersemantics" of the complete unit.

Nevertheless, the possibility of using a wider context is useful in some cases. We have already mentioned anaphoric resolution in analysis. During transfer or generation, it also happens that a sentence of the source text is segmented into several shorter sentences, for stylistic reasons.

All dynamic grammars are written by using production rules (not phrase structure rules) of the various kinds available in the SLLPs. An important feature of ARIANE-78 is that all steps (from morphological analysis to morphological generation) may be ultimately considered as describing transducers, not analyzers.

5 Computational Techniques

5.1 Dictionaries

Dictionaries are written in the SLLPs, and then compiled into some internal representation that includes a fast access method. At execution time, the dictionaries reside in virtual memory.

ATEF dictionaries use a two-step hash-coding scheme, followed by an ordered-table representation (for morphs of the same length sharing the same initial or final character). Access to a given item involves less than 100 machine operations.

TRANSF dictionaries use a quasi-perfect hash-coding scheme. SYGMOR dictionary access relies on dichotomy for the lexical units and on sequential search for other variables. But, then, the latter dictionaries are always small and of bounded size anyway: they contain the prefixes, affixes, and endings.

As a matter of fact, due to the compactness of the internal coding and to the speed of the access methods, dictionaries don't raise any computational problem.

5.2 Grammars

In ATEF, the grammar describes a finite-state non-deterministic transducer. It is implicitly divided into as many subgrammars as "morphological formats" (classes). Each item in a dictionary has such a format, which contains some static grammatical information, and is also referenced in the left-hand-side (l.h.s.) of one of several rules, which will be called in a non-deterministic way.

The underlying mechanism for handling non-determinism is simple backtrack. However, heuristic functions may be called by the rules. Their effect is to "prune" the search space in several predetermined ways. For instance, one of these functions says something like: if the application of the current rule leads to some solution, then don't compute the solutions that might be obtained from segments of strictly shorter length than the current one beginning at the same character. Another heuristic function is used to simply state that, if the rule leads to a solution, this solution should be the only one; previously computed solutions are discarded, and further possibilities are not examined.

In ROBRA, there are several levels of control. First, a given transformational system (TS) has a given store of transformational rules (TR), which operate by substitution. Then there is a collection of grammars (TG), each made of an ordered subset of the TRs. The order is local to the grammar, and is interpreted as a priority order. Each TR may contain a recursive call to a (sub)TG or to a transformational subsystem (sub-TS). The top level of control corresponds to the TS (and its sub-TSs), and is described by means of a **control graph** (CG). The nodes of the CG are the TGs, and a special "exit grammar" (&NUL). Arcs bear conditions of the same type as l.h.s. of rules.

ROBRA's interpreter submits the input tree to the initial grammar of the considered (sub)TS, and uses a built-in back-tracking mechanism to find the first path leading from this initial node to the next node, thereby applying the TGs found in the nodes, and traversing the arcs only if the attached conditions are verified by the current tree. In case of success, the result is the tree that reaches &NUL. In case of failure, the output is set equal to the input.

A "simple" execution of a given TG is carried out in two steps. First, a parallel application of the TRs of the TG is performed, by selecting the maximal (according to some parameters) family of non-overlapping occurrences of rule schemas (l.h.s.) and applying the corresponding rules. Then, the recursive calls, if any, are executed by submitting the appropriate subtrees to the called sub-TG or sub-TS.

The execution of a TG in "exhaustive" mode consists in iterating simple executions of this TG until no rule is applicable any more. In "controlled" mode, a marking algorithm is used in order to strictly diminish the number of possible occurrences of rules at each iteration, ensuring termination of the process. Hence, it is possible for the compiler to statically detect possible sources of undecidability, just by checking the modes of the TGs, testing for loops in the CG, and verifying a simple condition on the form of the recursive calls.

This kind of organization makes it possible to use text-driven strategies, which will operate differently on different parts of (the tree corresponding to) the unit of translation.

The case of SYGMOR is simpler, because the underlying model is a finite-state deterministic transducer. For each new node (leaf of the input tree), the interpreter selects the first rule whose l.h.s. is verified and executes it. Then, it uses the control part of the rule, which consists of an ordered sequence of rules to be applied, some of which may be optional. Usually, SYGMOR grammars are fairly small.

5.3 Efficiency

The basic software is programmed at various levels. The compilers and interpreters of the SLLPs are written in assembler (ASM360) or PL360, the monitor and the macros for the editor (XEDIT) in EXEC/XEDIT (IBM's VM/CMS's shell language). We can say something about efficiency on two levels.

First, the efficiency of the programming itself. Applications such as Russian-French use roughly 1 to 1.5 Mipw (million instructions per word translated) of VCPU (virtual CPU), measured on a 4331, a 370, a 3081, or an Amdahl. More than 88% of this is used by RO-

BRA's pattern-matching mechanism, and less than 10% by the "dictionary phases" (morphological analysis and generation lexical transfer). Translation is performed using 2.5 Mbytes of virtual memory, without any access to secondary storage during processing itself.

Recently, we made a comparison with Kyoto University's system, whose design is similar to ARIANE-78's. In particular, the bulk of the computing time is used by GRADE, a SLLP of the ROBRA family. The system is programmed in UTILISP and runs on a FACOM computer (Fujitsu), which is IBM-compatible and very fast (20 Mips).

It turns out that this MT system executes roughly 100 times as many instructions as ARIANE-78, and takes 40 times more space. Taking into account the fact that there is only 4 Mbytes of virtual memory (divided by 2 for the purpose of garbage collection), that the garbage collector gobbles up 40% of the VCPU, and that the runtime access to the 30 to 40 Mbytes of secondary storage (holding the lingware) takes 20% more, we end up with the net result that *a LISP implementation* (of this type of system) *is 40 times more voracious in computer time and space than a low-level implementation.*

Of course, the amount of programming and maintenance effort is higher for the latter type of implementation. At this point, it is worth remembering that in France, contrary to many countries, research labs usually have access to severely limited computer resources, and must pay for it. Natural Language Processing is very much an experimental science, and the designers of ARIANE-78 have felt they couldn't provide the linguists with a system they might use for experimentations only about one or two weeks a year because of financial constraints.

One possible reward of this painful kind of implementation is that it seems possible to run the complete system on the PC/XT370, according to the specifications and descriptions published in Europe.

A second level of comparison is by the computational methods used. For that, we may use old data from the former CETA system (before 1971), or data from current systems such as METAL (University of Texas at Austin), or KATE (KDD, Tokyo), based on augmented context-free formalisms. From some demonstrations and private communications, we got again the figure of 1 to 1.5 Mipw, for systems written in LISP, and about 40 times less for assembler-level implementation of the basic software.

Our (perhaps too hasty) conclusion is that *pattern-matching-based techniques are roughly 40 times costlier in VCPU than classical combinatorial methods* (if programmed in a smart way, of course).

However, we have tried the latter kind of approach in the past, and ended up finding it quite difficult to maintain a large scale system and to raise its overall quality. See Section 7 for further comments.

6 Practical Experience; Experimental Results

6.1 Cost of System Maintenance and Extension

This cost is quite low, in terms of computer resources and of human effort. The compilers are quite efficient, the structure of dictionary and annex tools is designed to simplify indexing and correcting and the modular character of the grammars makes it quite easy to modify and debug them.

6.2 How is Testing Performed?

Take the Russian-French application as an example. For testing, we use a set of corpora we retranslate each time a significant set of modifications has been incorporated in the lingware, and of course we translate new corpora that have just been inputted and checked for spelling errors. We then compare old and new translations of the first set, and revise the second.

6.3 What is Measured?

6.3.1 Speed

As mentioned earlier, we measure the VCPU time and deduce from it an estimate in terms of Mipw, which has proven to be quite stable over a variety of machines. Due to the differences in real memory size and processing speed, the real time (even in a single-user situation) may range anywhere from 100 words per hour to 5 words per second.

6.3.2 Quality

This is a difficult thing to measure. During revision, we do such a qualitative evaluation by detecting all translation errors and trying to find their origin, hence their gravity.

However, we would prefer to simply measure the time for human revision (without error hunting), as compared with the time for human revision of an average human rough translation of the same text. This kind of experiment has yet to be performed in a meaningful way.

6.4 Cost Effectiveness, Subjective Factors

This has to be measured in some real situation, as said earlier. We strongly hope that the setting of the National Project will allow that kind of measurement to take place in a systematic way.

7 Arguments re: Chosen Techniques

7.1 Against Alternative Methods

7.1.1 Interlingua

First of all, we have tried an approximation of the interlingua ("pivot") approach, and found it wanting. In the former CETA system, the pivot representation was of a hybrid sort using as vocabulary the lexical units of a given natural language, and as relations so-called "universals" corresponding to our current logical and semantic relations, plus abstract features such as semantic markers, abstract time and aspect, and so on. The problem here is threefold.

- It is very difficult to design such a pivot in the first place, and even more so if the vocabulary must also be independent of any particular natural language.

- The absence of surface-level information makes it impossible to use contrastive knowledge of two languages to guide the choice between several possible paraphrases at generation time.

- If the high-level representation cannot be computed on part of the unit of translation, the whole unit gets no representation, and hence no translation, or a word-by-word translation. This is already bad enough at the sentence level, and quite insufferable if the units are larger in order to access more context.

7.1.2 PS-Rules

Phrase structure (PS) grammars don't seem adequate for our purposes, even with all (not so recent) additions and niceties such as attributes, validation/invalidation between rules, attached transformations, etc. This is mainly so because the structures associated with the strings are grammar-dependent, although they should be language-dependent invariants.

Another problem comes from the monolithic aspect of such grammars, which makes them very difficult and ultimately impossible to understand and modify, although everything seems right at the beginning, with a few hundred rules. Stratification of the grammar in the METAL sense is just a device allowing conservation of results obtained in simple cases while rules are added to take care of more complex situations. For the latter, the grammar is still the collection of all rules, with no modularity.

7.1.3 Purely Combinatorial Methods

Ambiguity is a fundamental problem in Natural Language Processing. Combinatorial methods tend to compute all possibilities, perhaps weighting them, and to filter out the first one, the N one, or all of them. No heuristic programming is possible.

If more than one result of analysis (or transfer) is produced, the source of the ambiguity is lost, so that the system must produce several distinct translations for the unit. Again, this is difficult to accept at the sentence level, and certainly unacceptable at the paragraph level.

7.2 For Chosen Methods

7.2.1 Constrastivity and Transfer Approach

If we are some day to attain the level of performance of an average or good translator, it is necessary to sometimes rely on "rules of thumb," which use surface-level information, and embody some contrastive knowledge of the languages at hand.

Moreover, if the units of translation grow larger, the probability that some part cannot be completely analyzed at the most abstract levels of interpretation approaches certainty.

Hence, we feel that the use of one (and not several) so-called "multilevel structure" for representing each unit is appropriate. As a matter of fact, we consider such a structure as a generator of the various structures that have been implicitly computed at each level of interpretation.

This technique may be compared with the "blackboard" technique of some AI systems. During analysis, the different levels of linguistic knowledge are used in a cooperative way, and not sequentially, as in previous systems.

For example, some semantic information may be used to disambiguate at the syntactic level, as in the following sentences:

John drank a bottle of beer.

John broke a bottle of beer.

7.2.2 Transducers rather than Analyzers

Although procedural programming is notoriously more difficult than writing a collection of static rules used by a standard algorithm, leading to a yes or no answer, we consider it a lot better in the situation of incomplete and fuzzy knowledge encountered in MT. It happens that the same position has recently gained ground in AI, with the construction of "expert systems" that embody a lot of knowledge in their control and domain-specific heuristics.

In our case, this amounts to using our SLLPs for "lingware engineering," in much the same way as usual programming languages are used for software engineering. Starting from a kind of functional specification (expressed by means of static grammars), the computational linguist constructs a corresponding transducer in the time-honoured way of top-down decomposition and step-wise refinement.

7.2.3 Text-Driven Heuristic Programming

Heuristic programming and text-driven strategies seem more adequate than the use of a very complex grammar, whose rules are all tried, even in simple cases. Experiments have shown that the flow of control (from TG to TG) is significantly different on different parts (subtrees) of the translation units.

7.2.4 Fail-Soft Mechanisms

In the setting of second-generation systems, based on implicit rather than explicit understanding, a parallel can be made with compilers for programming languages. We don't want our "supercompilers" (for natural language, that is) to stop and produce nothing if they encounter an ill-formed clause somewhere in the unit of translation.

Rather, we want them to produce the best translation they can, under all circumstances, annotating it with special marks, analogous to error and warning messages, to be used later during the post-editing and technical revision of the document.

The "safety net" consisting of multiple levels of interpretation for the same structure makes it possible to use a broad spectrum from high-level to word-by-word translation.

8 Future Directions

8.1 Application Plans

Immediate application plans are all essentially those of the French National Project. As the first target, certain kinds of aircraft manuals have been selected for translation from French into English. Computer manuals to be translated from English into French may follow.

We also hope to develop current cooperative efforts and initiate new ones.

8.2 Research Plans

Lexical knowledge processing is one of the most important research topics, from a practical point if view. We aim at designing a kind of "integrated dictionary" where the "coded" and "natural" aspects are mixed. Such dictionaries could be used as reference or interface structures, *e.g.*, to generate coded dictionaries in different SLLPs for various steps of MT, or for other tasks, such as spelling correction, etc.

Grammatical knowledge processing is being investigated. The formalism of static grammars is being refined and experimented with for the string-to-tree correspondences, and a small team is currently designing a set of software tools to handle a data base of static grammars. The formalism should also be extended to tree-to-tree correspondences. Many useful ideas can be taken over from current work on specification, proof, and validation of programming languages.

A promising topic is the introduction of expert system components into second-generation MT systems in order to add some level of "explicit understanding" in the form of domain-specific "extralinguistic knowledge" and typology-specific "metalinguistic knowledge."

Research on better data- and control-structures for adequate SLLPs has been carried out. It should be continued and experimented with.

References

Bachut, D. and Verastegui, N. (1984), Software Tools for the Environment of a Computer-Aided Translation System. *Proceedings of COLING-84*. Stanford, California.

Boitet, C. (1976), Un essai de résponse à quelques questions théoriques et pratiques liées à la Traduction Automatique. Définition d'un système prototype. Thèse d'Etat. Grenoble.

Boitet, C. (1984), Research and Development on MT and Related Techniques at Grenoble University (GETA). Lugano Tutorial on Machine Translation.

Boitet, C. and Gerber, R. (1984), Expert Systems and Other New Techniques in MT. *Proceedings of COLING-84*, Stanford, California.

Boitet, C., Guillaume, P., and Quézel-Ambrunaz, M. (1978), Manipulation d'arborescences et parallélisme: le système ROBRA. *Proceedings of COLING-78*, Bergen.

Boitet, C., Guillaume, P., and Quézel-Ambrunaz, M. (1982), ARIANE-78; an Integrated Enviroment for Automated Translation and Human Revision. *Proceedings of COLING-82*, Prague.

Boitet, C. and Nedobejkine, N. (1981), Recent Developments in Russian-French Machine Translation at Grenoble. *Linguistics* 19: 199-271.

Chappuy, S. (1983), Formalisation de la description des niveaux d'interprétation des langues naturelles. Thèse de 3è cycle. Grenoble.

Chauché, J. (1974), Transducteurs et arborescences. Etude et réalisation de systèmes appliqués aux grammaires transformationnelles. Thèse d'Etat. Grenoble.

Clemente-Salazar, M. (1982), Etudes et algorithmes liées à une nouvelle structure de données en TA: les E-graphes. Thèse de Docteur-Ingénieur. USMG and INPG, Grenoble. See also *Proceedings of COLING-82*, Prague.

Gerber, R. (1984), Etude des possibilités de coopération entre un système fondé sur des techniques de compréhension implicite (système logico-syntaxique) et un système fondé sur des techniques de compréhension explicite (système expert). Thèse de 3è cycle. Grenoble.

Mozota, T. (1984), Un formalisme d'expressions pour la spécification du contrôle dans les systèmes de production. Thèse de 3è cycle. Grenoble.

Vauquois, B. (1975), *La Traduction Automatique à Grenoble.* Document de Linguistique Quantitative 29. Dunod, Paris.

Vauquois, B. (1979), Aspects of Automatic Translation in 1979. Scientific Program. IBM, Japan.

Vauquois, B. (1983), Automatic Translation. *Proceedings of the Summer School "The Computer and the Arabic Language,"* Rabat: Chapter 9.

Verastegui, N. (1982), Étude du parallélisme appliqué à la traduction automatisée par ordinateur. STAR-PALE: un système parallèle. Thèse de Docteur Ingénieur. USMG and INPG, Grenoble. See also *Proceedings of COLING-82*, Prague.

The LRC Machine Translation System

Winfield S. Bennett
Siemens Communication Systems, Inc.

Jonathan Slocum
Microelectronics and Computer
Technology Corporation (MCC)

Abstract

The Linguistics Research Center (LRC) of the University of Texas at Austin is currently developing METAL, a fully-automatic high quality Machine Translation (MT) system. Following an outline of the history and status of the project, this paper discusses the system's projected application environment and briefly describes our general translation approach. After detailing the salient linguistic and computational techniques on which METAL is based, we consider some of the practical aspects of such an application, including experimental results which imply that the system is now ready for production use. Two exhibits are appended: a German original text and its raw METAL translation, produced in 1984. (This is not the best translation ever produced by METAL, but it is better than the average for its time.) We close by indicating some future directions for the project.

1 History and Status

MT research at the University of Texas began in 1959; the Linguistics Research Center (LRC) was founded as a host organization for this project in 1961. For much of the history of this research, funding came from the U.S. Air Force's Rome Air Development Center and other U.S. government agencies. In January, 1979, Siemens AG began funding the current development phase of the METAL system; the project at that time comprised 1 full-time and 5 or 6 half-time workers. As a result of Siemens' support, the existing system was scrapped and a new implementation effort was undertaken in the Spring of that year; the project staff grew slowly at first, but with a recent substantial increase now numbers 6 full-time and 4 half-time workers at the LRC, plus others in Munich. The first "production" version of the system was delivered to the sponsor for testing in January, 1985.

The current operational system translates only from German into English, although experiments have been conducted with other Target Languages (Spanish and Chinese), and work on a second Source Language (English) is underway at the LRC. (Other applications, mentioned below, are underway elsewhere.) The German grammar in its present form contains more than 500 rules; the lexicon has well in excess of 20,000 monolingual entries for German and English, and is expected to double in size in the near future.

2 Application Environment

Like any modern MT system, METAL is to be used in a technical translation environment where human revision of the output is expected – just as is the case with human translation around the world. The justification for using an MT system is a combination of pure economics (cost reduction) and necessity (to achieve the desired speed, perhaps required to get the job done at all); the trade-off between these two differs, depending on the organization and circumstance. In general, we expect that the LRC MT system must prove cost-effective in order to gain user acceptance: speed per se will be a secondary consideration. This means that the cost of using METAL for draft translation, and a human revisor thereafter, must be significantly (not marginally) less than the cost of using humans for draft translation, and a human revisor thereafter; the cost of "using" METAL must include its full amortization, etc.

In an environment of technical translation, particularly of operation and maintenance manuals, one of the big problems is text format. As a glance at any technical manual will show, it is not the case that all material in a document must or can be translated. Large portions of a formatted text (up to 50% of the characters, in our experience) may not be translatable; the bulk of this may fall outside "sentence" boundaries, but some will fall within them. Thus, it is necessary for a text to be marked, or annotated, to distinguish that which is to be translated (*e.g.*, tables of contents, instructions, prose paragraphs) from that which is not (*e.g.*, flowchart box boundaries, sentence-internal formulas and acronyms, and various attention-focussing devices). The translatable units (not always "complete sentences") must then be extracted, translated, and finally reconstituted so as to appear like the original text.

In the LRC MT system, special programs have been developed to handle the formatting problems associated with technical manuals. This software automatically marks texts and extracts translatable units for input to METAL, and reformats the translation afterwards [Slocum and Bennett, 1982; Slocum *et al.*, 1984]. The only human intervention expected prior to translation is checking and correcting the output of the routines which mark translatable units; the human does not, for example, resolve anaphora or disambiguate homographs or word senses. Nothing in the LRC MT system provides for human intervention during the actual translation phase.

At the LRC, text processing and post-editing are presently done on a DEC-2060, and the actual translation on Symbolics Lisp Machines. For the foreseeable future a Lisp Machine will continue to be used as the "translation engine." For production use, the project sponsor will employ personal computers supporting OCR devices, floppy-disk drives, printers, etc., on which texts will be prepared and sent to the batch translation unit, and on which the output will be reformatted and revised; software specially suited to text preparation and post-editing is being programmed. Thus, the production version will constitute a complete translation environment.

3 General Translation Approach

In METAL, translation proper consists of four successive phases: Analysis (parsing), Integration, Transfer, and Synthesis (generation). The Integration phase works with analysis tree structures, performing (at the present time) inter- and extra-sentential anaphora resolution. Until recently, the Transfer and Synthesis phases were essentially a single phase, but work is in progress to split this phase, and introduce a much more powerful Synthesis phase. In this section we describe "Transfer" and defend it as our general translation approach; in the next section we discuss our linguistic techniques more fully.

It is frequently argued that translation should be a process of analyzing the Source Language (SL) into a "deep representation" of some sort, then directly synthesizing the Target Language (TL) (*e.g.*, [Carbonnel *et al.*, 1978]). We and others [King, 1981] contest this claim – especially with regard to "similar languages" (*e.g.*, those in the Indo-European family). One objection is based on large-scale, long-term trials of the "deep representation" (in MT, called the *pivot language*) approach by the CETA group at Grenoble [Boitet and Nedobejkine, 1980]. After an enormous investment in time and energy, including experiments with massive amounts (400,000 words) of text, it was decided that the development of a suitable pivot language (for use in Russian-French translation) was not yet possible. Another objection is based on practical considerations: since it is not likely that any NLP system will in the foreseeable future become capable of handling unrestricted input – even in the technical area(s) for which it might be designed – it is clear that a "fail-soft" technique is necessary. It is not obvious that such is possible in a system based solely on a pivot language; a hybrid system capable of dealing with shallower levels of understanding seems necessary in a practical setting. This being the case, it is better in near-term applications to start off with a system employing a "shallow" but usable level of analysis, and deepen the level of analysis as experience dictates, and theory plus project resources permit.

The standard alternative, which we have adopted, is to have a *transfer* component that maps "shallow analyses of sentences" in the SL into "shallow analyses of equivalent sentences" in the TL, from which synthesis then takes place. This assumes the form of a transfer dictionary and a transfer grammar. While we and the rest of the NLP community continue to explore the nature of an adequate pivot language (*i.e.*, the nature of deep semantic models and the processing they entail), we can, we believe, proceed to construct usable systems amenable to progressive enhancement as linguistic theory becomes able to support deeper models.

4 Linguistic Techniques

Our distinction between "linguistic techniques" and "computational techniques" (discussed in the next major section) is somewhat artificial, but it has some validity in a broad sense, as should become clear from an overview of the points considered. In this section we discuss our use of the following linguistic techniques: (a) allomorphic lexical analysis; (b) a phrase-structure grammar; (c) syntactic features; (d) semantic features; (e) scored interpretations; (f) transformations indexed to specific rules; and (g) attached procedures to effect translation.

4.1 Allomorphic Lexical Analysis

Entries in METAL monolingual dictionaries are indexed by both *canonical form* (the usual spelling one finds in a printed dictionary) and *allomorph* (the stem, without productive affixes). The affixes themselves are separate dictionary entries; although their semantics is necessarily different in kind from content morphemes, they are treated identically by the system software. If a particular stem exhibits internal inflection (*e.g.*, German nouns that umlaut in the plural), or varies for other reasons, then multiple entries are stored, one for each stem variation (allomorph). At first this may seem wasteful, but the majority of such cases in our dictionaries are German strong verbs – which sometimes behave differently, depending on inflection, and thus would require separate entries anyway.

At system-generation time, the allomorphs are entered into a "letter tree" which is searched during lexical analysis. The analysis of a word occurrence, then, is normally one or more sequences of morphemes (stems and affixes, mixed), each morpheme being an allomorph corresponding to one or more dictionary entries. These are fed to the parser as if they had been separate, alternative sequences of "words" in the text (except that each morpheme is marked according to whether it was word-initial and/or word-final), which parses them back into words while it is parsing the words into a sentence. Lexical ambiguity (including homography and polysemy, as well as ambiguity in morphological decomposition) is tolerated as a natural phenomenon in the system, and is resolved according to a scoring scheme, discussed below, which handles syntactic ambiguity as well.

4.2 Phrase-Structure Grammar

In the LRC MT system we employ a phrase-structure grammar, augmented by strong lexical controls and extensive use of transformations. The LRC MT system is currently equipped with over 500 PS rules describing the best-developed Source Language (German), and well over 10,000 lexical entries in each of the two main languages (German and English). The current state of our coverage of German is that the system is able to parse and acceptably translate the majority of sentences in previously-unseen texts, within the subject areas bounded by our dictionaries. We have recently begun the process of adding to the system an analysis grammar of the current TL (English), so that the direction of translation may be reversed; we anticipate bringing the English grammar up to the level of the German grammar in a few years' time. We do not feel constrained to account for every possible sentence form in such texts – and certainly not for sentence forms never found in such texts (as in the case of poetry) – since the required effort would not be cost-effective, whether measured in financial or human terms, even if it were possible using current linguistic techniques (which we doubt).

4.3 Syntactic Features

Our use of syntactic features is relatively noncontroversial, given our choice of the PS rule formalism. We employ syntactic features for two purposes. One is the usual practice of using such features to restrict the application of PS rules (*e.g.*, by enforcing subject-verb number agreement). The other use is perhaps peculiar to our type of application: once an analysis is achieved, certain syntactic features are employed to control the course (and outcome) of translation – *i.e.*, generation of the TL sentence. The "augmentations" to our PS rules include operators that manipulate features by restricting their presence, their values if present, etc., and by moving them from node to node in the "parse tree" during the course of the analysis. As is the case with other researchers employing such techniques, we have found this to be an extremely powerful (and, of course, necessary) means of restricting the activities of the parser.

4.4. Semantic Features

We employ simple semantic features, as opposed to complex models of the domain. Our reasons are primarily practical. First, features seem sufficient for at least the initial stage of our application. Second, the thought of writing complex models of even one complete technical domain is staggering: one set of operation and maintenance manuals we have worked with (describing a digital telephone switching system) is part of a document collection that is expected to comprise some 100,000 pages of text when complete. A typical NLP research group would not even be able to read that volume of material, much less write the "necessary" semantic models subsumed by it, in any reasonable amount of time. (The group members would also have to become electronics engineers, in all likelihood, in order to understand the text.) If such models are indeed required for our application, we will never succeed.

As it turns out, we are doing surprisingly well without such models. In fact, our semantic feature system is not yet being employed to restrict the analysis effort at all; instead, it is used during Transfer to improve the quality of the translations, primarily of prepositions. We look forward to extending the use of semantic features to other parts of speech, and to substantive utilization during analysis; but even we have been surprised at the results achieved using only syntactic features during analysis.

4.5 Scored Interpretations

It is a well-known fact that NLP systems tend to produce many readings of their input sentences (unless, of course, constrained to produce the first reading only – which can result in the "right" interpretation being overlooked). The LRC MT system may produce multiple interpretations of the input "sentence," assigning each of them a score, or plausibility factor [Robinson, 1982]. This technique can be used, in theory, to select a "best" interpretation from the available readings of an ambiguous sentence. We base our scores on both lexical preferencing and grammatical phenomena – plus the types of any spelling/typographical errors, which can sometimes be "corrected" in more than one way.

Scoring begins at the lowest level of the tree – at the morpheme level, based on lexical preference coded for dictionary entries (one per allomorph) and any spelling correction factors – and propagates upwards as the analysis proceeds. Homography and polysemy are dealt with as a natural consequence of the selection, from among all alternatives, of the most plausible (*i.e.*, highest scoring) reading(s). Thus, nowhere in the system is there special provision for dealing with these problems: all sources of ambiguity are handled by the identical mechanism.

Our experiences relating to the reliability and stability of heuristics based on this technique are decidedly positive: we employ only the highest-scoring reading for translation (the others are discarded), and our informal experiments indicate that it is rarely true that a better translation results from a lower-scoring analysis. (Surprisingly often, a number of the higher-scoring interpretations will be translated identically. But poorer translations are frequently seen from the lower-scoring interpretations, demonstrating that the technique is indeed effective.) This does require some careful "tuning" by the linguists, but this has been a manageable problem.

4.6 Indexed Transformations

We employ a transformational component, during both the analysis phase and the translation phase. The transformations, however, are indexed to specific syntax rules, or even lexical entries, rather than loosely keyed to syntactic constructs. (Actually, both styles are available, but our linguists have never seen the need or practicality of employing the open-ended variety.) It is clearly more efficient to index transformations to specific rules or words when possible; the import of our findings is that it seems to be unnecessary to have open-ended transformations – even during analysis, when one might intuitively expect them to be useful. A transformation tied to a particular syntactic rule may be written as part of that rule, or called by name if the linguist wishes several rules to share the same transformation (*e.g.*, an ab-ba constituent reversal is common).

4.7 Attached Translation Procedures

Our Transfer procedures (which effect the actual translation of SL into TL) are tightly bound to nodes in the analysis (parse tree) structure [Paxton, 1977]. They are, in effect, suspended procedures – parts of the same procedures that constructed the corresponding parse tree nodes to begin with. We prefer this over a more general, loose association based on, *e.g.*, syntactic structure because, aside from its advantage in sheer computational efficiency (search for matching structural transfer rules is eliminated), it prevents the "wrong" procedure from being applied to a construct. The only real argument against this technique, as we see it, is based on space considerations: to the extent that different constructs share the same transfer operations, wasteful replication of the procedures that implement said operations (and editing effort to modify them) is possible. We have not noticed this to be a problem. For a while, our system load-up procedure searched for duplicates of this nature and automatically eliminated them; however, the gains turned out to be minimal: different structures typically do require different translation operations.

5 Computational Techniques

Again, our separation of "linguistic" from "computational" techniques is somewhat artificial, but nevertheless useful. In this section we discuss our use of the following computational techniques: (a) a "some-paths," parallel, bottom-up parser; (b) associated rule-body procedures; (c) spelling correction; (d) another fail-soft analysis technique; and (e) recursive parsing of parenthetical expressions.

5.1 Some-paths, Parallel, Bottom-up Parser

Among all our choices of computational techniques, the use of a "some-paths," parallel, bottom-up parser is probably the most controversial. Our current parser operates on the sentence in a well-understood parallel, bottom-up fashion; however, the notion of "some-paths" will require some explanation. In the METAL system, the grammar rules are grouped into "levels" indexed numerically (0, 1, 2...), and the parser always applies rules at a lower level (*e.g.*, 0) before applying any rules at a higher level (*e.g.*, 1). Thus, the application of rules is partially ordered. Furthermore, once the parser has applied all rules at a given level it halts if there exist one or more "sentence" interpretations of the input; only if there are none does it apply more rules – and then, it always starts back at level 0 (in case any rules at that level have been activated through the application of rules at a higher level, as can happen with a recursive grammar). Thus, the rule-application algorithm is Markov-like, and the system will not necessarily produce all interpretations of an input possible with the given rule base. Generally speaking, the lower-level rules are those most likely to lead to readings of an input sentence, and the higher-level rules are those least likely to be relevant (though they may be necessary for particular input sentences, in which case they will eventually be applied). As a result, the readings derived by our parser are the "most likely" readings (as judged by the linguists, who assign the rules to levels). This works very well in practice.

Our evolving choices of parsing methodologies have received our greatest experimental scrutiny. We have collected a substantial body of empirical evidence relating to parsing techniques and strategy variations. Since our evidence and conclusions would require lengthy discussion, and have received some attention elsewhere [Slocum, 1981], we will only state for the record that our use of a some-paths, parallel, bottom-up parser is justified based on our findings. First of all, all-paths parsers have certain desirable advantages over first-path parsers (discussed below); second, our some-paths parser (which is a variation on an all-paths technique) has displayed clear performance advantages over its predecessor technique: doubling the throughput rate while increasing the accuracy of the resulting translations. We justify our choice of technique as follows: first, the dreaded "exponential explosion" of processing time has not appeared, on the average (and our grammar and test texts are among the largest in the world), but instead processing time appears to be linear with sentence length – even though our system may produce all possible readings; second, top-down parsing methods suffer inherent disadvantages in efficiency; third, it is difficult to persuade a top-down parser to continue the analysis effort to the end of the sentence, when it blocks somewhere in the middle – which makes the implementation of "fail-soft" techniques having production utility that much more difficult; and lastly, the lack of any strong notion of how to construct a "best-path" parser, coupled with the raw speed of well-implemented parsers, implies that a some-paths parser which scores interpretations and can continue the analysis to the end of the sentence, come what may, may be best in a contemporary application such as ours.

5.2 Associated Rule-body Procedures

We associate a procedure directly with each individual syntax rule, and evaluate it as soon as the parser determines the rule to be (seemingly) applicable [Pratt, 1973; Hendrix *et al.*, 1978] – hence the term "rule-body procedure." This practice is equivalent to what is done in ATN systems. From the linguist's point of view, the contents of our rule-body procedures appear to constitute a formal language dealing with syntactic and semantic features/values of nodes in the tree – *i.e.*, no knowledge of LISP is necessary to code effective procedures. Since these procedures are compiled into LISP, all the power of LISP is available as necessary. The chief linguist on our project, who has a vague knowledge of LISP, has employed OR and AND operators to a significant extent (we didn't bother to include them in the specifications of the formal language, though we obviously could have), and on rare occasions has resorted to using COND. No other calls to true LISP functions (as opposed to our formal operators, which are few and typically quite primitive) have seemed necessary, nor has this capability been requested, to date. The power of our rule-body procedures seems to lie in the choice of features/values that decorate the nodes, rather than the processing capabilities of the procedures themselves.

5.3 Spelling Correction

There are limitations and dangers to spelling correction in general, but we have found it to be an indispensable component of an applied system. People do make spelling and typographical errors, as is well known; even in "polished" documents they appear with surprising frequency (about every page or two, in our experience). Arguments by LISP programmers about INTERLISP's DWIM (Do What I Mean) aside, users of applied NLP systems distinctly dislike being confronted with requests for clarification – or, worse, unnecessary failure – in lieu of automated spelling correction. Spelling correction, therefore, is necessary.

Luckily, almost all such errors are treatable with simple techniques: single-letter additions, omissions, and substitutions, plus two- or three-letter transpositions account for almost all mistakes. Unfortunately, it is not infrequently the case that there is more than one way to "correct" a mistake (*i.e.*, resulting in different corrected versions). Even a human cannot always determine the correct form in isolation, and for NLP systems it is even more difficult. There is yet another problem with automatic spelling correction: how much to correct. Given unlimited rein, any word can be "corrected" to any other. Clearly there must be limits, but what are they?

Our informal findings concerning how much one may safely "correct" in an application such as ours are these: the few errors that simple techniques have not handled are almost always bizarre (*e.g.*, repeated syllables or larger portions of words) or highly unusual (*e.g.*, blanks inserted within words); correction of more than a single error in a word is dangerous (it is better to treat the word as unknown, hence a noun); and "correction" of errors which have converted one word into another (valid in isolation) should not be tried.

5.4 Fail-soft Grammatical Analysis

In the event of failure to achieve a comprehensive analysis of the sentence, a system such as ours – which is to be applied to hundreds of thousands of pages of text – cannot indulge in the luxury of simply replying with an error message stating that the sentence cannot be interpreted. Such behavior is a significant problem, one which the NLP community has failed to come to grips with in any coherent fashion. There have, at least, been some forays. Weishedel and Black [1980] discuss techniques for interacting with the linguist/developer to identify insufficiencies in the grammar. This is fine for system development purposes. But, of course, in an applied system the user will be neither the developer nor a linguist, so this approach has no value in the field. Hayes and Mouradian [1981] discuss ways of allowing the parser to cope with ungrammatical utterances; such work is in its infancy, but it is stimulating nonetheless. We look forward to experimenting with similar techniques in our system.

What we require now, however, is a means of dealing with "ungrammatical" input (whether through the human's error or the shortcomings of our own rules) that is highly efficient, sufficiently general to account for a large, unknown range of such errors on its first and subsequent outings, and which can be implemented in a short period of time. We found just such a technique several years ago: a special procedure (invoked when the analysis effort has been carried through to the end of the sentence) searches through the parser's chart to find the shortest path from one end to the other; this path represents the fewest, longest-spanning phrases which were constructed during the analysis. Ties are broken by use of the standard scoring mechanism that provides each phrase in the analysis with a score, or plausibility measure (discussed earlier). We call this procedure "phrasal analysis."

Our phrasal analysis technique has proven to be useful for both the developers and the end-users, in our application: the system translates each phrase individually, when a comprehensive sentence analysis is not available. The linguists use the results to pin-point missing (or faulty) rules. The users (who are professional translators, editing the MT system's output) have available the best translation possible under the circumstances, rather than no usable output of any kind. Phrasal analysis – which is simple and independent of both language and grammar – should prove useful in other applications of NLP technology; indeed, IBM's EPISTLE system [Miller *et al.*, 1980] employs an almost identical technique [Jensen and Heidorn, 1982].

5.5 Recursive Parsing of Parenthetical Expressions

Few NLP systems have ever dealt with parenthetical expressions; but MT researchers know well that these constructs appear in abundance in technical texts. We deal with this phenomenon in the following way: rather than treating parentheses as lexical items, we make use of LISP's natural treatment of them as list delimiters, and treat the resulting sublists as individual "words" in the sentence; these "words" are "lexically analyzed" via recursive calls to the parser, which, of course, actually performs grammatical analysis. Besides sheer elegance, this has the added advantage that "ungrammatical" parenthetical expressions may undergo Phrasal Analysis and thus become single-phrase entities as far as the analysis of the encompassing sentence is concerned; thus, ungrammatical parenthetical expressions need not result in ungrammatical (hence poorly handled) sentences.

6 Practical Considerations

From a user's viewpoint, there are four aspects on which MT systems should be judged: text preparation, dictionary update, actual translation, and post-editing. Other than dictionary update, these aspects are discussed elsewhere in this paper. We will therefore comment on our lexical maintenance procedures, and the users' acceptance thereof, before proceeding to our experimental results.

6.1 Lexical Maintenance

The factors important to the terminologists who maintain lexical databases include the kinds of information that one is required to supply, and the method used to enter that information in the dictionary

[Slocum and Whiffin, 1984]. If the lexical coding process is too complex, semantic errors will multiply and translation quality will suffer. Menu schemes wherein one selects the proper value of a feature from a short (at most, 10-item) list of options are greatly preferred over long lists of options or, worse, a scheme wherein one must volunteer the information via type-in. Even better is a scheme wherein the system, with minimal clues (*e.g.*, root form and part of speech) generates an entry likely to be mostly correct, which the terminologist then verifies and edits (again, via menu selection) as necessary. Needless to say, arcane codes which one must have a manual to keep track of are to be avoided at all cost.

The lexicon for METAL is stored in an on-line DBMS written in LISP. Input of lexical entries is facilitated by an INTERCODER, a menu-driven interface that asks the user for information in English and converts the answers into the internal form used by the system. An integral part of the INTERCODER is the "lexical default" program which accepts minimal information about the particular entry (root form and lexical category) and heuristically encodes most of the remaining necessary features and values. Entries may also be created using any text editor, without the aid of the INTERCODER or lexical defaulter.

Interfacing with the lexical database is done by means of a number of functions which permit the user to access, edit, copy, and/or delete entries individually, in small groups (using specific features), by entire categories, or in toto (essentially no longer done for reasons of size). In order to assure a high degree of lexicon integrity the METAL system includes validation programs which identify errors in format and/or syntax. The validation process is automatically used to check lexical items which have been edited or added, to ensure that no errors have been introduced.

Our terminologists indicate substantial subjective satisfaction with METAL's lexical coding scheme. Performance measurements indicate that, for categories other than verbs, a very few (2-5) minutes is all that is required to enter a pair of terms (in two languages, thus three dictionaries including Transfer); for verbs, the process is more complex, requiring as much as 20 minutes per word pair. But these times include the terminology research per se – *i.e.*, the process of discovering or generating a proper translation of a term – so the overall burden of lexical maintenance seems quite acceptable, and cost-effectiveness is not adversely affected.

7 Experimental Results

In the last five years, METAL has been applied to the translation into English of over 1,000 pages of German telecommunication and data processing texts. To date, no definitive comparisons of METAL translations with human translations have been attempted. (It is not obvious that this would be relevant, or of significant benefit.) However, some stimulating quantitative and qualitative statistics have been gathered.

Measuring translation quality is a vexing problem – a problem not exclusive to machine translation or technical texts, to be sure. In evaluating claims of "high-quality" MT, one must carefully consider how *quality* is defined: "percentage of words (or sentences) correct (or acceptable)," for example, requires definition of the operative word, *correct.* A closely related question is that of *who* determines correctness. Acceptability is ultimately defined *by the users, according to their particular needs*: what is acceptable to one user in one situation may be quite unacceptable in another situation, or to another user in the same situation. For example, some professional post-editors have candidly informed us that they actually look forward to editing MT output because they "can have more control over the result." For sociological reasons, there seems to be only so much that they dare change in human translations; but as everyone knows (and our informants pointed out), "the machine doesn't care." The clear implication here is that "correctness" has traditionally suffered where human translation is concerned; or, alternately, that "acceptability" depends in part on the relationship between the translator and the revisor. Either way, judgements of "correctness" or "acceptability" by post-editors are likely to be more harsh when directed toward MT than when directed toward human translation (HT). It is not yet clear what the full implications of this situation are, but the general import should be of some concern to the MT community. Since the errors committed by an MT system seldom resemble errors made by human translators, the possibility of a "Turing test" for an MT system does not exist at the current time.

For different (and obvious) reasons, qualitative assessments by MT system vendors are subject to bias – generally unintentional – and must be treated with caution. But one must also consider other circumstances under which the measurement experiment is conducted: whether (and for how long, and in what form) the text being translated, and/or its vocabulary, was made available to the vendor before the experiment; whether the MT system was previously exercised on that text, or similar texts; etc. At the LRC, we conduct two kinds of measurement experiments: "blind," and "follow-up." When a new text is acquired from the project sponsor, its vocabulary is extracted by various lexical analysis procedures and given to the lexicographers who then write ("code") entries for any novel words discovered in the list. The linguistic staff never sees the text prior to a blind experiment. Once the results of the blind translation are in, the project staff are free to update the grammar rules and lexical entries according to what is learned from the test, and may try out their revisions on sample sentences from the text. Some time later, the same text is translated again, so that some idea of the amount of improvement can be obtained.

7.1 Translation Speed

On our Symbolics 3600 LISP Machine, with 512K 32-bit words of physical memory, preliminary measurements indicate an average performance of about 2+ seconds (real time) per input word; this is already 10 times the speed of a human translator, for like material. The paging rate indicates that, with added memory, we could expect a significant boost in this performance ratio; for other (predictable) reasons, as well, further speed increases are anticipated.

7.2 Correctness

In addition to collecting some machine performance statistics, we count the number of "correct" sentence translations and divide by the total number of sentence units in the text, in order to arrive at a "correctness" figure. (For our purposes, "correct" is defined as "noted to be unchanged for morphological, syntactic, or semantic reasons, with respect to the original machine translation, after revision by professional post-editors is complete." Non-essential stylistic changes are not considered to be errors.) In the course of experimenting with over 1,000 pages of text in the last five years, our "correctness" figures have varied from 45% to 85% (of full-sentence units) depending on the individual text and whether the experiment was of the "blind" or "follow-up" variety. During a recent "blind" test, for example, METAL achieved a 75% "correctness" figure on a moderately long text (ca. 10 pages).

8 Interpretation of the Results

Certain objections have been raised concerning the present feasibility of MT. It has been argued that, unless an MT system constitutes an almost perfect translator, it will be useless in any practical setting [Kay, 1980]. As we interpret it, the argument proceeds something like this:

1. there are classical problems in Computational Linguistics that remain unsolved to this day (*e.g.*, anaphora, quantifiers, conjunctions);
2. these problems will, in any practical setting, compound on one another so as to result in a very low probability that any given sentence will be correctly translated;
3. it is not in principle possible for a system suffering from malady (1) above to reliably identify and mark its probable errors;
4. if the human post-editor must check every sentence to determine whether it has been correctly translated, then the translation is useless.

We accept claims (1) and (3) without question. We consider claim (2) to be a matter for empirical validation – surely not a very controversial contention. As it happens, a substantial body of empirical evidence gathered at the LRC to date refutes such claims: the "correctness" figures reported above (measured by our sponsor's post-editors) establish this contention. (In point of fact, we consider "correctness" figures to be virtually meaningless, aside from being unreliable, as will become obvious. But Kay's claim (2) assumes that "correctness" is a valid measure, and thus falls in either case.)

Regarding (4), we embrace the assumption that a human post-editor will have to check the entire translation, sentence-by-sentence; but we argue that Kay's conclusion ("then the translation is useless") is again properly a matter for empirical validation. Meanwhile, we are operating under the assumption that this conclusion is patently false – after all, where translation is taken seriously, human translations are routinely edited via exhaustive review, but no one claims that they are therefore useless! In other words, Kay's claim (4) also falls, based on empirical evidence that relates to HT directly – but, by extension, to MT as well.

8.1 Acceptance and Cost-Effectiveness

There *is* a meaningful, more-or-less objective metric by which any MT system can and should be judged: *overall* (human/machine) *translation performance*. The idea is simple. The MT system must achieve two simultaneous goals: first, the system's output must be acceptable to the post-editor for the purpose of revision; second, the cost of the total effort (including amortization and maintenance of the hardware, the software, and the dictionaries) must be less than the current alternative for like material – human translation followed by post-editing.

Regarding user acceptance, we can relate that the editors revising METAL translations over the past few years have recently stated that the system has achieved a level of quality that they find acceptable for their day-to-day work [Whiffin, personal communication]. From our experimental evidence, it would seem that this is a harder goal to reach than mere cost-effectiveness; *i.e.*, "cost-effectiveness" can be demonstrated in experimental settings, with an output quality that the editors will not accept on a daily basis. In addition, translators have noted that the time required to create a triple of METAL dictionary entries – monolingual German term, monolingual English equivalent, and bilingual Transfer pair – varies from 2-20 minutes, depending on the part of speech and the amount of terminology research required. (The latter is needed for human translation in any case.) On an on-going average basis, a new term can be expected once per page of text.

Until METAL is evaluated by unbiased third parties, taking into account the full costs of translation and revision using METAL *vs.* conventional (human) techniques, the question of METAL's cost-effectiveness cannot be answered definitively. However, we have identified some performance parameters that are interesting. Our sponsor has calculated that METAL should prove cost-effective if it can be implemented on a system supporting 4-6 post-editors who can sustain an average total output of about 60 revised pages/day. At 275 words/page, and 8 hours/day, this works out to 1.7 seconds/word, minimum real-time machine performance. Our mid-1984 real-time performance figure of 2+ seconds/word on a Symbolics 3600 approached this goal; it also compares very favorably with the human translation rate (experienced at Siemens, for decades) of 4-8 pages/day for like material. If this level of performance could be slightly increased while maintaining a high enough standard of quality that an individual revisor can indeed edit 10-15 pages/day, on a daily basis, METAL should have achieved cost-effectiveness. By early 1986 real-time performance had increased, to just over 1 second/word.

Most important, we have also measured revision performance: the amount of time required to edit texts translated by METAL. In the first such experiment, conducted late in 1982, two Siemens post-editors revised METAL's translations at the rate of 15-17 pages/day (depending on the particular editor). In a second experiment, conducted in mid-1983, the rates were only slightly higher (15-20 pages/day), but the revisors nevertheless reported a significant improvement in their subjective impression of the quality of the output. In a third experiment, conducted in early 1984, the editors reported further improvement in their subjective impression of the quality of the output, and their revision rates were much higher: almost 30 pages/day. In a fourth experiment, conducted in mid-1984, their average revision rate climbed to over 40 pages/day; this figure also compares favorably with the revision rate of human translations experienced at Siemens: 8-12 pages/day for like material (not including original translation time: 4-6 pages/day). These MT revision figures are surely biased by virtue of the experimental setting itself (*i.e.*, one-shot measures of post-editing performance on human translations would be significantly higher than the on-going 8-12 average quoted above), but nevertheless these numbers indicate that we have probably reached the goal of cost-effectiveness.

9 Future Directions

The METAL German-English configuration was ready for market testing by pilot groups in Fall 1986, with full commercial introduction planned for Fall 1987. Current plans are to continue improving this system and working on an English-German system at the LRC, while developing a bidirectional Dutch-French, French-Dutch system in Belgium. Work on a German-Spanish version is underway in Barcelona.

Technically speaking, we anticipate retaining most of the system as-is, aside from the usual sorts of maintenance modifications; however, as mentioned above, we are in the process of upgrading the power of the Synthesis component. In addition, there are plans to change the format and content of Transfer lexical entries so as to standardize their format (verbs are structured differently from other parts of speech) and increase their ability to control structural transfer. These changes, we anticipate, will allow further improvement in the quality of the raw output of the LRC MT system, and so further enhance its attraction and cost-effectiveness.

References

Boitet, Ch., and N. Nedobejkine (1980), "Russian-French at GETA: Outline of the Method and Detailed Example," *Proceedings of the 8th International Conference on Computational Linguistics*, Tokyo, Sept. 30 - Oct. 4.

Carbonnel, J., R. E. Cullingford, and A. V. Gershman (1978), "Knowledge-Based Machine Translation," Research Report #146, Dept. of Computer Science, Yale University, Dec. 1978.

Hayes, P. J., and G. V. Mouradian (1981), "Flexible Parsing," *AJCL* 7 (4), Oct-Dec., pp. 232-242.

Hendrix, G. G., E. D. Sacerdoti, D. Sagalowicz, and J. Slocum (1978), "Developing a Natural Language Interface to Complex Data," *ACM Transactions on Database Systems* 3 (2), June 1978, pp. 105-147. Reprinted in J. A. Larson and H. A. Freeman (eds.), *Tutorial: Data Base Management in the 1980's.* IEEE Computer Society Press, Los Alamitos, California, 1981, pp. 89-131.

Jensen, K., and G. E. Heidorn (1982), "The Fitted Parse: 100% Parsing Capability in a Syntactic Grammar of English," Research Report RC-9729 (#42958), Computer Sciences Department, IBM Thomas J. Watson Research Center, Yorktown Heights, New York, December.

Kay, M. (1980), "The Proper Place of Men and Machines in Language and Translation," Technical Report, Xerox PARC, Palo Alto, California.

King, M. (1981), "Design Characteristics of a Machine Translation System," *Proceedings of the 7th International Joint Conference on Artificial Intelligence* [7th IJCAI], Vancouver, B.C., Canada, Aug. 1981, v. 1, pp. 43-46.

Lehmann, W. P., W. S. Bennett, J. Slocum, *et al.* (1981), "The METAL System," Final Technical Report RADC-TR-80-374, Rome

Air Development Center, Griffiss AFB, New York, January 1981. Available as Report AO-97896, National Technical Information Service, U.S. Department of Commerce, Springfield, Va.

Miller, L. A., G. E. Heidorn, and K. Jensen (1980), "Text-Critiquing with the EPISTLE System: An Author's Aid to Better Syntax," Research Report RC 8601 (#37554), Behavioral Sciences and Linguistics Group, Computer Sciences Dept., IBM Thomas J. Watson Research Center, Yorktown Heights, New York, December.

Paxton, W. H. (1977), "A Framework for Speech Understanding," Ph.D. dissertation available as Technical Note 142, Artificial Intelligence Center, SRI International, Menlo Park, California, June.

Pratt, V. R. (1973), "A Linguistics Oriented Programming Language," *Proceedings of the 3rd International Joint Conference on Artificial Intelligence* [3rd IJCAI], Stanford University, California, August, pp. 372-381.

Robinson, J. J. (1982), "DIAGRAM: A Grammar for Dialogues," *CACM* 25 (1), January, pp. 27-47.

Slocum, J. (1981), *A Practical Comparison of Parsing Strategies for Machine Translation and Other Natural Language Processing Purposes.* University Microfilms International, Ann Arbor, Michigan.

Slocum, J., and W. S. Bennett (1982), "The LRC Machine Translation System: An Application of State-of-the-Art Text and Natural Language Processing Techniques to the Translation of Technical Manuals," Working Paper LRC-82-1, Linguistics Research Center, University of Texas, July.

Slocum, J., *et al.* (1984), "METAL: The LRC Machine Translation System," presented at the ISSCO Tutorial on Machine Translation, Lugano, Switzerland, 2-6 April 1984. Also available as Working Paper LRC-84-2, Linguistics Research Center, University of Texas, April 1984.

Slocum, J., and L. Whiffin (1984), "Machine Translation: Viewpoints from Both Sides," *AILA Bulletin* (last issue), pp. 27-58. Also available as Report AI-010-85, Microelectronics and Computer Technology Corporation (MCC), Austin, Texas, February 1985.

Weischedel, R. M., and J. E. Black (1980), "If the Parser Fails," *Proceedings of the 18th Annual Meeting of the ACL*, University of Pennsylvania, June 19-22.

Appendix A: a German DP Text

Einteilung des Plattenspeichers

Blockstruktur

Die kleinste adressierbare Informationseinheit ist ein Block = 1 Sektor. Zu jedem Block gehoert ein Header. Der Header enthaelt die gesamte Adresse, sowie Angaben ueber den Zustand des Blockes (Benutzbarkeit!). Zur Sicherung der Header-Information und der Daten befindet sich am Ende des Headers und des Datenfeldes ein Pruefzeichen von 16 Bit.

Vor dem Headerfeld befindet sich eine Praeambel von 42 Byte Laenge fuer den Ausgleich aller Toleranzen.

Vor dem Datenfeld befindet sich eine Praeambel von 5 Byte Laenge zur Aufsynchronisierung der Leseverstaerker. Vor und hinter dem Datenfeld befindet sich eine Luecke. Die Luecken sind aus folgenden Gruenden notwendig:

Luecke 1: 56 Bit wegen Schreib-Loesch-Kopfabstand. Zu Beginn der Daten-Schreiboperation muss gewaehrleistet sein, dass der Loeschkopf den Header nicht zerstoeren kann.

Luecke 2: 316 Bit im Normalmodus wegen der Toleranzen in der Umdrehungsgeschwindigkeit. Es muss die Moeglichkeit beruecksichtigt werden, dass das Schreiben des Blockes (Header + Datenfeld) an der unteren und oberen Grenze der Umdrehungsgeschwindigkeit erfolgen kann. Im Spezialmodus wird diese Luecke wegen der kleineren Bloecke 1340 Bit lang.

Am Ende des Header- und Datenfeldes befindet sich 1 Postambel von 8 Bit Laenge.

Spurstruktur

Eine Spur wird eingeteilt in 4 bzw. 8 Sektoren. Die Unterteilung der Spur in Sektoren erfolgt durch Index- und Sektormarken.

Die Indexmarke wird magnetisch durch einen Schlitz auf der untersten Platte des Plattenstapels erkannt und dient als allgemeiner Bezugspunkt fuer den Aufbau der Spurstruktur. Vom Indexpunkt ausgehend wird die Spur mit einem eigens dafuer vorgesehenen Dienstprogramm (oder Simulator!) mit Headern beschrieben. Die Bitzahl fuer das Datenfeld wird so bemessen, dass auch bei unguenstiger Drehzahl (= 2448 U/min) immer noch 4 bzw. 8 vollstaendige Bloecke Platz finden. (Siehe Abschnitt 4.1 Luecke 2). Je nachdem bei welcher Geschwindigkeit die Spur beschrieben wird, entsteht zwischen Ende des Datenfeldes und Indexmarke bzw. Sektormarke eine mehr oder weniger grosse Luecke.

Sektormarkierung

Die Sektormarke wird ebenso wie die Indexmarke von der Schlitzplatte, die sich als Bodenplatte an jedem Plattenstapel befindet, magnetisch abgenommen. Im Handel werden Plattenstapel mit 32 und mit 20 Schlitzen angeboten. Im vorliegenden Fall soll der Plattenstapel mit 20 Schlitzen beim WSP 411 und mit 32 Schlitzen beim WSP 414 verwendet werden. Eine Maske, dargestellt durch einen Zaehler blendet aus den 20 bzw. 32 Sektormarken 4 bzw. 8 aus, so dass 4 bzw. 8 gleich grosse Sektoren entstehen. Die Maske bzw. der Zaehler wird von der Herstellerfirma (CDS) in jeden Wechselplattenspeicher fest eingebaut.

Speicherstruktur

Dargestellt ist die Struktur des WSP 411.

Ein Plattenstapel umfasst 6 bzw. 11 Platten mit 10 bzw. 20 benutzbaren Oberflaechen. Pro Oberflaeche befindet sich ein Kopf. Jeder Kopf ueberstreicht 203 Spuren. Die Gesamtheit aller Spuren mit gleichem Radius nennt man Zylinder.

Der Plattenstapel umfasst also 203 Zylinder. Die Zylinder haben die Adressen 000-202, die Koepfe haben entsprechend den Plattenseiten die Adressen 0-9 bzw. 0-19.

Bei einer fortlaufenden Uebertragung wird die Adresse in der Reihenfolge Sektor, Kopf, Zylinder erhoeht.

Appendix B: a raw METAL Translation

Division of disk storage

Block structure

The smallest addressable information unit is a block = 1 sector. A header is part of every block. The header includes the entire address, sowie specifications about the state of the block (usability!). A check character of 16 bits is found for the saving of the header information and the data at the end of the header and the data field.

A preamble of 42 byte length for the adjustment of all tolerances is found in front of the header field.

A preamble of 5 byte length is found in front of the data field for the synchronization of the read amplifier. A gap is found in front of and behind the data field. The gaps are necessary from the following reasons:

Gap 1: 56 Bit because of distance between write and erase heads. At the beginning of the data write operation it must be guaranteed, that the erase head can not destroy the header.

Gap 2: 316 Bit in the normal mode because of the tolerances in the rotational speed. The possibility must be considered that writing the block (header + data field) at the lower and upper limit/boundary of the rotational speed can occur. This gap becomes 1340 bits long in special mode because of the smaller blocks.

The 1 postamble of 8 bit length is found at the end of the header and data field.

Track structure

A track is divided into 4 and/or 8 sectors. The subdivision of the track into sectors occurs through index label and sector marks.

The index label is recognized magnetically by a slot on the lowest disk of the disk pack and is used for the track structure as the general reference point for establishing. By the index point, the track with a utility program designated especially for that (or simulator!) is described with headers. The number of bits for the data field is calculated then that always still 4 and/or 8 complete blocks do also find space with unfavorable rotational speed/number of revolutions (= 2448 r.p.m.s). (See section 4.1 gaps 2.) Depending on with which speed the track is described, a more or less large gap occurs between the end of the data field and index label and/or sector mark.

Sector marker

Likewise the index label is read in the sector mark as by the slot disk which is found as a bottom disk at every disk pack magnetically. The disk packs with 32 and with 20 slotting are offered on the market. The disk pack should be used in this case with the 20 slots with the WSP 411 and with the 32 slots with the WSP 414.

A mask, represented through a counter masks out 4 and/or 8 from the 20 and/or 32 sector marks so that large sectors result similar to 4 and/or 8. The mask and/or the counter is incorporated by the Herstellerfirma (CDS) into every removable disk storage.

Storage structure

The structure of the WSP 411 is represented.

A disk pack contains the 6 and/or 11 disks with 10 and/or 20 usable surfaces. A heading is found per surface. Every heading covers 203 tracks. The entirety of all tracks with same radius calls one cylinder.

Therefore the disk pack contains 203 cylinders. The cylinders have the addresses 000-202, the headings have the addresses 0-9 and/or 0-19 corresponding to the disk surfaces.

Sector, heading, cylinder is increased the address during a continuous transfer in the sequence.

The Japanese Government Project for Machine Translation

Makoto Nagao, Jun-ichi Tsujii, and Jun-ichi Nakamura
Department of Electrical Engineering
Kyoto University
Sakyou-ku, Kyoto, Japan 606

1 Outline of the Project

The project is funded by a grant from the Agency of Science and Technology through the Special Coordination Funds for the Promotion of Science and Technology, and was started in fiscal 1982. The formal title of the project is "Research on Fast Information Services between Japanese and English for Scientific and Engineering Literature." The purpose is to demonstrate the feasibility of machine translation of abstracts of scientific and engineering papers between the two languages, and as a result, to establish a fast information exchange system for these papers. The project term was initially scheduled for three years with a budget of about seven hundred million yen, but, due to the present financial pressures on the government, the term has been extended to four years, up to fiscal 1986.

The project is conducted by the close cooperation between four organizations. At Kyoto University, we have the responsibility of developing the software system for the core part of the machine translation process (grammar writing system and execution system); grammar systems for analysis, transfer and synthesis; detailed specification of what information is written in the word dictionaries (all the parts of speech in the analysis, transfer, and generation dictionaries), and the working manuals for constructing these dictionaries. The Electrotechnical Laboratories (ETL) are responsible for the machine translation text input and output, morphological analysis and synthesis, and the construction of the verb and adjective dictionaries based on the working manuals prepared at Kyoto. The Japan Information Center for Science and Technology (JICST) is in charge of the noun dictionary and the compiling of special technical terms in scientific and technical fields. The Research Information Processing System (RIPS) under the Agency of Engineering Technology is responsible for completing the machine translation system, including the man-machine interfaces to the system developed at Kyoto, which allow pre- and post-editing, access to grammar rules, and dictionary maintenance.

The project is not primarily concerned with the development of a final practical system; that will be developed by private industry using the results of this project. Technical know-how is already being transferred gradually to private enterprise through the participation in the project of people from industry. Software and linguistic data are also being transferred in part. Finally, complete technical transfer will be done under the proper conditions.

The Japanese source texts being used are abstracts of scientific and technical papers published in the monthly JICST journal *A Current Bibliography of Science and Technology.* At present, the project is only processing texts in the electronics, electrical engineering, and computer science fields. English source texts will be abstracts from INSPEC in these fields. The sentence structures used in abstracts tend to be complex compared to ordinary sentences, with long nominal compounds, noun-phrase conjunctions, mathematical and physical formulas, long embedded sentences, and so on. The analysis and translation of this type of sentence structure is far more difficult than ordinary sentence patterns. However, we have not included a pre-editing stage because we wanted to find the ultimate limitations on handling this type of complex sentence structure.

Our system is based on the following concepts:

1. The use of all available linguistic information, both surface and syntactic. The writing of as detailed as possible syntactic rules. The development of a grammar writing system that can accept any future level of sophisticated linguistic theory.

2. The introduction of semantic information wherever necessary

to enable the syntactic analysis to be as accurate as possible. The importance of semantic information not over-estimated; a well-balanced usage of both syntax and semantics. Heavily semantics-oriented analysis is very attractive and effective for sentences within narrow limits, but a system of that type cannot cope with the complicated structures found in descriptions of the wider world where semantic description becomes almost impossible.

3. There are many exceptional linguistic phenomena that are more word-specific than explainable in general linguistic theory. The system should be able to accept word-specific rules. In our system, these rules are written into the lexical entries, with the priority given to these grammar rules in the analysis, transfer, and synthesis phases. This mechanism allows the system to be upgraded step by step by the accumulation of linguistic facts and word-specific rules in the dictionary and effectively bypasses any deadlock in system improvement.

4. The system must be able to produce an output with an imperfect sentence structure and containing untranslated original words rather than fail completely in cases where the analysis was imperfect. From the post-editor's point of view, an imperfect output is far preferable to no output at all.

Many other concepts and methods have been developed in our machine translation system, and these are explained in the sections following. This paper concentrates on the main features of the Japanese to English translation system. Details of the English to Japanese system, which is also included in our national machine translation project, are being developed, and the results will be published shortly.

2 The Grammar Writing System, GRADE

2.1 Objectives of the Software System

In developing a machine translation system, the grammar rules should accurately reflect the intention of the grammar writer. This is fundamental to the achievement of a good grammar system. One of the basic necessities of any machine translation system is a programming language to write the grammar, composed of the language for specifying the grammar rules and the accompanying execution system.

A grammar-writing language for machine translation that is powerful must fulfill the following requirements:

1. The language must allow manipulation of linguistic characteristics in both source and target languages. The linguistic structure of Japanese differs greatly from that of English. For example, in Japanese the restrictions on word order are not so strong, and some syntactic components can be omitted. A grammar writer must be able to reflect these sorts of characteristics.

2. It is desirable that the grammar-writing language use the same framework for writing the grammars in the analysis, transfer, and synthesis phases. The grammar writer should not be forced to learn several different systems for the different translation stages.

With these points in mind, we developed a new software system for machine translation comprising the language used to specify the grammar rules and the execution system. We call it GRADE (GRAmmar DEscriber).

2.2 The Structure of GRADE

The data format used to express the structure of a sentence during the analysis, transfer, and generation phases has a large influence on the design of the grammar-writing language. GRADE uses an annotated tree structure to represent the sentence structure during the translation process. Grammatical rules in GRADE are described in the form of tree-to-tree transformations with each node annotated. An annotated tree in GRADE is a tree structure whose nodes are annotated by sets of property-value pairs. This tree-to-tree transformation gives a great power of expression to rewriting rules that can be used in the grammars for the analysis, transfer, and synthesis phases of the machine translation system. Annotation parts can be used to express information such as syntactic category, number, semantic markers, and other properties. They can also be used as flags to control rule application.

A *rewriting rule* in GRADE consists of a declaration part and a main part. The *declaration part* has the following four components:

- *Directory entry part*, containing the grammar writer's name, the version number of the rewriting rule, and the last revision date. This part is not used at execution time. The grammar writer can access the information using the HELP facility in GRADE.

- *Property definition part*, where the grammar writer declares the property names and their possible values.

- *Variable definition part*, where the grammar writer declares the names of the variables.

- *Matching instruction part*, where the grammar writer specifies the mode of application of the rewriting rule to an annotated tree.

The *main part* specifies the transformation in the rewriting rule, and has the following three parts:

- *Matching condition part*, which describes the conditions for the structure of trees and the property values of nodes.

- *Substructure operation part*, which specifies the operations for the parts of the annotated tree that match the conditions written in the matching condition part.

- *Creation part*, which specifies the structure and the property values of the transformed annotated trees.

The matching condition part allows the grammar writer to specify not only a specific structure for an annotated tree but also structures that may repeat several times, structures that are optional, and structures where the order of the substructures is unrestricted.

The substructure operation part specifies operations on the parts of the annotated tree that match in the matching condition part. It allows the grammar writer to assign a property value to a node, or to assign a variable to a tree or property value. The variable is declared in the variable declaration part. It also allows one to call a subgrammar, a subgrammar network (which is explained below), a dictionary rule, a built-in function, or a LISP function. In addition, the grammar writer can specify a conditional operation using the IF-THEN-ELSE statement.

The structure and the property values of the transformed annotated tree are written in the creation part. The transformed tree is described by node labels that are used in the matching condition part or the substructure operation part.

The matching instruction part of a rewriting rule specifies the application path through the annotated tree. Paths through the trees are specified by combinations of the four basic modes: left-to-right, right-to-left, bottom-to-top, and top-to-bottom.

GRADE allows the grammar writer to divide the whole grammar into several subgrammars and to describe the phases of the translation process separately. A subgrammar may correspond to a grammatical unit such as the parsing of a simple noun phrase or the parsing of a simple sentence. The network of subgrammars forming the whole grammar allows the grammar writer to control the translation process in detail. If the subgrammar network in the analysis phase consists of the subgrammar for a noun phrase (SG1) and the subgrammar for a verb phrase (SG2) in this sequence, the GRADE executor first applies SG1 to the input sentence, and then applies SG2 to the result.

2.3 Some Specific Features of GRADE

GRADE allows a grammar writer to write word-specific grammar rules as a subgrammar at the word dictionary entry level. A subgrammar written in a dictionary entry is called a dictionary or lexical rule. A dictionary rule is specific to a particular word in the dictionary.

A dictionary rule is called by the CALL-DIC function in the substructure operation part. When CALL-DIC is executed by an entry word and rule identifier as keys, the dictionary rule is retrieved and is applied to the part of the annotated tree specified by the grammar writer.

Any grammar-writing language must be able to resolve the syntactic and semantic ambiguities found in natural languages. GRADE allows the grammar writer to merge the results of all possible tree-to-tree transformations for a particular subgrammar. However, it must avoid any combinatorial explosion when it encounters ambiguities.

For instance, let us take the case where a grammar writer writes a subgrammar to analyze the case frame of a verb, containing two rewriting rules; one rule is to construct a VP (verb phrase) from a V and NP (verb and noun phrase), and the other is to construct a VP from a V, NP, and PP (verb, noun phrase, and prepositional phrase). When he specifies the NONDETERMINISTIC-PARALLELED mode for the subgrammar, the GRADE executor applies both rewriting rules to the input tree, constructs two transformed trees, and merges them into a new tree whose root node has the special PARA property. The root node is called a para node and the subtrees under this node are the trees that have been transformed by the rewriting rules. Figure 1 shows this mode applied to create a para node.

The grammar writer can select the most suitable subtree under the para node by applying a subgrammar that assigns a priority value to each subtree and using a built-in function that orders the subtrees according to their values.

A para node is treated the same as other nodes in the current implementation of GRADE. The grammar writer can use the para node as he wants, and can select a subtree under a para node at a later application of the grammar rule.

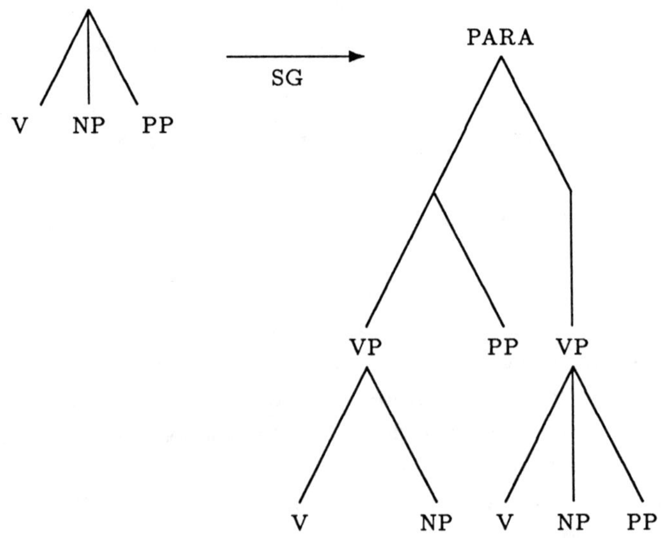

Figure 1. Example of para node formation.

2.4 System Configuration and Environment

The system configuration of GRADE is shown in Figure 2. Grammar rules written in GRADE are first translated by the GRADE translator into internal forms, expressed as S-expressions in LISP. The internal forms of the grammar rules are applied to the input tree that is output by the morphological analysis program. The rules are applied by the GRADE executor, and the results are sent to the morphological generation program.

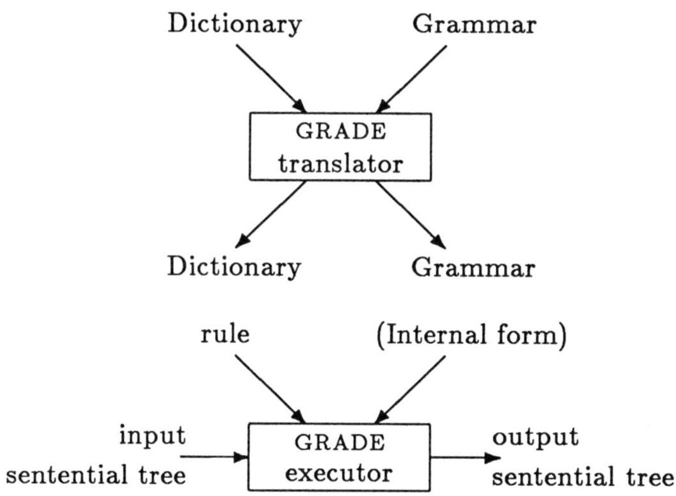

Figure 2. System configuration of GRADE.

The GRADE system program is written in UTILISP (University of Tokyo Interactive LISP) and implemented on a FACOM M382 computer, which can handle Chinese characters. The system will also run on the Symbolics 3600. The system program contains about 10,000 lines.

3 The Dictionaries

Because our system is based on the "transfer" approach, there are three separate dictionaries (for analysis, transfer, and synthesis). In this project, Japanese words are classified into 12 major categories (parts of speech) and 46 subcategories according to their morpho-syntactic behavior. English words are classified into 14 major categories and 28 subcategories. The outline of the dictionaries of different kinds is explained in this section. The details are available in the Japanese literature.

3.1 The Japanese Analysis Dictionary

3.1.1 Analysis Dictionary for Verbs

Some Japanese verbs are used in a wide range of circumstances, each usage expressing a subtly different "meaning." These must all be translated into English differently. Distinguishing these different usages requires careful investigation of the context around the verb. As described in Section 2, GRADE allows the definition of grammar rules that are applied only to specific lexical items. We use this capability to discriminate between verb usages. However, many verbs have only two or three different usages at most. We prepared a fixed format for the lexical coding of these verbs. Descriptions in this format are converted to internal representation in GRADE automatically by a program. For verbs that have a wide range of usages, where the rules need to be written based on a variety of heuristic information, the grammar rules can be written directly in GRADE, bypassing the fixed format. In the fixed format, a verb can have several case frames corresponding to different usages. A case frame in Japanese is represented as a set of triplets like:

(Surface-Case-Mark Deep-Case Constraints-on NP)

<SCM> <DC> <CON>

SCM is a set of postpositional case particles, one of which follows the noun phrase to fill the case. DC expresses the deep case interpretation of the relationship between the verb and the noun phrase. CON specifies a set of semantic markers that the noun phrase to fill the case should have. Note that the deep case interpretation of the same surface case particle changes depending on the verb.

We listed 103 postpositional case particles and 33 deep case relations in Japanese, and 32 deep case relations in English (Table 1), which we believe to be sufficient for Japanese to English translation. Figure 3 gives a list of semantic markers used for semantic specification of the nouns in CON.

Table 1. English case labels.

1.	AGenT	17.	RANge
2.	Causal-POtency	18.	COmpaRison
3.	EXPeriencer	19.	TOOl
4.	OBJect	20.	PURpose
5.	RECipient	21.	Space-FRom
6.	ORIgin	22.	Space-AT
7.	SOUrce	23.	Space-TO
8.	GOAl	24.	Space-THrough
9.	COntent	25.	Time-FRom
10.	PARtner	26.	Time-AT
11.	OPPonent	27.	Time-TO
12.	BENeficiary	28.	DURation
13.	ACCompaniment	29.	CAUse
14.	ROLe	30.	CONdition
15.	DEGree	31.	RESult
16.	MANner	32.	COnCession

Since one case frame corresponds to one usage of a verb, and each usage corresponds to a different "meaning" of the verb, the lexical properties of verbs are represented by the properties of each case frame. The following properties are coded for each case frame.

a. Aspectual features: stative, semi-stative, durative, resultant, transitional.

b. Volition: volitional verb, non-volitional verb.

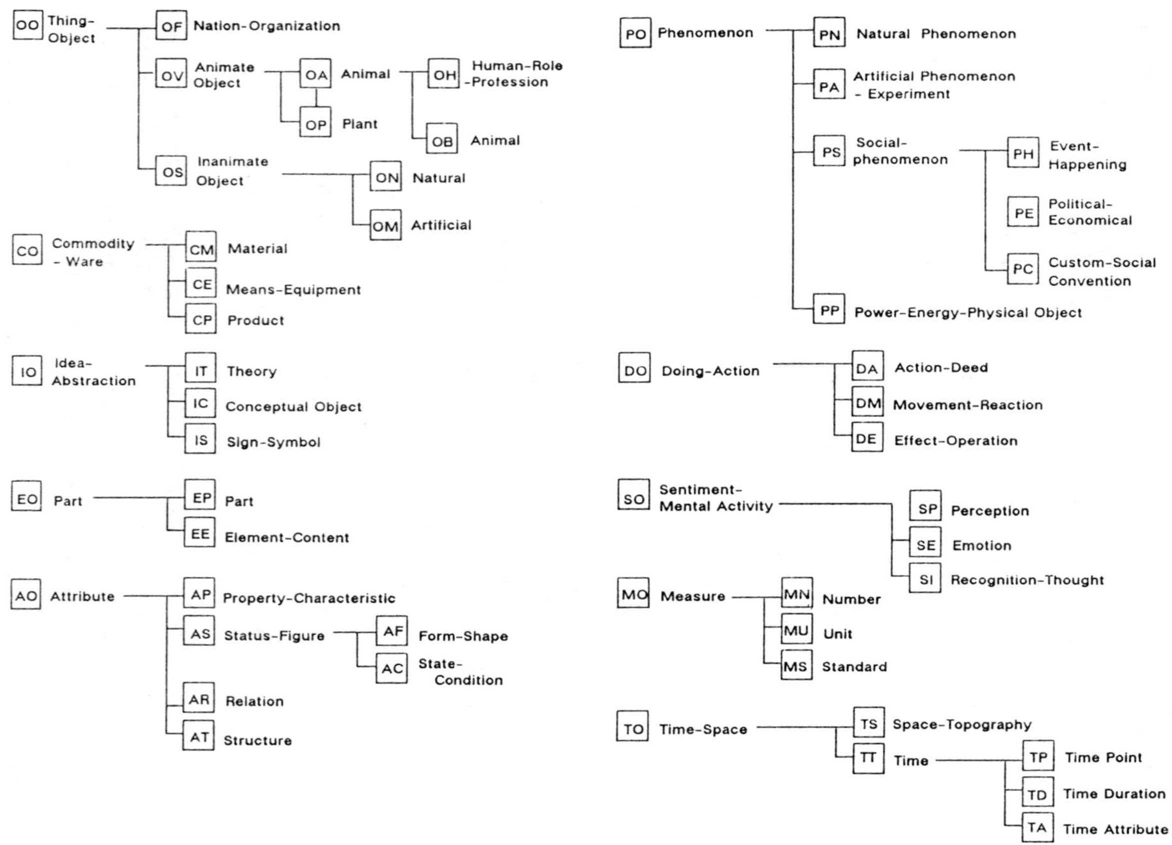

Figure 3. System of semantic primitives for nouns.

c. Possible transformations of surface case markers: Some auxiliary verbs that follow the verb and express passive, or causative voice, etc., change the surface case marking; that is, the postpositional case particles described in SCM are changed. Which auxiliary verbs can follow, and what transformation of surface case markers is caused by an auxiliary verb, depend on the verb itself, and so are marked as a lexical property of the verb.

d. Idiomatic expressions: Information on collocation; for example, which nouns and adverbs are often collocated with the verb are described in this column.

e. Lexical entry in transfer dictionary: As described before, a verb may have more than one case frame, each of which corresponds to one "meaning" of the verb. The transfer dictionary contains an entry for each meaning. Thus a single surface verb in Japanese may correspond to several different entries in the transfer dictionary. On the other hand, certain usages of different surface verbs may be reduced to a single entry in the transfer dictionary, if they are synonymous.

f. Semantic class: This property is used for semantic classification of verbs such as "mental-action," "physical-transfer," etc.

g. Miscellaneous properties: Several other minor properties are coded in the current dictionary.

3.1.2 Analysis Dictionary for Nouns

The following properties are described using the fixed noun format:

a. Subcategorization of nouns: proper noun, common noun, action noun, adverbial noun, postpositional noun, conjunctive noun, complementizer.

b. Semantic codes: The semantic codes shown in Figure 3 are used.

c. Information on collocation: Adjectives, nouns, etc., which often occur together with a noun are specified. This information plays a role similar to the case frame of a verb, and is effective in discriminating the different usages and meanings of nouns.

We also have fixed formats for words in the other morpho-syntactic classes. All words in the dictionary have, besides the above information, the properties listed in Table 2.

Table 2. Properties of Japanese words in the dictionary.

lexical item	subject code
word length	lexical entry in the transfer dictionary
word stem	semantic codes (for nouns, verbs)
pronunciation	thesaurus codes (for nouns)
part of speech	idiomatic expressions
sub-categorization of part of speech	case frames (for verbs, adjectives)
conjugation	
synonym	
derivations (noun, verb, adjective, adverb)	
related words	

3.2 The Japanese to English Transfer Dictionary

3.2.1 Transfer Dictionary for Verbs

Different verb usages are discriminated during the analysis phase. This means that usage ambiguities are partially resolved before the transfer phase. However, the concept of "meaning" (usage) applied to a single word is very vague and in fact depends greatly on the language pairs we have for translation. For example, the verb *NOMU* in Japanese can be used in the following ways:

Tabako-wo NOMU	→	smoke a cigarette
Kusuri-wo NOMU	→	take medicine
Mizu-wo NOMU	→	drink water

These three cases should be translated differently. In a similar way, the English verb *to wear* is used as:

Wear a suit	→	Suutsu-wo KIRU
Wear black shoes	→	Kuroi Kutsu-wo HAKU
Wear spectacles	→	Megane-wo KAKERU
Wear a wristwatch	→	Udedokei-wo SURU

These four cases should be translated differently into Japanese. Some might claim that these verbs are very ambiguous and have different meanings; but this contradicts the intuitive conclusion that suggests it is reasonable to consider that the target language simply has more specific verbs in these cases. In other words, discrimination in meaning at the analysis stage is not necessarily sufficient to select the appropriate target verb.

The verb transfer dictionary is divided into two parts: a word selection part and a mapping part. The word selection part is used to choose appropriate target verbs by referring to semantic markers of the case elements. The semantic markers currently being used appear to be insufficient to decide appropriate target verbs in certain cases. We cannot, for instance, distinguish *medicine* and *cigarette* with the current set of semantic markers, which is relevant to choosing appropriate English verbs for *NOMU*. However, we can treat such problems by specifying word selection rules in the noun transfer dictionary.

The mapping part gives the correspondence of the deep cases in Japanese and English. In most cases, the Japanese deep case maps to the same deep case in English. There are, however, certain deep cases that are interpreted differently in the two languages.

Sometimes a single Japanese verb can not be translated into a single English verb and has to be paraphrased using a combination of a verb and another element such as a noun or a prepositional phrase. For example:

SHISAKUSURU → develop (something) on a trial basis

Such linguistic expressions are also treated in the mapping part.

Although many verbs in the transfer dictionary are coded in this fixed format and converted to lexical rules in GRADE by a program, we also write lexical rules directly for verbs that have a wide range of usages.

3.2.2 Transfer Dictionary for Nouns

Some Japanese words that behave morpho-syntactically as nouns have to be translated into English words in other morpho-syntactic classes. Such class conversions should be treated in the transfer dictionary, because they are highly dependent on the lexical item. For example:

(i) TAIWA-KEISHIKI-de JIKKOUSURU
(interaction) (to execute)
→ to execute interactively

(ii) PUROGURAMU-MOODO-de JIKKOUSURU
(program mode) (to execute)
→ to execute in program mode

The above two examples have exactly the same structures in Japanese (where the noun phrases *TAIWA-KEISHIKI-de* and *PUROGURAMU-MOODO-de* fill the same deep case, "manner") but translate to different English structures simply because an appropriate lexical item exists for (i) but not for (ii).

The fixed format for nouns includes the following items:

a. Conditions on the sequence of words in the preceding part:
A set of default rules that translate Japanese postpositional case particles to English prepositions is provided in the transfer

grammar. However, these default rules are often violated, because certain English nouns require specific prepositions. This kind of information is coded in this column.

b. Conditions on the sequence of words in the succeeding part: Postpositions often give a clue to the morpho-syntactic class conversion.

c. Collocation with verbs:
Certain combinations of nouns and verbs in Japanese are translated into English as single verbs, and certain combinations of nouns and verbs such as *kusuri* (medicine) and *NOMU* (to smoke, to drink, to take) require specific translation of the verb *(to take)*. This is the kind of information coded here.

3.3 English Generation Dictionary

The format for verbs includes the following items:

a. Components: In the transfer phase, certain Japanese verbs are translated into English expressions containing not only verbs but also prepositional phrases and/or adverbial particles *(off, up,* etc.). These complex expressions have separate entries in the generation dictionary, and the structural descriptions for the complex expressions are given here.

b. Verb patterns: The verb codes from the *Longman Dictionary of Contemporary English* are used to specify the syntactic patterns a verb can take.

c. Aspectual features: stative, transitive, process, completive, momentary.

d. Voice: usually passive, can be used in passive voice, cannot be used in passive voice.

e. Volition: volitional verb, non-volitional verb.

f. Agent of *to*-infinitive: SUBject (*I promise him to go*). OBJect (*I want him to go*).

g. Case frames: A case frame of a verb is expressed by a set of quadruplets like:

Surface-Case	Deep-Case	Syntactic-Form	Semantic-Code
SC	DC	SF	SEC

SF is a list of numbers, each of which expresses one syntactic form the case element can take:

1. noun phrase
2. infinitive without *to*
3. *to*-infinitive
4. *-ing*
5. *that*-clause
6. *wh*-clause
7. adjective
8. *-ed*

The formats for other parts of speech are described in the Japanese literature.

4 Japanese Sentence Analysis

4.1 Analysis Strategies

As pointed out by Wilks [1973], semantic information cannot be used as constraints on single linguistic structures; it can be used only as preference cues to help choose the most feasible interpretation from among all the syntactically possible interpretations. We believe that many types of preference cues, besides semantic ones, exist in real texts and these cannot be captured by Context-Free Grammar (CFG) rules. By making use of various types of preference cues, our analysis grammar for Japanese can work almost deterministically to give the most preferable interpretation at the first output, without extensive semantic processing.

In order to integrate heuristic rules based on various levels of cues into a unified analysis grammar, we have introduced the following principles in the analysis of Japanese sentences:

1. Explicit control of rule application: Heuristic rules can be ordered according to their strength.

2. Multiple relation representation: Various levels of information including morphological, syntactic, semantic, and logical are expressed in a single annotated tree and can be manipulated at any time during the analysis. This is required not only because many heuristic rules are based on heterogeneous levels of cues but also because the analysis grammar should be able to perform semantic/logical interpretation of sentences at the same time, and the rules for these phases should be written using the same framework as the syntactic analysis rules.

3. Lexicon-driven processing: We can write heuristic rules specific to a single or a limited number of words, such as rules concerned with collocation among words. These rules are strong in the sense that they almost always succeed. They are stored in the lexicon and invoked at the appropriate time during the analysis without decreasing efficiency.

4. Explicit definition of analysis strategies: The whole analysis phase can be divided into steps. This makes the whole grammar efficient, natural, and easy to read. Furthermore, strategic consideration plays an essential role in preventing undesirable interpretations from being generated.

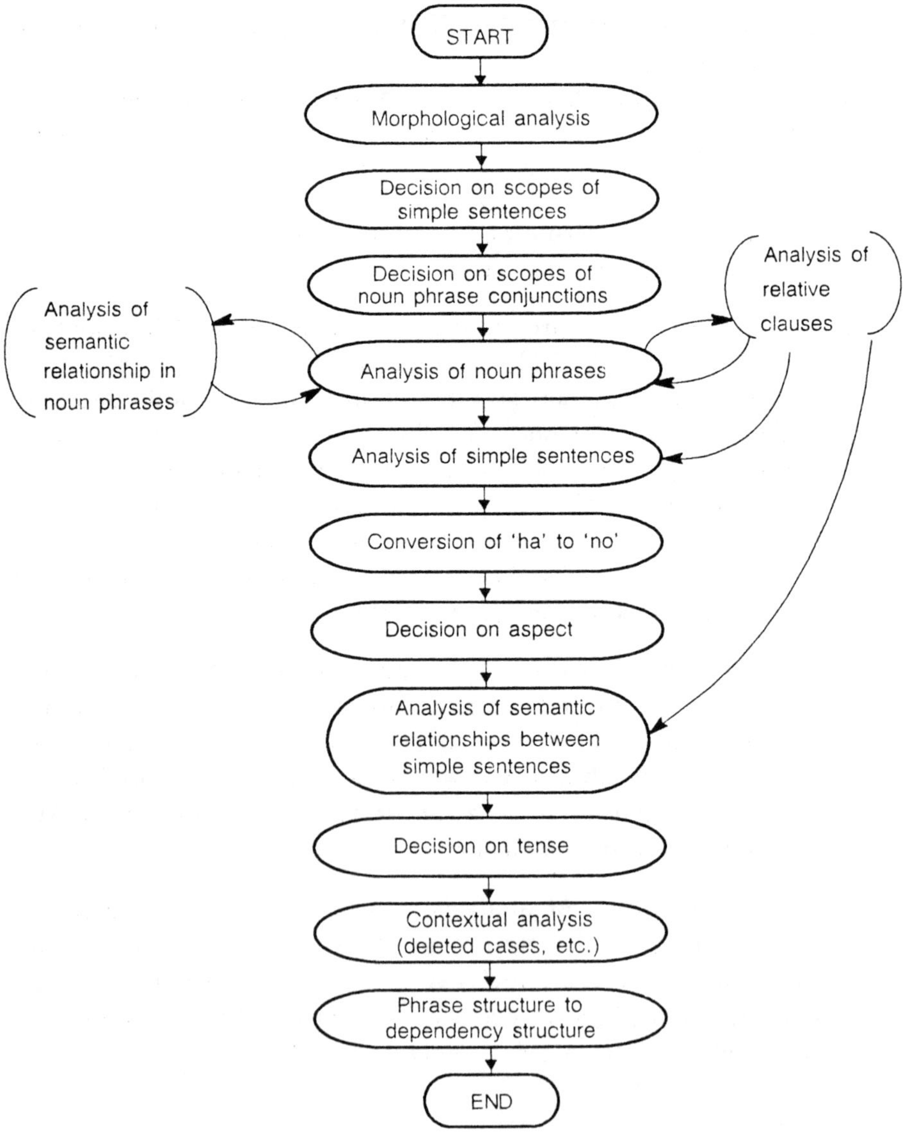

Figure 4. Basic flow of processing.

Figure 4 shows the overall organization of our current analysis grammar. The main components are:

1. Morphological Analysis
2. Analysis of Simple Noun Phrases
3. Analysis of Simple Sentences
4. Analysis of Embedded Sentences (relative clauses)
5. Analysis of Sentence Relationships
6. Analysis of Outer Cases
7. Contextual Processing (processing of omitted case elements, interpretations of *ha,* etc.)

The analysis produces dependency tree structures showing the semantic relationships between the words in the input sentence.

4.2 Typical Steps in the Analysis Grammar

4.2.1 Simple Sentences

As described in 3, the analysis dictionary for verbs contains verb case frames that are expanded to GRADE rules with unrestricted word order to obtain a match with the input sentence structure. Certain verbs such as *ARU, NARU, SURU, MOTSU,* etc., which have a wide range of usages, are discriminated by directly coding SGN in the dictionary.

4.2.2 Relative Clauses

Relative clause constructions in Japanese express several different relationships between modifying clauses (relative clauses) and their antecedents. Some relative clause constructions cannot be translated into English as relative clauses. We classified Japanese relative clauses into four types, according to the relationship between the clause and its antecedent. Because these four forms of relative clauses have the same surface forms, like

- - - - - - - - - - -(verb) (noun)

Relative Clause Antecedent,

careful processing is required to distinguish between them. We have developed a sophisticated analysis procedure that uses the various levels of heuristic information.

4.2.3 Noun Phrase Conjunctions

Noun phrase conjunctions often appear in abstracts of scientific and technical papers. It is important to analyze them correctly, especially in determining the scope of the conjunction, because they often lead to a proliferation of the analysis results. We have many heuristic rules based on various types of information. Some are based on surface lexical items, some on word morphemes, and some on semantic information. They are used differently in different conjunctive structures. We can distinguish strong heuristic rules (that is, rules that almost always give correct scopes when applied) from others. In fact, there is some ordering of heuristic rules according to their strength. In GRADE we can define arbitrary ordering of rule applications by using subgrammar networks and also by ordering rewriting rules inside a subgrammar. This capability of being able to control the rule application sequence is absolutely necessary in integrating heuristic rules based on heterogeneous types of information into a unified set of rules.

4.2.4 Sentence Relationships and Outer Case Analysis

In Japanese there are several different syntactic constructions corresponding to English subordinators and coordinators like *although*, *in order to*, *and*, and so on. The correspondence between forms of Japanese and English sentence constructions is not straightforward. Some postpositional particles in Japanese express several different semantic relationships between sentences, and therefore should be translated into different subordinators in English according to the semantic relationships. The postpositional particle *TAME* can express either a "purpose-action" relationship or a "cause-effect" relationship. In order to resolve the ambiguity in the semantic relationships expressed by *TAME,* a set of lexical rules is defined in the dictionary for the entry *TAME.* The rules are roughly as follows, where the sequence (S1, S2) is assumed:

(i) If S1 expresses a completed action or a stative assertion, the relationship is "cause-effect."

(ii) If S1 expresses neither a completed action nor a stative assertion, and S2 expresses a volitional action, the relationship is "purpose-action."

Note that whether S1 expresses a completed action or not is determined in a preceding phase by using rules that utilize the aspectual features of the verbs described in the dictionary, and auxiliary verbs following the verb. We have heuristic rules for 57 postpositional particles for sentence conjunctions like *TAME.*

Postpositional particles that express case relationships are also very ambiguous in the sense that they express several different deep cases. Although the interpretations of inner case elements are directly given in the verb dictionary as the form of mapping between surface case particles and their deep case interpretations, the outer case elements should be semantically interpreted by referring to the semantic categories of noun phrases and the verb properties. Lexical rules for 62 case particles have also been implemented and tested.

5 Transfer and Generation of English

In principle we use the deep case dependency structure to represent a sentence semantically. Theoretically it is possible to assign a unique case dependency structure to each input sentence. In practice, however, the analysis phase may fail, or it may assign the wrong structure. Therefore, as an intermediate representation, we use a structure that makes it possible to annotate multiple possibilities as well as multiple levels of representation. Properties at a node are represented as vectors, so that this complex dependency structure is flexible in the sense that different interpretation rules can be applied to the structure.

Transfer and generation rules are organized along the principle that "if a better rule exists, then the system uses it; otherwise, the system attempts to use a standard rule; if that fails, the system uses a default rule." The grammar involves a number of stages of application of heuristic rules. Figure 5 shows the process flow for the transfer and generation phases.

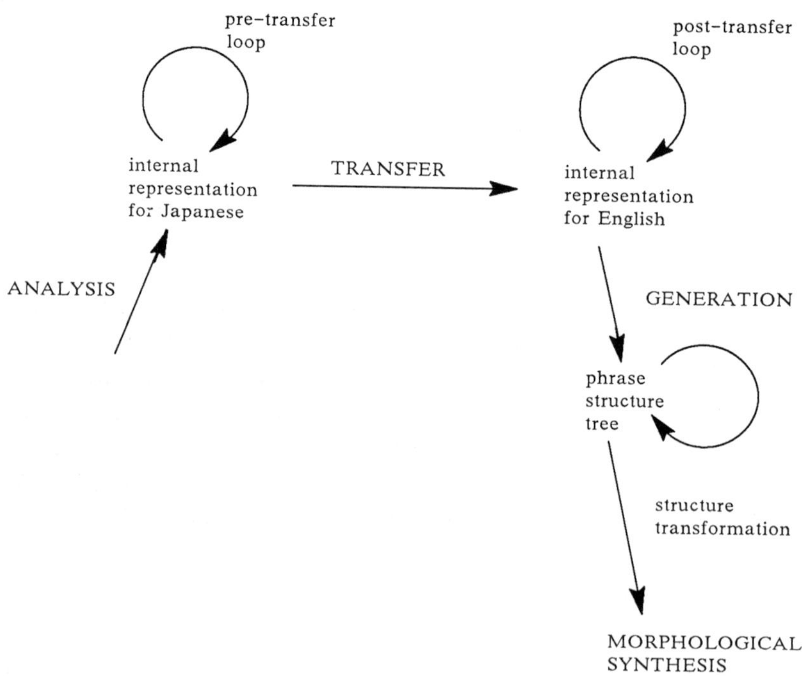

Figure 5. Process flow for the transfer and generation phases.

To obtain a more neutral (or target-language oriented) structure, some heuristic rules are activated immediately after the standard analysis of the Japanese sentence is finished. We call such activation the pre-transfer loop. Semantic and pragmatic interpretations are done in the pre-transfer loop. The larger the number of heuristic rules applied in this loop, the better the results.

5.1 Word Selection in English Using Semantic Markers

Word selection in the target language is a big problem in machine translation. There are varieties of choices for translation of a word in the source language. The main principles adopted by our system are:

1. Area restriction using field codes, such as electrical engineering, nuclear science, medicine, and so on.

2. Semantic codes are attached to a word in the analysis phase and used for the selection of the proper target language word or phrase.

3. The sentence structure involving the word to be translated is sometimes effective in determining the proper word or phrase in the target language.

Table 3 shows an example of part of the verb transfer dictionary. Selection of the English verb is done from the semantic categories of the nouns related to the verb. A number (i) attached to the verb, like form-1 or produce-2, labels the i-th usage of the verb. When semantic information on the nouns is not available, the column labelled 0 is applied to produce a default translation.

The expressive power of format-oriented descriptions is, however, insufficient for a number of common verbs such as *SURU* "to make, to do, to perform..." and *NARU* "to become, to consist of, to provide..." In such cases, we can write the transfer rules directly in GRADE. There must be a constant effort to list varieties of usages with their corresponding English sentence structures and semantic conditions.

A postposition in Japanese represents a case slot for a verb, but it has a variety of usages; thus determination of the English preposition corresponding to each Japanese postposition is quite difficult. It also depends on the verb that governs the noun phrase having that postposition.

Table 3. Word selection in target language by using semantic markers.

生ずる	Xが生ずる	X	non-living substance structure	form-1	form X(obj)
			social phenomena	take place	X take place
			action, deed, movement reaction	occur-1	X occur
			standard, property state, condition relation	arise-1	X arise
			∅	produce-2	produce X
	XがYを生ずる	Y	non-living substance structure	form-1	X form Y
			phenomena, action	cause-1	X cause Y
			∅	produce-2	X produce Y
上げる	XがYを上げる	Y	property	improve-1	X improve Y
			measure	increase-2	X increase Y
			∅	raise-1	X raise Y

↑ Semantic marker for X/Y

Table 4. Default rule for assigning a case label of English to the Japanese postposition *ni*.

J-SURFACE-CASE	J-DEEP-CASE	E-DEEP-CASE	Default Preposition
に(ni)	RECipient	REC, BENeficiary	to (REC — to, BEN — for)
	ORIgin	ORI	from
	PARticipant	PAR	with
	TIMe	Time-AT	in
	ROLe	ROL	as
	GOAl	GOA	to
	...	...	...

Table 4 illustrates part of a default table for determining deep and surface case labels when no higher-level rule applies. This sort of table is defined for all case combinations. In this way, we guarantee at least one translation to be assigned to an input. The particular usage of a preposition for a particular English verb is written in the lexical entry for the verb, and the information is used for English sentence generation.

Many odd structures are still left after the pre-transfer loop and the lexical selection, and the internal English representation must be adjusted further into more natural forms. We call this part the post-transfer loop.

Global sentence structures are completely different in Japanese and English, and correspondingly the internal structures are also completely different. The fundamental differences between the internal representation of Japanese and of English are absorbed in the pre-transfer loop. But before the English generation phase, some structural transformations are still required for cases such as (a) embedded sentence structures, and (b) complex sentence structures. These structural adjustments are performed in the post-transfer loop. The steps comprising the transfer phase are shown in Figure 6.

5.2 English Surface Structure Generation

After transferring from the Japanese deep dependency structure to the English one, the structure is converted to a phrase structure tree with all the surface words attached to the tree.

The conversion is performed top-down from the root node of the dependency tree to the leaf. Therefore, when a governing verb demands a noun phrase expression or a *to*-infinitive expression for its dependent phrase, a structural change must be made to the phrase. Noun-to-verb transformations and noun-to-adjective transformations are often required due to the difference in expressions between Japanese and English. This process moves down from the root node to all the leaf nodes.

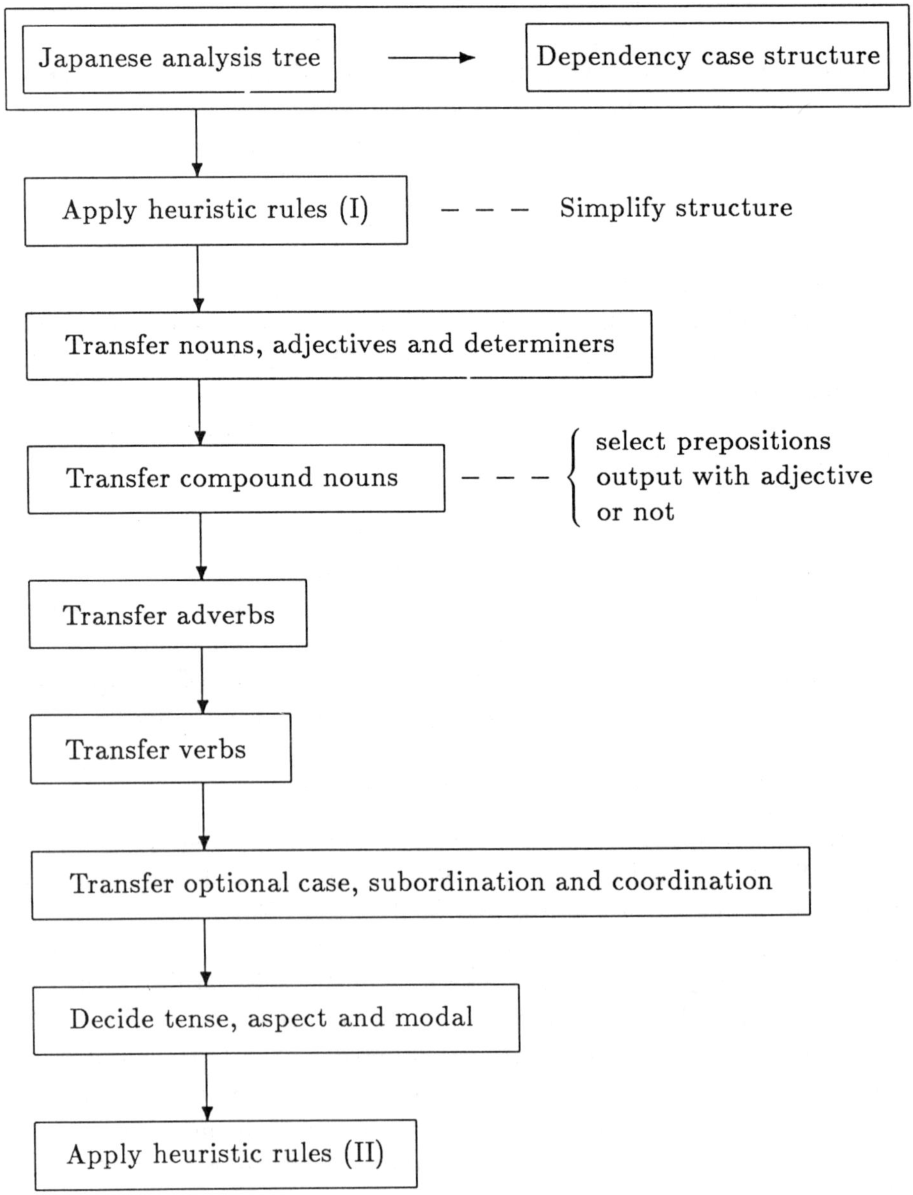

Figure 6. Outline of the transfer phase.

After this phrase structure generation process, some sentential transformations are performed. For example:

- When the agent is missing, a passive transformation is applied.
- When the agent and the object are both missing, the predicative verb is nominalized and made the subject by supplementing verb phrases such as *is made* or *is performed.*
- When the subject phrase has a big tree, the anticipatory subject *it* is introduced.
- In compound and complex sentences, redundant subject nouns are pronominalized.
- Duplication of head nouns in conjunctive noun phrases is eliminated. For example, "uniform component and non-uniform component" is reduced to "uniform and non-uniform components."

Any big structural transformations required in the translation come from the essential differences between English, which is a *DO*-language, and Japanese, which is a *BE*-language. In English, case slots such as tool, cause/reason, and some others often appear in the subject position, while in Japanese such expressions are never used. Transformations of this kind are incorporated in the generation grammar as shown in Figure 7. They produce more natural English expressions. The stylistic transformation part of the process is still very primitive. We need to accumulate much more linguistic knowledge and lexical data before we can produce really natural English expressions.

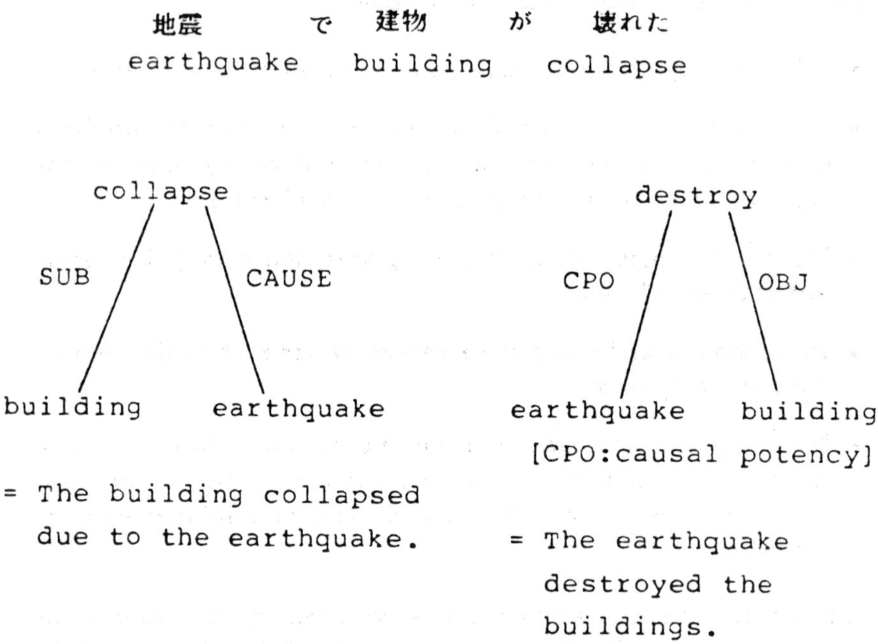

Figure 7. An example of structural transformations in the generation phase.

6 Evaluation of Translation Quality

The following two aspects of the machine translation output have been adopted to evaluate translation quality. They are to some extent independent indicators.

1. Intelligibility: An evaluation of the extent to which the translated text can be understood by a native speaker of the target language. In Japanese-to-English translation, we evaluate the extent to which an average British or American reader can un-

derstand the output without any reference made to the Japanese original.

2. Accuracy: The degree to which the translated text conveys the meaning of the original text is evaluated, and a measure of the amount of difference between the input and output sentences. The evaluation is done by Japanese translators specializing in Japanese-to-English translation.

6.1 Intelligibility

Evaluation of intelligibility is based on a scale of 1 to 5; the categories are described below. (See Appendix A for translation examples.)

1. The meaning of the sentence is clear, and there are no questions. Grammar, word usage, and style are all appropriate, and no rewriting is needed.

2. The meaning of the sentence is clear, but there are some problems in grammar, word usage, and/or style, making the overall quality less than 1.

3. The basic thrust of the sentence is clear, but the evaluator is not sure of some detailed parts because of grammar and word usage problems. The problems cannot be resolved by any set procedure; the evaluator needs the assistance of a Japanese evaluator to clarify the meaning of those parts in the Japanese original.

4. The sentence contains many grammatical and word usage problems, and the evaluator can only guess at the meaning after careful study, if at all. The quickest solution will be a retranslation of the Japanese sentence because too many revisions would be needed.

5. The sentence cannot be understood at all. No amount of effort will produce any meaning.

As the evaluation number increases on the above scale from 1 to 5, intelligibility decreases. The evaluator uses the above scale to evaluate the output sentence without any reference to the Japanese original in the first place. When the output sentence contains untranslated words in Japanese, the English translation of those words is provided by a Japanese rewriter before the evaluation. This evaluation work has been carried out to date by one British and one American evaluator, neither of whom has the ability to read or evaluate Japanese. Both evaluators have one year's experience in proofreading and checking translations of general scientific and technical literature, but neither has specialized knowledge in the field of electrical engineering, which has been used for the input material up to now.

6.2 Accuracy

Accuracy is evaluated on a scale of 0 to 6; that is, seven categories. (See Appendix B for translation examples.)

0. The content of the input sentence is faithfully conveyed to the output sentence. The translated sentence is clear to a native speaker and no rewriting is needed.

1. The content of the input sentence is faithfully conveyed to the output sentence, and can be clearly understood by a native speaker, but some rewriting is needed. The sentence can be corrected by a native speaker without referring to the original text. No Japanese language assistance is required.

2. The content of the input sentence is faithfully conveyed in the output sentence, but some changes are needed in word order.

3. While the content of the input sentence is generally conveyed faithfully in the output sentence, there are some problems with things like relationships between phrases and expressions, and with tense, voice, plurals, and the positions of adverbs. There is some duplication of nouns in the sentence.

4. The content of the input sentence is not adequately conveyed in the output sentence. Some expressions are missing, and there

are problems with the relationships between clauses, between phrases and clauses, or between sentence elements.

5. The content of the input sentence is not conveyed in the output sentence. Clauses and phrases are missing.
6. The content of the input sentence is not conveyed at all. The output is not a proper sentence; subjects and predicates are missing. In noun phrases, the main noun (the noun positioned last in the Japanese) is missing, or a clause or phrase acting as a verb and modifying a noun is missing.

As the evaluation number increases on the above scale from 0 to 6, the accuracy decreases. This part of the evaluation was done by four Japanese translators, each of whom has one or two years experience in Japanese to English translation. The whole evaluation process is monitored by a Japanese translation specialist with extensive experience in translation work.

6.3 Results of Evaluation

We describe here the results of the evaluation of the translation of 1,682 sentences taken from the monthly JICST journal *A Current Bibliography of Science and Technology.* Of these, 791 were selected for the development of the analysis grammar, and the remaining 891 were reserved for final testing. (The 791 sentences forming the first group were originally selected out of 1,000 after eliminating 120 that contained ungrammatical Japanese expressions, and a further 90 that contained long mathematical or chemical formulae. The deletion of the latter was because, in the early stages, the analysis grammar that would deal with formulae had not been completed.) All sentences were input to the machine translation system without pre-editing.

Tables 5 and 6 present the evaluation results for intelligibility and accuracy for the two groups of abstracts. Table 7 gives a comparison of the two groups. As the system was not tuned to the sentences in the second group, there were many unknown grammatical structures and missing words in the dictionary, which made the evaluation result worse than the first group.

As these tables show, when the accuracy of translation goes down, so too does the intelligibility. We did not find any examples of intelligibility being low when accuracy was high, but we did find a reasonable number of cases where the translation accuracy was evaluated as low, but intelligibility was rated high. Table 8 lists typical sample sentences for each evaluation type.

Just as there are no clear and objective criteria for evaluating the quality of Japanese to English translations done by humans, standard criteria for judging the results of machine translation have yet to be established. The evaluation methods proposed in this paper are still in the trial stage, and much more refining and improving is still needed.

The translation quality and the amount of post-editing needed is closely related to the quality and nature of the original text. It is quite natural to expect that simple sentences can be translated accurately and intelligibly. We need to develop some way to evaluate the degree of difficulty of the original text along with the translation evaluation. Only within this wider context can accuracy and intelligibility be meaningfully discussed.

The JICST abstracts used in this project were written primarily with the aim of condensing as much information as possible into a few sentences. This means that there are many long sentences, many of which are not very correct from a linguistic point of view. This is one obvious factor contributing to the poor evaluation results shown in Tables 5 to 7.

Evaluation of the quality of machine-translated sentences is closely linked to the way in which the machine translation output is to be used, hence to the ease with which post-editing can be done. Only a minimum of post-editing will be necessary to convey the technical meaning of the original to a specialist in the particular field for the purpose of information acquisition. However, when the translated text is for wide circulation or publication (for example, technical manuals), style and naturalness of sentential expressions, as well as exact meaning, become more important. Depending on these situations, the yardstick for intelligibility will change as well.

Table 5. Evaluation results, first group (791 abstracts).

intellig.	accuracy									
	0	1	2	3	4	5	6	defect.	tot.	pct.
1	98	0	9	4	1	2	2	0	116	14.7
2	0	186	8	28	22	11	4	0	259	32.7
3	0	1	135	45	42	17	16	3	259	32.7
4	0	0	20	19	26	10	24	1	99	12.5
5	0	0	5	2	8	6	36	1	58	7.3
total	98	187	177	98	98	46	82	5	791	
pct.	12.4	23.6	22.4	12.4	12.4	5.8	10.4	0.6		

Table 6. Evaluation results, second group (891 abstracts).

intellig.	accuracy									
	0	1	2	3	4	5	6	defect.	tot.	pct.
1	61	0	7	5	0	3	7	0	83	9.3
2	0	142	22	27	8	13	9	0	221	24.8
3	0	0	138	68	44	26	17	4	297	33.3
4	0	0	10	24	35	16	37	4	126	14.1
5	0	0	0	1	6	7	149	1	164	18.4
total	61	142	177	125	93	65	219	9	891	
pct.	6.8	15.8	19.9	14.0	10.4	7.3	24.6	1.0		

Table 6a. More recent evaluation (September 1985).

intellig.	accuracy										
	0	1	2	3	4	5	6	7	defect.	tot.	pct.
1	256	1	34	13	6	6	2	0	0	318	24.5
2	1	274	36	31	26	11	1	0	1	381	29.3
3	0	0	157	87	79	26	29	0	6	384	29.5
4	0	0	19	39	60	16	24	1	3	162	12.5
5	0	0	2	3	18	2	10	0	0	35	2.7
?				1	1				18	20	1.5
total	257	275	248	174	190	61	66	1	28	1300	
pct.	19.8	21.2	19.1	13.4	14.6	4.7	5.1	0.1	2.2		

Table 7. Comparison between first and second groups for intelligibility.

intelligibility	first group 791	second group 891
1	14.7%	9.3%
2	32.7%	24.8%
3	32.7%	33.3%
4	12.6%	14.1%
5	7.3%	18.4%

Table 8. Typical sample sentences in different evaluation categories.

accuracy	first group 791	second group 891
0	12.4%	6.8%
1	23.6%	15.8%
2	22.4%	19.9%
3	12.4%	14.0%
4	12.4%	10.4%
5	5.8%	7.3%
6	10.4%	24.6%
	0.6%	1.0%

Acknowledgements

We are deeply indebted to Professor Toyoaki Nishida (Kyoto University), Mr. Yoshiyuki Sakamoto (ETL), Tsuyoshi Toriumi (JICST), and Masayuki Sato (JICST) for taking part in this project, and to many other people from private companies for their help in the development of the system. We are grateful to the Science and Technology Agency and to the Agency of Engineering Technology for their constant funding of and guidance for the project. Professors Yutaka Kusanagi, Shinobu Takamat-su, Makoto Hirai, and others gave us comments during the development of the system.

References

Nagao, Makoto, Nishida, Toyoaki and Tsujii, Jun-ichi (1984), "Dealing with the Incompleteness of Linguistic Knowledge in Language Translation," *Proceedings of COLING-84*, Stanford University, California, pp. 420-427.

Nakamura, Jun-ichi, Tsujii, Jun-ichi and Nagao, Makoto (1984), "Grammar Writing System (GRADE) of Mu-Machine Translation Project and its Characteristics," *Proceedings of COLING-84*, Stanford University, California, pp. 338-343.

Sakamoto, Yoshiyuki, Satoh, Masayuki, and Ishikawa, Tetsuya (1984), "Lexicon Features for Japanese Syntactic Analysis in Mu-Project-JE," *Proceedings of COLING-84*, Stanford University, California, pp. 42-47.

Tsujii, Jun-ichi, Nakamura, Jun-ichi and Nagao, Makoto (1984), Analysis Grammar of Japanese in the Mu-Project, in *Proceedings of COLING-84*, Stanford University, California, pp. 267-274.

Wilks, Yorick (1973), "An Artificial Intelligence Approach to Machine Translation," in R. C. Schank and K. M. Colby (eds.), *Computer Models of Thought and Language*. W. H. Freeman, San Francisco, pp. 114-151.

Appendix A: Sample Output and Intelligibility Scores

Intelligibility = 1

高周波非自続放電中のドリフト電流の大きさ，荷電粒子密度，電場の分布を数値的に研究した。

Distributions of size, charged particle density and electrical fields of drift currents during the high frequency non-self-sustaining discharge were studied numerically.

安定した同時動作アークを実現するための条件を非平衡ブリッジ回路として解析し，計算機を用いて解く。

Conditions for realizing stabilized simultaneously-operated arcs are analyzed as non-balanced bridge circuits, and the solution is made by using computers.

質量，電荷，運動量およびエネルギー保存式を適当な境界条件下で反復有限差分法によって解く。

Mass, charges, momentum and energy preservation formulas are solved by the iterative finite differential method under appropriate boundary conditions.

Intelligibility = 2

真空中の誘電体板に入射する平面波の回折により生じる表面波の複素振幅と等価表面電流分布を積分方程式の数値解により見出す。

Complex amplitudes and equivalent surface current distribution of the surface waves formed by the diffraction of the plane wave emitted to dielectric plates in vacua are found by numerical solutions of integral equations.

平面波到達方向が切線に近いほど不規則部近傍での解の非一様成分振幅は増大，縁による散乱の寄与が増大する。

As the plane wave arrival direction is close to tangents, the nonuniform component amplitude of solutions in the neighborhood of the irregular section is increased, and the number of contributions of the scattering by edges increases.

強度ゆらぎに凍結仮説が成立するとき光電子増倍管電流スペクトル密度二乗平均値は周期性をもつ。

Multiplier photo tube current spectrum root-mean-square values have the periodicity when freezing hypotheses are established in the intensity fluctuation.

Intelligibility = 3

幾何光学理論を反射波の計算に用いる場合，波源と観測点を与えた時の導体面上の反射点を知る必要がある。

Specular points of the conductor surfaces when wave sources and observation points are given have to be known when geometrical optics theories are applied to the calculation of reflected waves.

荷電粒子の運動は準静的共振モードＨ００の周波数の近くに周波数スペクトルが集中した回折放射バーストをともなうことを明らかにした。

It was done that the motion of charged particles accompanies the diffractive radiation bursts which frequency spectra concentrated in the neighborhood of frequencies of quasi-static resonance mode H OO be obvious.

放射エネルギーは粒子が共振器結合スロット上を飛ぶとき最大で粒子固有電磁場の非一様性を反映する。

As for the radiation energy it is maximum when particles fly resonator coupled slots, and the nonuniformity of the particle intrinsic electromagnetic field is reflected.

Intelligibility = 4

電荷の発生原因は生活環境，産業環境のいたる所にあり，材料や運動経過の他に表面の形状状態や導電率，誘電率，湿度などが重要である。

ある as for causes of generation of charges in every place of the living environment and the industrial environment, and forms, conductivity, dielectric constants, humidity of surfaces, and so on are important as well as materials and movement.

実機には軸対称と言えない部分が存在する場合が多いが，この場合のモデル化には補正係数を導入し，それを非線形反復計算の中に組み入れた。

There were many cases in which the parts exist which 言える in real machine be axi-symmetric but correction factors were introduced for the modeling of this case, and it was incorporated in nonlinear iterative computations.

真横および配列方向から入射した場合，円柱間隔および円柱半径に対する前方，後方散乱断面積および円柱近傍における空間的な合成電界および磁界の等振幅分布を示し，散乱波の特性を明らかにした。

The equiamplitude distribution of the spatial composite electric fields and magnetic fields to intervals of the conducting cylinders and radii of the conducting cylinder in front rear scattering cross section and the neighborhood of the cylinder was shown, and characteristics of scattering waves were done be obvious when the emission was made from sides and array directions.

Intelligibility = 5

手作業から自動整形そう入機械までの各種そう入機械を紹介。

The various insertion machine till automatic forming machines is introduced by the manual operation.

プリント配線自体は集積回路化が進んだが，マザーボード裏の配線は主に巻付け配線である。

Integrated circuits proceed in the printed wiring itself, and the wiring of the mother board reverse is mainly the wire wrapping.

自動機による配線の比率が増大し，手作業の２倍以上になった。

Ratios of the wiring by automatic machines increased, and they became more than two twice of the manual operation.

Appendix B: Sample Output and Accuracy Scores

Accuracy = 0

小規模不均質性をもつ平面不均質媒質からの空間変調波の反射を研究。

The reflection of space modulated waves from the plane nonhomogeneous medium with small-scale heterogeneity is studied.

ランダム不均質成層媒質からの周期変調信号の反射特性を研究。

Reflection characteristics of periodically modulated signals from media of random nonhomogeneous layers are studied.

2つのはん関数の順序積の平均値。

Mean values of ordered products of two functionals.

Accuracy = 1

応答の高次平均が順序キュミュラントで表現され，物理系のＧａｕｓｓ特性を最大限利用できる。

High-order averages of responses are expressed by the ordinal cumulant, and the Gauss characteristic of physical systems can be utilized to the utmost.

横波の半影域内での電磁場の一様漸近特性。

Uniform asymptotic characteristics of electromagnetic fields in half shadows of transversal waves.

反射場ポテンシャルの正解の漸近特性の解析により横波の半影域からの任意の距離で成立する場の一様漸近式を得た。

Uniform asymptotic equations of the fields established in arbitrary distances from the half shadow region of transversal waves by the analysis of asymptotic characteristics of correct answers of the reflection field potential were obtained.

Accuracy = 2

加速された荷電場のブラデオン部分とタキオン部分への分解。

The analysis of accelerated charged fields to bradyonic and tachyonic parts.

円形加速機中の電子の角度分布を知ることが電子ビームの動力学の研究及びいくつかの応用にとって重要である。

It is important from research and several applications of dynamics of electron beams to know the angle distribution of electrons in circular accelerators.

カットオフ下の電流密度は電圧とギャップ距離の関数で与えられ実験と相反する。

The current density under the cutoff is given by functions of voltages and gap distances, and the current density under the cutoff contradicts experiments.

Accuracy = 3

実現条件には行列が含まれ，多変数と単一変数の回路網間の基本的差を強調する。

Realization conditions include matrices, and basic differences between single-variable networks are stressed multivariable.

スレーブ側の結線方法，スレーブへの要請など概要を述べた後，いくつかの論理構成の例を示す。

Several examples of the logical composition are given after describing outlines such as methods for connection of the slave side and requests for slaves.

次に，診断機能について議論した後，将来の拡張性及びシステム素子の生産販売状況について述べる。

Next, production and marketing situations of the future expansibility and system elements are described after discussing diagnostic functions.

Accuracy = 4

次にスレーブ論理を実行するはん用のアドレス論理回路とデータ制御回路を示す。

The 汎用だ address logical circuits and data control circuits executing the slave logic next are shown.

測定端出力をディジタル化処理して誤差修正を行うが，ケーブルコネクタ間の反射係数，不整合時の損失などの測定例を述べ，精度にも言及した。

The error correction is carried out by processing the measuring terminal output digitally, and measurement examples such as reflection coefficients of cable connectors and losses at the time of the mismatching are described, and the accuracy is also refered to.

方法としては有限差分法を用い，関連式は電磁界法則の積分形によった。

Related equations were based on the integral type of laws of electromagnetic field as methods by using finite differential methods.

Accuracy = 5

ＤＣ解の一意性，自励振動回路網のある与えられた領域での漸近安定性を論ずることができる。

The asymptotic stability in the regions by which there is an unique self-excited vibration network of the DC solution and for giving the unique self-excited vibration network of the DC solution can be discussed.

この条件は，よく知られている線形，時不変，集中定数ｎポート回路網の時間域，周波数域の受動性，無損失性条件の非線形な場合への拡張となっている。

This condition becomes the expansion of passivity and losslessness conditions of time region and frequency region of linear and time-invariable well known concentrated constant n-port networks to nonlinear cases.

この方法では電気回路の解析は主としてシステム方程式を使って行う。

Electric circuits are 解析する ed by using system equations mainly in this method.

Accuracy = 6

全体で１００ｋｍ以上のＡｌ管の長さになるが，接合及び施工法を示し，Ａｌの特徴を生かした応用例として紹介。

It becomes the length of AL tubes of more than 100 km in wholes, and junctions and installation methods are shown, and introduced as application examples utilizing features of the AL.

在来の対話式システムと異なり，ピン位置を人手でディジタル化，入力する必要がない。

Unlike conventional interactive systems, pin positions are digitized be manual, and they do not have to be inputted.

ピン位置，ピン数，電流容量によるピン寸法を自動的に最適化する。

Pin dimensions by pin positions, number of pins and current capacity are optimized automatically.

はんだ付けにさいし界面で標記の化合物が形成される。

The soldering forms above-mentioned compounds in interfaces.

SPANAM and ENGSPAN: Machine Translation at the Pan American Health Organization

Muriel Vasconcellos and Marjorie León

1 Project History and Current Status

1.1 Overview

Machine translation has been supporting the activities of the Pan American Health Organization (PAHO) since 1980. SPANAM, the system that translates from Spanish into English, began to produce texts for requesting offices within the Organization in 1980, and the English-Spanish system, ENGSPAN, became operational in 1984. As of December 1985, SPANAM had produced 2,614,779 words of translation (10,459 pages) in response to 872 job orders, while ENGSPAN had translated 612,973 words (2,452 pages), of which 594,293 words (2,377 pages) were production texts, requested under 146 orders. The translation programs run on PAHO's mainframe computer (now an IBM 4381 running under DOS/VSE/SP), which is used for many other purposes as well. A version of the program is also available for the IBM 3081 (OS/MVS). Texts are submitted and retrieved using the ordinary word-processing workstation (Wang OIS/140) as a remote job-entry terminal. Production is in batch mode only. The input texts come from the regular flow of documentation in the Organization, and there are no restrictions as to field of discourse or type of syntax. Specially trained translators, working at the word-processing screen, produce polished output of standard professional quality at a rate between two and three times as fast as traditional translation (4,000-10,000 words a day for post-editing *vs.* 1,500-3,000 for human

---

SPANAM and ENGSPAN are trademarks of the Pan American Health Organization.

translation). The output is ready for delivery to the requesting office with no further preparation required.

The translation programs and their supporting software are currently written in PL/I. SPANAM's speed on the mainframe has been registered at 1,500 words per minute in clock time (495,000 words an hour in CPU time), while that of ENGSPAN has reached 836 wpm in clock time (102,000 wph CPU). They run with size parameters of 215K and 800K, respectively. As of December 1985, the dictionaries for SPANAM had 61,282 source entries and 58,485 target entries, while those of ENGSPAN had 45,614 and 47,545, respectively. These reside on permanently mounted disks and occupy from 7 to 10MB each.

SPANAM and ENGSPAN use essentially the same modular system architecture. ENGSPAN is more advanced linguistically, however, since it has an ATN parser and separate lexical and syntactic transfer modules. The overall policy is to regularly upgrade SPANAM as breakthroughs become available in the more sophisticated ENGSPAN. In this way it has been possible to maintain ongoing production with SPANAM while its capabilities are gradually enhanced and expanded. Because of this dynamic mode of development, information about the theoretical status of either SPANAM or ENGSPAN is necessarily short-lived.

1.2 Early History: 1976-1979

The Pan American Health Organization, with headquarters in Washington, D.C., is the specialized international agency in the Americas that has responsibility for action in the field of public health. It comes under the umbrellas of both the Inter-American System and the United Nations family, serving in the latter instance as Regional Office of the World Health Organization. In addition to its headquarters staff of 533 in Washington, PAHO has a field staff of 657 that supports both the operational programs in its 10 Pan American centers and 29 other offices in the field serving the 38 member countries.

Business may be conducted in any of the four official languages: Spanish, English, Portuguese, and French. The translation demand is greatest into Spanish, which over the years has corresponded to more than half the total workload (average 57 percent), and, after that, into English. The demand for Portuguese is considerably smaller, and there is only an occasional requirement for French.

In 1975 the Organization's administrators undertook a feasibility study and determined that MT might be a means of reducing the expenditure for translation. There was already a mainframe computer, then an IBM 360, at the headquarters site, and the decision was made to develop an MT system that would run on this installation on a time-sharing basis. Work was to focus on the Spanish-English and English-Spanish combinations. The effort was to be supported under the Organization's regular budget.

The intention from the outset was that MT should articulate with the routine flow of text in PAHO. Post-editing was considered to be unavoidable, since the system would have to deal with free syntax, with any vocabulary normally used in the Organization, and, in time, with a large range of subjects and different genres of discourse. No serious thought was given to a mode of operation that would require pre-editing.

Initial efforts began in 1976. A team of three part-time consultants worked under contract for the Organization for two years, and one of these consultants remained with the project on a part-time basis for a third year. In the beginning the translation strategy reflected some of the principles that had been applied at Georgetown University in the late 1950's and early 1960's in the course of work on the Russian-English system. It should be stressed, however, that the project's theoretical orientation has evolved significantly, and that the algorithm now reflects up-to-date linguistic and computational approaches.

The consultants chose to address the Spanish-English direction first because they recognized that results could be available earlier than if they had started with English as the source. Parallel efforts were concentrated on the architecture of the system itself and the extensive supporting software. The period 1976-1978 saw the mounting of this architecture and the writing of a basic algorithm for the translation of Spanish into English. At the end of three years the Spanish-English algorithm was in place, as well as a set of PL/I support programs that performed a variety of related tasks. The Spanish source dictionary had been built to a level of 48,000 entries, with corresponding English glosses in the separate target dictionary. Work on the dictionaries was supported by mnemonic, user-friendly software developed in 1978-1979 to facilitate the operations of updating, side-by-side printing, and retrieval of individual records. A corpus of about 50,000 words had been translated from Spanish into English.

Human resources during the period 1976-1978 consisted of the three part-time consultants together with PAHO's contribution in the form of dictionary manpower (total 24 staff-months in the three-year period) and, starting in 1977, half-time participation of the staff terminologist, who assumed the responsibility of coordination. A computational linguist was recruited and assigned to the project at the end of 1979.

The year 1980 was a turning-point for MT at PAHO. Advances came together which made it possible to move into a production mode. With the computational linguist on board, the programs were greatly improved, and the operational problems of text input, the most serious impediment to production, were resolved. An interface established between the IBM mainframe and the Organization's word-processing facility (then a Wang System 30) enabled MT to take its place in the text-processing chain and tap into a large body of text that had been made machine-readable for other purposes. A program was written to convert the Wang text for processing on the IBM mainframe, and thereafter any Spanish text that had been keyed into the word-processor, regardless of the purpose for which it was entered, was available for machine translation.

1.3 Operational Phase: 1980-present

Today the machine translation activity functions as a component of the Organization's newly merged Language Services, and the human translators in both languages post-edit machine output directly on the screen. However, progress toward this end has been gradual.

In 1981, the increasingly steady flow of requests for translation justified the assignment of a full-time post-editor. The rising demand was matched by an expanded volume of texts prepared originally in machine-readable form. Whereas word processing had previously been restricted to special services provided by a typing pool, the installation of word-processing hardware (Wang OIS/140) throughout the headquarters building brought all the program units into the text-processing chain. Furthermore, an optical character reader (then a Compuscan Alphaword II) was interfaced with the word-processing system; thus, existing typewriters could also be used as input devices, and this meant that texts could be prepared in the field, and scanned in Washington for subsequent input to SPANAM.

With accelerated production, improvements to SPANAM followed in tandem. From the beginning it was the policy, and continues to be so today with both SPANAM and ENGSPAN, that the output from production serves not only to meet the purpose for which it was requested but also to provide feedback for further development of the algorithm and dictionaries. As post-editing proceeds, the translator makes note of recurring problems at all levels on a side-by-side version of the output (for every translation two outputs are generated, the side-by-side hard copy and the word-processing document on the screen). The messages noted by the translators serve as a basis both for updating the dictionaries and for making enhancements, as feasible, in the algorithm. The capture of this information at the time of post-editing saves much work later on.

This mode of operation has brought the dictionaries to their current size. The totals correspond largely to base, or stem, entries, rather than fully inflected forms. For example, in SPANAM's Spanish source dictionary of 61,282 entries, 94% were stems and 6% were full forms. For both systems the incidence of not-found words in random text is well under 1 percent – limited usually to proper names, scientific names, new acronyms, and nonce formations. Through coordination with the terminology side of the program, the glosses have been increasingly tailored to the specific requirements of PAHO. In addition, microglossaries have been established for various users, so that specialized glosses can be elicited.

Further details about the working environment are given in Sections 2 and 6 below.

1.4 SPANAM/ENGSPAN Development: 1981-present

In early 1981 a long-range strategy was decided on for the continued improvement of SPANAM and the development of a parallel system from English into Spanish. Two consultants from Georgetown University, Professors R. Ross Macdonald and Michael Zarechnak, undertook separate evaluations of SPANAM at that time. Their recommendations led to the adoption of a combined working mode in which improvements were to be introduced in SPANAM according to a predetermined schedule while at the same time development began on the other system, ENGSPAN. Recognizing that each language combination imposed a different set of linguistic priorities, the consultants nevertheless emphasized that greatly expanded parsing was needed in both cases, especially in the analysis of English as a source language. Such parsing, in turn, called for revision of the dictionary record in order to allow for a broader range of syntactic and semantic coding. It was felt that the basic modular architecture of SPANAM, as well as the dictionary record in its essential format, should be used for ENGSPAN as well. A common architecture for the two systems meant that they could continue to share the same supporting software. Thus, improvements could migrate readily from one system to the other; it would be easy for them to cross-fertilize.

Having adopted this approach to development, with each side to benefit systematically from the work being done on the other, the project addressed its attention in 1981 to the enhancements that had been recommended for SPANAM. Then, as the SPANAM effort tapered off, time was devoted increasingly to ENGSPAN. By the end of 1982 the ENGSPAN program and dictionaries (about 40,000 source entries, most of them with acceptable glosses in the Spanish target) were in place.

Translation from English into Spanish has special importance for public health in the developing countries, and this fact provided the incentive for seeking extrabudgetary support from the U.S. Agency for International Development (AID). In August 1983 AID gave the Organization a two-year grant for the accelerated development of ENGSPAN. This funding made it possible to have a second computational linguist for the grant period, as well as consultants and part-time dictionary assistants who undertook specific tasks within the approved plan of work.

With the added manpower, the project made significant progress on the English-Spanish algorithm. Particular focus was placed on the development of a parser using an augmented transition network (ATN), which as of April 1984 was integrated into the rest of the ENGSPAN program. The dictionary record was modified without any increase in its overall size, so that it can now accommodate 211 fields, as compared with 82 in the 1980 version of SPANAM. Introduction of the new syntactic and semantic codes in the English dictionary was completed in 1985.

2 Application Environment

2.1 Pre-editing Policy

As indicated above, it has always been expected that the output of SPANAM and ENGSPAN would have to be post-edited. There was no application of MT at PAHO for which a customized language would be feasible. Nor was it to be expected in the near future that either of its source languages would be the front end of other language pairs. In these circumstances, there were few advantages to be gained from pre-treatment of the input. Since post-editing was inevitable, it was felt that an additional pre-editing step would be uneconomic: the advantages would not be sufficient to offset the added cost of a second human pass. Moreover, in order for pre-editing to be worthwhile, the process would have to draw on a high degree of linguistic sophistication, and adequate manpower for this purpose was scarce.

Thus, pre-editing in the linguistic sense has been ruled out for SPANAM and ENGSPAN. In theory, a document can be sent for execution by SPANAM without being seen by any human eyes. If the operator has keyed in the original Spanish document using normal in-house typing conventions, no adjustments should be required. With inexperienced operators, the precaution is taken to check the format, particularly the line-spacing and page width, since deviations from the standard at that level can disrupt the work of the algorithm. OCR input also needs to be reviewed for accuracy.

Production texts are usually run only once. For long projects, particularly with ENGSPAN, the translation is run in several parts, additions or changes being made to the dictionaries after each section is processed. Demonstrations are always performed on random text.

2.2 Post-editing Policy

2.2.1 General Position

It is a firm rule at PAHO that post-editing is done by professional translators who have been specially trained in the techniques of handling machine output. The strictness of this rule is balanced against a flexible standard for the degree of post-editing required.

The decision as to the extensiveness of post-editing takes into account:

- the purpose of the translation,
- the user's own resources for editing,
- the time frame, and
- structural linguistic considerations in the text itself.

A text may be needed for information only, for publication, or for a variety of uses between these two extremes. If it is to be edited by the requesting office, only the most glaring problems are dealt with by the translator. On the other hand, if it is to be published without much further review, the translator devotes careful attention to the quality of the text. These factors are determined in consultation with the user at the time the job is submitted. As to time constraints, it may happen that the work has to be delivered under considerable pressure: information-only translations of 20-25 pages may have to be delivered within a couple of hours, and once a 40-page proposal for funding was delivered in polished form the same day it was requested. With translation for publication, however, longer periods are negotiated.

Contrary to what might be deduced from the nature of PAHO's mission, SPANAM and ENGSPAN are asked to cope with a wide range of subject areas and types of text. There have been: documents for meetings, international agreements, technical and administrative reports, proposals for funding, summaries and protocols for international data bases, journal articles and abstracts, published proceedings of scientific meetings, training manuals, letters, lists of equipment, material for newsletters – even film scripts. They are certainly what Lawson (1982:5) would call "try-anything" systems.

The fact that SPANAM and ENGSPAN have such highly varied applications makes it particularly necessary to use trained professional translators as post-editors. Whereas Martin Kay (1982:74) suggests that the person who interprets machine output "would not have to be a translator and could quite possibly be drawn from a much larger segment of the labor pool," experience in the PAHO environment suggests that this conclusion would be valid only for technical experts working on a text for information purposes – a circumstance that is rare at PAHO.

Only an experienced translator will be aware of the words whose variable meanings are dependent on extralinguistic context. For example, *proyecto* in Spanish can be translated as "project," "proposal," or "draft," and the choice depends on full knowledge of the situation to which the text refers. *Esperar* can be translated as "hope" or "expect," and the difference is significant in English – sometimes even crucial. Such ambiguities require the attention of a translator with training, experience, good knowledge of the subject-matter vocabulary in both languages, and a technical understanding of what is meant by the text. Only a person with this combined background is in a position to make the choices that will fully reflect the intention of the original author. Another area in which the translator's role is important is in interpretation of the degree of intensity associated with relative terms. For example, *trascendente* in Spanish can have much less force than its English cognate, and the entire tone of a message may be over- or underdrawn depending on the interpretation given to a key term of this nature. Indeed, it has been the experience of SPANAM that users, even technical experts, can misinterpret the glosses appearing in the machine output and assign an altogether incorrect meaning in the process of "correcting" the text. The role of the experienced translator is not to be underestimated.

It was these considerations that led PAHO to form a combined language service, effective as of November 1984, under which all translators would ultimately be expected to devote part of their time to the post-editing of MT output. Fortunately, at the time of the merger there were six translator vacancies, and for four of these posts arrangements were made to include post-editing, and also dictionary maintenance, in the job description and in the announcement that listed the duties of the staff being recruited. This policy will be continued with future vacancies. Thus the incoming translators are aware from the outset that their duties will include post-editing.

2.2.2 Linguistic Strategies

In addition to experience in the interpretation of nuances, the post-editor needs a strong linguistic background in order to master the particular strategies that have proven to be effective in the recasting of certain unwieldy constructions that frequently recur – with SPANAM, for example, the result of translating a verb that was in sentence-initial position in Spanish. For the translator untrained in post-editing, the most time-consuming task is the recasting of such constructions. For problems of this kind a series of "quick-fix" post-editing expedients (QFP) have been developed. At the same time, there is a series of word-processing aids that help to speed up the physical process of editing and to deal with pragmatic decisions in the output which are not handled by syntactic rules.

To follow through with the example mentioned above, certain maneuvers are suggested as being useful with fronted verb constructions in Spanish, which occur frequently and present difficulties for the SVO pattern typically required for English. The purpose of the QFP is to minimize the number of steps that are required in order to make the sentence work. Since it was a V(S)O construction that triggered the problem in the first place, any solution that avoids reordering will necessarily depart from one-on-one syntactic fit. In other words, in the example of the fronted verb, one might try to see if the opening phrase, which will be a discourse adjunct, a cognitive adjunct (terms from Halliday 1967), or the main verb itself, could be nominalized so that it can serve as the subject of the sentence in English. Such an approach manages to preserve in the theme position (Halliday 1967) the cognitive material which had been thematic in the source text, usually with a parallel effect on the focus position as well (Vasconcellos 1985b). For this reason, the result is often quite satisfactory, even compared with a translation that is syntactically more "faithful" – see Section 6 below, and (Vasconcellos 1986). The examples below compare QFPs with solutions that were actually proposed by translators new to post-editing (THT = traditional human translation).

In example (1) the semantic content of the fronted verb is reworked into a noun phrase that can serve as the subject of the sentence. Time is saved by leaving the rheme of the sentence untouched; only a few characters, highlighted inside the box, were changed. Moreover, additional speed was gained by making changes from left to right, in the same direction in which the text is being reviewed.

(1) Durante 1983 se inició ya la transformación paulatina de estos planteamientos en acciones.

MT: During 1983 ~~there~~ was initiated already the gradual transformation of these proposals into actions.

THT: During 1983 these proposals already began to be gradually transformed into actions. (62 keystrokes)

QFP: During 1983 progress began toward the gradual transformation of these proposals into actions. (27 keystrokes)

In example (2), on the other hand, the adjunct itself is nominalized, again with a significant saving of time and keystrokes:

(2) En este estudio se buscará contestar dos preguntas fundamentales:

MT: [In] this study [it will be sought] to answer two fundamental questions:

THT: In this study answers to two fundamental questions will be sought: (53 keystrokes)

QFP: This study [seeks] to answer two fundamental questions: (14 keystrokes)

Use of this approach, wherever feasible, as well as ones that have been devised for other troublesome differences between the source and target languages, adds up to substantial economy, with apparently little or no deterioration in the quality of the translation (see Section 6 below). However, knowing when and how to make such changes requires considerable skill. This is one more reason why the post-editor should have a strong background in translation and, if possible, in linguistics as well.

It has always been emphasized in the post-editing of SPANAM and ENGSPAN that editorial changes should be kept to the minimum that is needed in order to make the output intelligible and acceptable for its intended purpose.

2.2.3 Word-processing Strategies

The post-editors work directly on-screen. Experience has shown that post-editing on hard copy, with the changes entered by a "word-processing operator," is not a highly efficient mode. Accordingly, attention has also been given to speeding up the post-edit by automating as many of the recurring operations as possible.

The SEARCH-and-REPLACE function on the word processor is heavily used in post-editing. In addition, SPANAM and ENGSPAN have a series of special macros that have been developed for purposes of MT. Besides a full set of possible word switches ($1 \times 1, 1 \times 2, 2 \times 1, 2 \times 2, 1 \times 3, 3 \times 1, 3 \times 3$, etc.), there are macros that deal with the particular character strings that have to be changed most often in the output for pragmatic reasons. For example, with a single "glossary" keystroke it is possible to perform the following editorial operations in the English output:

SEARCH-and-DELETE:

the, *of*, *there*, *to*, *in order to*

SEARCH-and-REPLACE:

from replaces *of*, *for/of*, *for/by*, *in order to V/for Ving*, *a/the*, *which/that*, *who/that*, *every/each*, *among/between*, *such as/as*, *some of the/some*

The inventory can be changed or expanded at will.

2.2.4 Other Time-savers

From the discussion above it can be seen that speed in post-editing is achieved by a combination of strategies. Some of the points made may appear at first sight to be unimportant, but yet they can add up to a significant difference. One example of an apparently trivial factor is the method of positioning the cursor under the string to be modified. Delays at this point can add up to a surprising proportion of total time spent on post-editing, since they will occur with every change that is made. Informal experiments suggest that the most efficient approach for positioning the cursor is to always use the SEARCH key. (The "mouse" and light pencil remain to be fully investigated.) The slowest method, unfortunately, seems to be the one that is most often used, namely simple manual striking of the directional keys. Since people tend to rely on the directional keys unless otherwise trained, this point is emphasized with the post-editors who work on SPANAM and ENGSPAN.

The staff of the project are constantly on the lookout for new ways of saving time. All tasks are streamlined as much as possible. A series of programs has been developed on the word processor for automating the housekeeping support that has to be done apart from post-editing, and recently some of this work was made even more efficient by passing it on to the mainframe computer.

2.3 Post-editing vis-à-vis Other Aspects of the System

In the PAHO MT environment there is a close link between post-editing and the other aspects of the system. The translators are trained to update the dictionaries, and required changes in the dictionaries are proposed at the time of post-editing. This saves going through the text a second time, and it also captures ideas about the glosses and coding of a particular item when the translator has the entire text fresh in mind. This person, if adequately trained in updating, is in an excellent position to decide how to deal with the specific constructions that tend to recur in production translations.

The translators also alert the computational linguist to areas where the algorithm needs improvement.

2.4 Integration into a Complete Translation Environment

As of November 1985 the human and machine translation activities at PAHO, together with simultaneous interpretation, were merged into a single Language Services Unit. There is now centralized screening of incoming jobs. In addition, requestors are free to specifically request a machine translation if they wish. The triage makes it possible to maximize the effectiveness and efficiency of the respective modes. There is now a more rational utilization of the manpower available at any given time, with the staff being assigned to different duties depending on both needs and skills. Also, it is hoped to be able to ultimately reduce a given person's day in front of the word-processing screen from eight hours to six through the rotation of assignments. To date, however, there have been no complaints of eyestrain or other discomfort with the VDU.

In the area of management, the SPANAM/ENGSPAN programs on the mainframe computer are also helping with labor-intensive operations for which the human translation service is responsible: it is already performing automatic word counts, and spelling-check systems are being developed to reflect the Organization's highly technical vocabulary.

SPANAM/ENGSPAN can also help to lighten the load in the human translation process by retrieving technical and scientific terms in context. Considered from the standpoint of term retrieval, MT makes for an efficient lexical data base. With an ordinary LDB, the translator has to go to the terminal (which is not usually for his/her use alone), sign on, and initiate a search. After all the mechanical steps have been performed, there is still the possibility that the term is not in the data base at all, and that the effort will have been wasted. When this happens repeatedly over time, frustration builds up. With SPANAM/ENGSPAN, on the other hand, not only does the translator know immediately what translation has been assigned to the term, but he also knows its degree of reliability and whether or not a full terminological entry is available in the WHOTERM data base, which can be accessed from the same workstation. The status of a term is indicated by small superscript symbols which can be requested at the time the text is sent for translation.

WHOTERM's files normally contain: a definition of each term in English, translational equivalents in up to four languages besides English, synonyms if there are any, a reliability code for the primary term in each language, scope notes, and a subject code. In addition to the general file, it has files with: names of organizational entities, full equivalents for abbreviations, scientific names of pathogens, generic names of drugs in three languages, and chemical names of pesticides with trade names cross-referenced to them (Ahlroth and Armstrong-Lowe, 1983).

SPANAM/ENGSPAN can also aid the human translation process with the system of microglossaries for specialized subject areas (see Section 4.3 below). When a text is known to deal with a certain subject, the translator can request a corresponding microglossary which will contain alternative glosses. One or more of these microglossaries can be specified at the time the job is submitted. The post-editing translator can also have a microglossary of his/her own in which can be stored special glosses that he/she prefers to use.

It is possible for SPANAM/ENGSPAN to provide "slashed entries," *i.e.*, alternative choices in the output entry such as *project/proposal/draft*, *hope/expect*, *time/weather*, etc., although this is not the regular policy. These alternatives can be stored in a microglossary. In the output, the desired translation is saved and the rest is deleted with a single keystroke.

If the translator provides feedback in the form of suggested or requested changes in the dictionaries, the updating can be done immediately. Some of the requesting offices have developed the habit of providing regular feedback, and this means that their translations become increasingly tailored to their specific requirements.

While there is no doubt that SPANAM/ENGSPAN reach their maximum efficiency when post-edited on-screen, at the same time studies are being done on ways in which a translator can dictate the changes orally and then have a word-processing operator enter them, working from the audio tape.

The human translation service stands to benefit, also, from the macros that have been developed on the word processor in editing a text and from the word count and other support programs.

3 General Translation Approach

Since the bulk of the Organization's translation work involves only Spanish and English, the machine translation system was developed specifically for this pair of languages. No consideration was given to using the interlingua approach. The broad range of subject areas to be dealt with made it impractical to consider using a knowledge-based approach or one based on a representation of the meaning of the text. Although the systems are currently language-specific, significant portions of the algorithm could be adapted for use in a system involving Portuguese or French, the other official languages of the Organization. Because SPANAM and ENGSPAN were developed separately, they reflect different theoretical orientations and utilize different computational techniques. At the same time, they have many features in common.

SPANAM was originally designed as a direct translation system. The translation is produced through a series of operations which analyze the Spanish source string, transform the surface structure to produce a syntactic frame for the English target string, substitute the English glosses indicated by the results of the analysis, insert and/or delete certain grammatical morphemes, and synthesize the required endings on the English words. The principal stages involved in the translation algorithm are: morphological analysis and single-word lookup, gap analysis, multi-word unit lookup, homograph resolution, subject identification, treatment of prepositions, object pronoun movement, verb string analysis, subject insertion, *do*-insertion, noun phrase rearrangement, target lookup, target synthesis.

ENGSPAN is a lexical and syntactic transfer system based on the slot-and-filler approach to language structure. It performs a separate analysis of the English source string, applies transfer routines based on the contrastive analysis of English and Spanish, and then synthesizes the Spanish target string. The principal stages of this algorithm are: morphological analysis and single-word lookup, gap analysis, substitution and analysis unit lookup, sentence-level parse, lexical transfer, target lookup, syntactic transfer, and target synthesis. The program includes a backup module for homograph resolution, and backup strategies for verb string and noun phrase analysis, that are invoked if the sentence-level parse is unsuccessful.

4 Linguistic Techniques

4.1 Morphological Analysis

SPANAM's morphological lookup procedure makes it possible to find most Spanish words in their stem forms. The algorithm recognizes plural and feminine endings for nouns, pronouns, determiners, quantifiers, and adjectives; person, number, and tense endings for verbs; and derivational endings such as *-mente*/*-ly*. Bound clitic pronouns are separated from verb forms and any accent mark related to the presence of the clitic is removed. Another subroutine adds missing accent marks when the source word is written with an initial capital or in all capital letters. The components of compounds formed with hyphens or slashes are looked up as separate words. A few prefixes are also removed from words without a hyphen.

ENGSPAN's morphological analysis procedure, known as LEMMA, is called if the full-form is not found in the dictionary and the word consists of at least four alphabetic characters. This procedure checks for the presence of a number of different endings and contractions.

Each time an ending is removed, the new form of the word is looked up. LEMMA uses morphological and spelling rules and short lists of exceptions in order to determine when to remove or add a final *-e*, when the word ends in a double consonant, etc. If a lemmatized form of the word is found in the dictionary, its record is checked to make sure that its part of speech corresponds to the ending that was removed. If LEMMA exhausts all its possibilities, the word is checked against a list of prefixes and rules for British spelling. If these efforts are unsuccessful, a dummy record is created for the word and a gap analysis routine is called. Not-found words are initially considered to be common nouns (and proper nouns if capitalized) and given the possibility of also functioning as verbs and adjectives. Information from both LEMMA and derivational suffixes is used in order to confirm or reassign the main part of speech, as well as to confirm, remove, or add possibilities for ambiguities.

The lookup strategy used in both SPANAM and ENGSPAN keeps down the size of the dictionary while at the same time allowing a good deal of flexibility. The dictionary coder has the option of entering a word in its full form, in one or more of its inflected forms, or in its stem form. With irregular forms and homographs, the full form must be used. For example, in the Spanish source dictionary the only entries for the verb *esperar* are the stem *esper* and the verb/noun homograph *espera.* The English source dictionary contains an entry for *expect* and *unexpected*, but not for *expects*, *expected*, *expecting*, or *unexpectedly.*

4.2 Homograph Resolution

SPANAM deals with part-of-speech homographs at several different stages of the program. Ambiguities that can be resolved by morphological clues or capitalization are handled by the lookup procedure. Proper names are also identified at this stage. One-character words are distinguished from letters of the alphabet after the lookup has been completed. The homograph resolution module handles other types of homographs by examining the surrounding context.

The possible parts of speech for a word are indicated in the dictionary record in a series of bit fields which include: verb, noun, adjective, pronoun, determiner, numerative, preposition, modifier, adverb, conjunction, auxiliary, and prefix. Any combination of two or more bits may be coded. Other sequences of bit codes are used to distinguish between different types of pronouns, adverbs, and conjunctions: relative, interrogative, nominal, adverbial, connector, interruptive, compound, and coordinate.

The use of multiple-word substitution units reduces the number of lexical ambiguities which must be resolved by the algorithm. Analysis units may also be used to selectively specify the part of speech of any or all of the words covered by the unit.

ENGSPAN's front-line approach to homograph resolution is embodied in the ATN parser which is described below in Section 5.3. The English words can be coded for the same possible parts of speech as in SPANAM. Determination of the function of each word depends on the path taken through the network. The sequence of parts of speech which leads to the first successful parse is used as the basis for the transfer stage.

There are three ways in which lexical information from the dictionary is used to help the parser arrive at the correct analysis. Substitution units compress idioms into one record with a single part of speech. Analysis units can be used to indicate that a group of words can be expected to occur in collocation with a particular function. This information may be overridden, whenever necessary, by the parser. An individual word may also be coded to indicate which of its possible parts of speech is statistically most frequent. Again, the final decision is made by the parser based on the results of the sentence-level analysis.

4.3 Polysemy

SPANAM/ENGSPAN have two principal tools for dealing with polysemy: microglossaries and transfer units. Substitution units and analysis units are also used when common collocations are involved.

A microglossary is a subset of dictionary entries which can be selected for a particular subject area, discourse register, or user. Microglossary entries may be used in both the source and the target dictionaries. Glosses pertaining to the subject area of international public health form part of the main dictionary. Microglossaries are in use for special translations of terms in the fields of law, finance, sanitary engineering, agriculture, computer science, and biomedical research. The system may have up to 99 microglossaries with any number of entries in each one. The microglossaries to be consulted during the translation of a particular text are specified at run time. The existence of a specific microglossary entry is indicated in the main record for the word. Thus no time is wasted looking for special entries under every word. More than one microglossary may be activated for the same translation, in which event they are listed and consulted in order of priority.

The transfer unit is a lexical transfer rule which is stored in the source dictionary. The existence of a transfer unit is indicated in the record corresponding to the individual source word. A transfer unit specifies a condition to be tested and an action to be performed. Examples of conditions are:

- The subject of this verb has X feature(s) or is word W;
- The object of this verb (or preposition) has X feature(s) or is word W;
- This word modifies a word with X feature(s) or modifies word W;
- This word is modified by a word with X feature(s) or is modified by word W;
- This verb has N object(s);
- This verb governs preposition P and the object of P has X feature(s) or is word W;
- This verb has a complement of type T.

Transfer units are explicitly ordered in the dictionary. The action may either select an alternative translation, insert a word such as a preposition, or delete one or more words. The action also indicates whether or not additional transfer entries should be sought for the same word.

4.4 Syntactic and Semantic Features

The dictionary record for each lexical item (including substitution units) contains bit fields for storing information about its syntactic and semantic features. These features are used in all stages of the translation. For example, verbs and deverbal nouns are specified as occurring with one or more of the following possibilities: no object, one object, two objects, complement, locative, marked infinitive, unmarked infinitive, declarative clause, imperative clause, interrogative clause, gerund, adjunct, bound preposition, object followed by marked infinitive, object followed by clause, and object followed by bound preposition. Subject and object preferences can be specified as ±Human, ±Animate, and ±Concrete. Other fields can be made available for case frames at such time as they may be introduced. Features which can be coded for nouns include *count*, *bulk*, *concrete*, *human*, *animate*, *feminine*, *proper*, *collective*, *device*, *location*, *time*, *quantity*, *scale*, *color*, *nationality*, *material*, *apposition* (noun, infinitive, or clause), *body part*, *condition*, and *treatment.* Adjectives are coded for many of the same features mentioned above. In addition, they can be coded as *inflectable*, *optionally inflectable*, *comparable*, *general*, *temporary*, *resultative*, and *tough-movement.* Adverbs can be coded as *time*, *place*, *manner*, *motive*, *interruptive*, and *connector.* One of the references used in developing the coding scheme for the English entries was (Sager, 1981).

4.5 Annotated Surface Structure Nodes

In ENGSPAN, the structure produced by the parser consists of a graph of nodes corresponding to each clause and phrase. Each node has a table indicating its constituents, their roles, and their locations. If the constituent is a lexical item, the location is a word number; if it is a phrase or a clause, the location is the pointer to the appropriate node. Each node is annotated with features applicable to the type of phrase or clause involved. These features include *Type*, *Mood*, *Person*, *Number*, *Tense*, *Aspect*, and *Voice*.

Both the ATN formalism and the structural representation used in ENGSPAN draw heavily on the presentation of ATN parsers and systemic grammar in Winograd (1983). Winograd's discussion, in turn, is based on the work of Woods (1969 and 1971) and Kaplan (1973). Of course, the ATN parser has necessarily had to be adapted to the needs and computational environment of the PAHO project.

4.6 Spanish Verb Synthesis

The procedure for the synthesis of Spanish verb forms is based on principles of generative morphology and phonology. The program synthesizes all regular and most of the irregular verbs, in all tenses and moods except the future subjunctive, and in all persons except the second person plural. The verb is entered in the target dictionary in its stem form. Binary codes are used to specify the conjugation class and the 11 exception features that govern the synthesis of irregular forms. Only one dictionary entry is needed for each verb. A small number of highly irregular stems and full forms (74 in all) are listed in a table. The majority of "stem-changing" verbs require no special synthesis coding. The procedure consists of a series of morphological spellout rules; raising, lowering, diphthongization, and deletion rules based on phonological processes; stress assignment rules; and orthographic rules to handle predictable spelling changes.

Spanish verbs are also coded to permit the synthesis of the nominalization corresponding to "the action or process of." The verb synthesis procedure is invoked to produce nominalized forms which correspond to the first or third person present indicative or present subjunctive, or to the past participle or infinitival form of the verb. Other forms are produced by a combination of stem alterations and derivational affixes. Irregular forms require a separate target dictionary entry.

5 Computational Techniques

5.1 Dictionaries

The SPANAM/ENGSPAN dictionaries are VSAM files stored on a permanently mounted disk. The source and target dictionaries are separate files. The basic record has a fixed length of 160 bytes. The source entry is linked to its target gloss by means of a 12-digit lexical number (LEX). The first six digits of the LEX are the unique identification number which is assigned to each pair when it is added to the dictionary. The second half of the LEX is used to specify alternate target glosses associated with the same source entry. The main or default target gloss for each pair has zeroes in these positions.

5.1.1 Single-word Entries

The key for a source entry is the lexical item itself, which may be up to 30 characters in length. The source dictionary is arranged alphabetically. The key for a target entry is the LEX, and the target dictionary is arranged in numerical order.

Words may be entered in the source dictionary either with or without inflectional endings. Most nouns are entered only in the singular and adjectives only in the masculine singular. Verbs are entered as stems. Full-form entries are required for auxiliary verbs, words with highly irregular morphology, and homographs.

Several source items may be linked to the same target gloss by assigning them the same LEX. For example, irregular forms of the same verb or alternative spellings of a word require only one entry in the target dictionary. Likewise, more than one target gloss can be linked to the same source word through the lexical number. Each alternate gloss is distinguished by coding in the second half of the LEX. Two positions are used to designate terms belonging to microglossaries, two for glosses corresponding to different parts of speech, and two for context-sensitive glosses which are triggered by transfer units.

5.1.2 Multiple-word Entries

The dictionaries contain four types of multiple-word entries: substitution units (SU), analysis units (AU), delayed substitution units (DSU), and transfer units (TU). The key for a multiple-word entry in the source dictionary is a string consisting of the first six digits of the LEX for each word in the unit. With an SU or an AU, the words must occur consecutively in the sentence in order for the unit to be activated. A DSU or a TU can cover either a continuous or discontinuous string.

The basic SU contains from two to five words. A different record structure is used for longer entries, such as names of organizations and titles of publications. When an SU is retrieved, the dictionary records corresponding to the individual words are replaced with one record corresponding to the entire sequence. The gloss for the unit is also found in a single entry in the target dictionary. This type of unit is used in order to obtain the correct translation of names of organizations, titles of publications, slogans, etc., and is an efficient way of handling some fixed idioms, phrasal prepositions, and certain technical terminology. An SU record has the same format as a single-word entry. In addition, it contains a character string which indicates the part of speech of each of its members. This information can be used by the parser if it is unable to parse the sentence using the single part of speech specified for the unit. Examples of phrases which are entered as SUs are: *by leaps and bounds*, *International Drinking Water Supply and Sanitation Decade*, and *Health for All by the Year 2000.*

The AU, which also contains from two to five words, has several functions. At the very least, it alerts the analysis routines to the possible presence of a common phrase and provides information on its length and function. It can also be used to resolve the part-of-speech ambiguity of any of its members. Finally, it can specify an alternate translation for one or more of its parts. The AU is an entry in the source dictionary but has no counterpart in the target dictionary. The record for each source word is retained in the representation of the sentence, but the last two digits of its lexical number are modified if a translation other than the main gloss is desired. When the target lookup is performed, the gloss for each word is retrieved separately. This ensures that the rules for analysis and synthesis of conjoined modifiers will be able to access information about the individual words of the phrase. It also makes it possible for the parser to determine whether or not the individual words are being used as a unit in the given context. Examples of phrases entered as AUs are *drinking water* and *patient care*. The algorithm is still able to correctly analyze sequences such as *the children have been drinking water with a high fluoride content* and *it is essential that the patient care for himself.*

The DSU is used to handle lexical items such as phrasal verbs which are likely to occur as noncontiguous words in the input. The existence of a DSU is indicated in the source record of the first word of the unit. The unit is retrieved from the dictionary during the sentence-level parse. The decision of whether or not to accept the unit is based on both syntactic and semantic requirements of the parser. If the unit is accepted, it replaces the individual records and causes a different target gloss to be retrieved. Examples of DSUs are *look up*, *put on*, and *carry out*.

The TU is used to specify an alternate translation of a word or words which depends on the occurrence of a specific word or set of features in one of its arguments or in a specified environment. These entries are stored in the source dictionary only and are retrieved after the analysis has been completed. If the conditions specified in the transfer entry are met, the corresponding lexical numbers are modified so that the desired target gloss is selected during the target lookup. For example, if the object of *know* is coded as +Human, the verb is translated as *conocer* instead of *saber*. If *female* and *male* modify a noun coded as −Human, they are translated as *hembra* and *macho* instead of *mujer* and *hombre*.

5.2 Grammar Rules

SPANAM until recently used two basic types of grammar rules: pattern matching and transformations. Pattern matching is used for the recognition and reordering of noun phrases. The grammatical patterns are stored in a file which can be updated without recompiling the program. The patterns are applied by searching for the longest match first. Transformations are used to identify and synthesize the verb phrase and clitic pronouns. The rules are expressed in PL/I code and are grouped in modules according to the part of speech of the head word. Each group of rules is tested once for each sentence. The structural description of each rule is compared with the input string. The description may require a match of parts of speech, syntactic features, or specific lexical items. If a match is found, the rule is applied. The rule may permute, add, delete, or substitute lexical items or features associated with them.

ENGSPAN's analysis component takes the form of an augmented transition network. The network configuration indicates possible sequences of constituents. The rules governing the acceptability of any specific input string are contained in the conditions attached to the various arcs of the network. The building of the nodes of the structural representation and the assignment of features and roles is determined by actions associated with each arc. The conditions and actions are contained in separate modules which are part of the compiled program. The configuration of states and arcs is specified in a file which is updated on-line. The contents of this file also determine which of the conditions and actions are actually attached to specific arcs for a particular run.

As of December 1985, the ATN grammar had 11 networks: sentence, clause, noun phrase, verb phrase, sentence nominalization, hyphenated compound, prepositional phrase, comparative phrase, adverbial phrase, relative clause, and dependent clause. Each network consists of a set of states connected by arcs. Four types of arcs are used: CATEGORY arcs, which can be taken if the part of speech matches that of the input word; JUMP arcs, which can be taken without matching a word of the input; SEEK arcs, which initiate recursive calls to a network; and SEND arcs, which return control to the calling network after the successful parsing of a constituent. In all, there were 150 conditions and 60 actions as of December 1985.

5.3 Parsing Algorithm

The ENGSPAN algorithm performs a top-down, left-to-right sequential parse using a combination of chronological and explicit backtracking. The parser stops after completing the first successful parse. The path taken through the network depends on the ordering of the arcs at each state, the structural information already determined by the parser, and the codes contained in the dictionary record for each lexical item and multiple-word entry. Also available to the parser is information regarding sentence punctuation, capitalization, parenthetical material, etc., which has been gathered by an earlier procedure. The algorithm processes the words of the input string one at a time, moving from left to right. At each state, all arcs are tested to determine whether they may be taken for the current word. The possible arcs are placed on a pushdown stack and the top arc on the stack is taken. The parser continues through the input string as long as it can find an arc which it is allowed to take. If no arc is found for the current word, the parser backtracks. Which of the alternative arcs is taken off the stack depends on the situation that caused the parser to backtrack. If the end of the string is reached and the algorithm is at a final state in the network, the parse is successful. If no path can be found through the network, the parse fails.

Long-distance dependencies, such as those involved in relative clauses and WH-questions, are parsed using a *hold list*. When the parser encounters a noun phrase followed by a relative pronoun, a copy of the phrase is placed on the hold list. When a question is being parsed, the questioned element is placed on the list. When a gap is detected in the relative clause or interrogative sentence, the phrase on the hold list is used to fill the appropriate slot.

Whenever backtracking is required, a *well-formed phrase list* is used to save a copy of the phrases that have been completed but are about to be modified or rejected. For all SEEK arcs, the parser checks to see if a phrase of the appropriate type is already on the well-formed phrase list. If there are several phrases on the list that begin with the same word, the longest phrase is tried first. A new phrase is parsed only if there is nothing on the well-formed phrase list that satisfies the SEEK arc. In this way, large amounts of reparsing are avoided.

Conjoining is currently being handled by a configuration of arcs at the end of each subnetwork which allows additional phrases of the same type to be parsed recursively. When partial phrases are conjoined, the end of the subnetwork is reached by traversing one or more JUMP arcs.

The ATN parsing algorithm has been developed in an independent PL/I program, using the ENGSPAN input and dictionary lookup modules.[1] It is also totally compatible with SPANAM. The network grammar is read in at run time, making it possible to experiment with different network configurations without recompiling the program. Each time an enhanced version of the parser has been tested and debugged, it replaces the working version in the ENGSPAN program. The parser is being incorporated in a similar way into SPANAM as well.

Figure 1 shows the relationships between the major components of the translation algorithm and the data structures that it utilizes. A more detailed description of the ATN grammar and parser is found in a report submitted to the U.S. Agency for International Development (León and Schwartz, 1986).

5.4 Safety Net

In the event of an unsuccessful parse, ENGSPAN must still produce a Spanish text. A "safety-net" strategy has been built into the translation algorithm in order to enable the transfer component to operate with incomplete information from the analysis component. The quality of the translation obtained using the safety-net procedures is often quite acceptable. For many sentences, it may be comparable in accuracy and grammaticality to a translation based on a successful parse.

---

[1] A major portion of the parsing routines was developed by Lee Ann Schwartz

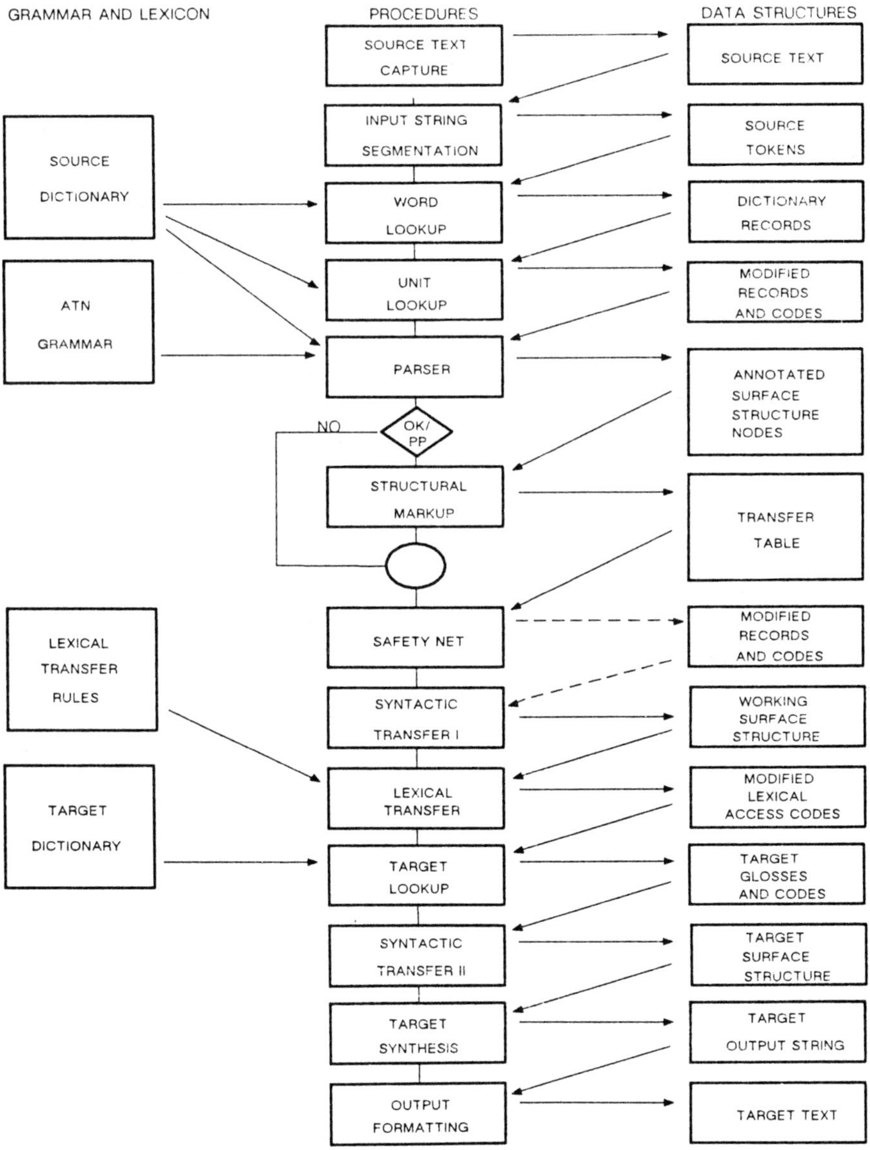

Figure 1. Major components of the translation algorithm.

The parser contributes to the safety net by keeping track of the longest path through the network whenever it is forced to backtrack. The amount of work done by the parser is limited by a parameter which can be specified at run time. If the limit is reached before the end of the input string, the parser stops and returns a partial parse. When a partial parse is produced, the surface structure nodes that are still active and have been assigned a headword are used as if they were part of a complete parse. Part-of-speech disambiguation for a word that does not belong to an active surface structure node is accomplished in one of two ways. If the word was parsed as part of the longest path, it is assigned the part of speech specified on the category arc originally traversed by the parser. A backup homograph resolution procedure determines the part of speech for words that were never accepted by the parser, *i.e.*, those that are not included in the longest path and all words within parentheses or dashes. The disambiguation procedure looks at a maximum of two tokens to the left and right, compares the syntactic environment with the coding of the word in question, and selects the most probable part of speech.

Other aspects of the safety net are incorporated in the procedures for lexical and syntactic transfer.

5.5 Transfer Component

5.5.1 Surface Structure Markup

When the parse is successful, the next step is to inspect the surface structure produced by the parser and derive additional information needed for translation. For example, noun phrases are assigned the semantic roles of *agent*, *object*, *experiencer*, or *beneficiary*. When a subject has been raised out of an embedded clause, the two roles of that noun phrase are indicated. For complements and reduced relative clauses, the modification relationships that were established by the parser are associated with specific lexical items. The result of this structural markup is a table which contains information about both the syntactic and semantic roles of the principal constituents of the sentence.

5.5.2 Lexical Transfer

The selection of alternate target glosses based on sentence context is governed by the AUs and TUs which are described in 4.3 above. Both these types of units offer the possibility of changing the LEX that is used for retrieval. AUs are applied before the sentence is parsed, while TUs are applied just prior to target dictionary lookup. Most types of TUs depend on the information produced by the parser, but the safety-net strategy allows some units to take effect even when the sentence cannot be parsed.

Lexical transfer itself is accomplished by retrieving from the Spanish target dictionary the record corresponding to the LEX of the English entry. This record is then examined to determine whether or not an alternate entry should be retrieved. Codes in the main target entry indicate the existence of additional records for microglossary entries, irregular plural nouns, irregular verb nominalizations, and adjectival translations for premodifying nouns and present participles.

5.5.3 Syntactic Transfer

The strategy for syntactic transfer is to utilize the surface structure of the source sentence, performing whatever operations are necessary in order to generate a grammatically correct and stylistically acceptable sentence in the target language. Whenever possible, the linear order of the phrasal units is preserved in order to maintain the overall cohesion of the text. Correct Spanish syntax is achieved through the manipulation of function words. Topicalization is also used to handle certain instances of preposed noun phrases. One situation that requires the postposing of the subject is that of a clause in which the finite verb is the final element.

The transfer component includes three different types of syntactic transfer rules. The first type is triggered by a lexical item in the English source text or the presence of a particular surface structure in English. The application of these rules generally results in a modification of the LEX used for retrieval of the Spanish gloss and therefore must be performed before the target lookup. The second type is a general syntactic transformation that converts a surface structure of

English to a surface structure of Spanish. These transformations are independent of the lexical items involved and can be performed either before or after target lookup. In ENGSPAN, they are performed prior to the target lookup. The third type of syntactic transfer rule depends on the characteristics of the lexical item in the Spanish target text and therefore must be applied after target lookup.

Examples of source-triggered rules are the transformation of *there* + *be* into the Spanish *haber* construction, and introduction of a first person subject in a sentence such as *Let us begin.* General rules include the ordering of the elements of the verb string, the insertion and ordering of clitic pronouns, the suppression of subject pronouns, and the nominalization of gerundive phrases that function as the object of a preposition. Examples of rules that require access to information about the target lexical items are subject-verb agreement, the ordering of the elements of the noun phrase, the triggering of the subjunctive mood and imperfect tense, and the transformation that reverses the syntactic roles of the subject and object with verbs such as *gustar* and *faltar*.

Syntactic transfer works best when the input string has been successfully parsed. Some rules, such as those that deal with subject-raising and subject postposition, can only be applied if the necessary information is available from the parse. For other rules, however, the transfer algorithm contains sufficient rules to make up for the lack of a complete parse. For example, verb strings with a limited amount of interruptive material can usually be restructured correctly. Most noun phrases, including many with multiple premodifiers and conjoined structures, can also be identified and rearranged into Spanish word order.

5.6 Synthesis Component

When the transfer component has completed its work, each target lexical item is associated with a group of features which specify the inflectional endings to be synthesized. Additional codes indicate whether the item is to receive a derivational prefix or suffix and whether the item is to be preceded by function words such as the definite article, personal *a*, or the preposition *de*.

Verb synthesis is performed first, since the resulting form may serve as the input to the other synthesis procedures. The next task is the generation of the surface forms of the reflexive, direct object, and indirect object pronouns. Then all elements of the noun phrase are inflected for gender and number. This step is followed by prefixation and the insertion of function words. The final steps in synthesis are the introduction of phonologically determined variants and the adjustment of capitalization and diacritics.

6 Practical Experience

6.1 System Maintenance

6.1.1 Dictionaries: SPANAM

As indicated earlier, the Spanish source dictionary had 61,282 entries and the English target 58,485 as of December 1985. The program for updating the SPANAM dictionaries is user-friendly. Many default codes are entered by the update program automatically. Even though there are now 211 possible fields in which codes can be entered, as opposed to the original 82, almost all of them can be specified using mnemonic descriptors and code names.

Today, updating is done largely on the basis of production text. Every job reveals ways in which the dictionaries can be improved, either with new glosses for individual words or idiomatic phrases, especially with technical terminology, or deeper coding of existing entries. The steady, ongoing development of the dictionaries (Table 1) has ensured both a decrease in unfound words, with advantages for program effectiveness, and closer correspondence to the type of language that is used in the Organization, leaving less work for the post-editor.

Table 1. Dictionary Sizes, PAHO MT Systems, 1976-1985

	SPANAM		ENSPAN	
Year	Spanish	English	English	Spanish
1976	4,000	3,500		
1977	7,836	7,341		
1978	38,506	38,376		
1979	48,289	53,303		
1980	50,921	55,792		
1981	53,785	51,187[1]	44,411[2]	44,998
1982	54,383	52,223	40,107	41,358
1983	56,247	53,326[3]	40,772	42,116
1984	61,240	58,440	43,585	45,125
1985	61,282	58,485	45,614	47,545

Table 2. Translation Speeds, SPANAM, 1979-1985

	Best clock time			Average CPU time	
Year	wpm	wph	pages/h	wpm	wph
1979	160	9,600	38	Not available	
1980	176	10,560	42	Not available	
1981	192	11,520	46	3,184	191,000
1982	580[4]	34,800	139	2,600	156,000
1983	700	42,000	168	2,880	172,800
1984	710	42,600	170	2,982	178,920
1985	1,500	90,000	360	8,250	495,000

[1] 7,000 unmatched target entries were deleted by a special-purpose program.

[2] Upon reversal of dictionaries, 4,500 duplicate source entries and corresponding target records were deleted by a special-purpose program.

[3] 1,000 irregular verb forms were deleted by a special-purpose program.

[4] Reflects change to VSAM lookup.

As indicated earlier, the translator notes the changes that are needed at the time of post-editing, and later updates the dictionaries. An hour is reserved for this work at the end of the day. If there is no production pending, the translator may spend extra time on dictionary work; on the other hand, if there is pressure, the dictionaries may have to be postponed for a while. Because of this integration of dictionary-building into the work of the translator, the post-editing cost is no longer an element that can be clearly identified.

6.1.2 Dictionaries: ENGSPAN

ENGSPAN has the same user-friendly software as SPANAM for updating its dictionaries. As of December 1985 the English source dictionary had 45,614 entries and the Spanish target had 47,545.

The AID support provided for two half-time dictionary assistants, one a linguist of English mother tongue and one a translator of Spanish mother tongue. A new deeply coded source entry costs from $.60 to $1.00; Spanish target glosses that require research are about the same. Simple changes in existing entries average about $.25 each. The semantic coding of medical terms was accomplished semi-automatically by using the SEARCH-AND-REPLACE function on the word processor, macros, and the Sort utility to identify and group terms that were morphologically related.

6.1.3 Other System Maintenance

The SPANAM and ENGSPAN programs, as well as the support software, are maintained by the two staff computational linguists, who carry out these tasks in addition to development work.

Hardware and system support are provided by the Pan American Health Organization. There is no separate charge for utilization of the computer, either for time or storage space. The programs execute in a partition of 1,024K and utilize 1MB on disk for work space, 8.5MB for program libraries, and 33.2MB for dictionaries and other permanently mounted files.

6.2 Testing

6.2.1 SPANAM

The output of SPANAM is subject to daily scrutiny by the project staff. In addition, frequent demonstrations are given for visitors using random text as input, and these results are examined as well.

An experimental version of the program is used to test and debug system enhancements resulting from production feedback and from the research and development being done for ENGSPAN. Before the experimental version of the program replaces the production version, a control test is performed by translating the same text with both programs and comparing the output using the Document Compare software available on the Wang OIS/140. The CPU time, throughput time, and number of disk I/O operations for both versions are also compared.

6.2.2 ENGSPAN

An experimental corpus of over 50,000 words was selected at the beginning of the project. Sentences are chosen from this corpus for the testing of specific program modules. Following every major enhancement of the algorithm or dictionary, the corpus texts are retranslated and the results compared with previous translations. Production texts, which no longer undergo any previous review by the project staff, are also used to supplement the original corpus. After the translation has been post-edited and delivered to the requesting office, the dictionary is updated by the addition of new words and missing codes, and the translation is then rerun. Problem sentences from these random texts are retained for use in subsequent development tasks.

6.3 Measurement Criteria

6.3.1 Speed: CPU/Throughput Time

The speed of SPANAM has steadily improved over the years (Table 2). When major changes are made in the program, care is always taken to make sure that they do not cause any significant degradation of speed. With the new 4381 computer, which executes 5 million instructions per second, CPU time has been measured at 8,250 words per minute and clock time at 1,500 words per minute. The best throughput speeds are obtained at night, when there are fewer users working on the computer. During the day, turnaround at peak periods can be considerably slower. The speed is adequate for the current load of production.

With ENGSPAN, the CPU and clock times are 1,700 and 836 words per minute, respectively. These speeds tend to decrease as the coverage of the ATN grammar is expanded.

6.3.2 Comparison with Human Translation Speed

With a trained post-editor, throughput time using SPANAM or ENGSPAN is never slower than that of a human translator. The range is from one and a half to four times as fast, with the average falling between two and three times as fast. The output of a translator working as post-editor ranges from 4,000 to 10,000 words a day, depending on all the factors mentioned earlier, as well as the actual difficulty of the text. On the other hand, human translators working in the international organizations commonly produce around 2,000 words a day, with some services reporting an average of 1,500 and others an average of 2,500. It is possible to reach 3,000 or even higher, but usually not on a regular basis. It should be kept in mind that these rates do not take into account the time of the staff who transcribe the translators' dictation. Freelance translators report higher rates (Leonard, 1985). Given the variability of both sets of figures, it would be difficult to make any hard-and-fast comparisons. However, for the same person using both modes it might be possible to draw some conclusions: one translator who post-edits for SPANAM reports that she consistently produces about three times as much output with MT as she does in the traditional way.

6.3.3 Quality: Correctness

No systematic analysis of errors produced by SPANAM or ENGSPAN has been done. Three consultants were engaged under different contracts to evaluate the overall status of the project: Professors Yorick Wilks (1978), R. Ross Macdonald (1981), and Michael Zarechnak (1981). While they commented on general characteristics of the output, they were more concerned with underlying processes that might produce the errors than the errors as such. Referring to the quality of the output, Professor Macdonald (1981:7) reported:

> The current output is rather good. If a human being had written it, perhaps the output would be considered to be defective in many respects. When it is known, however, that it was produced by a machine, the basis of judgment shifts, and the output seems really very presentable. Any person of good will can understand this output, and I assume that no misleading translations have been discovered that would vitiate the intent of any article.

At the end of the period of the AID grant, the status of ENGSPAN was also evaluated. Its practical implementation was assessed by Ruhl Information Management. The output of the parser was examined by Professor Naomi Sager, who reported as follows:

> An ATN English grammar of considerable coverage has been developed ... The number and complexity of constructions handled by the grammar has increased to the point where relatively few types of input sentences are not parsed adequately for subsequent translation ... While some grammar development remains to be done, it is impressive how much of the input material can be parsed with relatively few failures.

The Spanish synthesis was the subject of an evaluation by Professor William Cressey.

6.3.4 Postediting Effort vs. Human Translation Quality

The question of effort required for post-editing is inextricably tied up with standards for human translation. Both these issues are colored by subjective criteria. In Section 2.2 above there was a discussion of linguistic strategies for reducing the time spent on post-editing. The "quick-fix" post-edit definitely takes less time than a "syntactic" post-edit.

In an effort to see how translators would handle some of the same sentences that had been fixed up quickly in post-editing, a set of 17 Spanish source sentences was given to 12 trained translators who were asked to provide spontaneous human versions in English (Vasconcellos 1986). In the results, not one sentence was translated twice in the same way; apart from lexical differences, there were a variety of combinations and permutations in the ordering of the various phrasal elements. However, when the respondents were subsequently shown the "quick-fix" alternatives, they agreed that the latter were at least as good, and sometimes even better, than what they themselves had proposed (probably because there was greater cohesion in the presentation of the semantic components – Vasconcellos 1985b). This exercise underscored the difficulty of measuring the quality of a translation.

6.4 Cost-Effectiveness

Because of all the variables involved, including in particular the purpose of the translation, it is usually rather difficult to make clear-cut comparisons between MT production and traditional translation at PAHO. However, with one large project, carried out in 1980, such a comparison was possible. About half the document, *i.e.*, the part that was originally in Spanish, was fed to SPANAM, while the remaining half was farmed out for translation from English into Spanish by human translators who worked in the traditional mode. For 101,296 words of machine translation, the cost was $3,218, including a hypothetical cost for machine time, and 36 staff-days were devoted to the activity. Had the same number of words been farmed out to human translators, the cost would have been $8,296 and the number of staff- and contract-days (based on an output of 2,000 words a day) would have amounted to 65.75. Hence there was a monetary saving of $5,078, or 61 percent, and the staff-days were reduced by 29.5, or 45 percent.

Sometimes it is hard to know whether or not SPANAM and ENGSPAN are translating texts that would otherwise have been submitted for human translation. Quite possibly the user is less hesitant to request a machine translation than a human one. B. Dostert (1979) has reported such a phenomenon in a survey of 58 users of MT.

6.5 Subjective Factors

The SPANAM/ENGSPAN staff have come to the understanding that in the end an MT system will stand or fall depending on the human environment in which it is placed, and that some of the most important factors cannot be measured. In the broad sense, these include: long-term commitment, positive attitudes, innovative responses, creative problem-solving. At the more specific level they include also the real availability of input in machine-readable form, a cooperative spirit among the staff who must share the oversaturated word processing equipment, willingness on the part of the translator to use the word processor for long periods, resourceful post-editing, and a host of other factors of nonresistance that are seldom taken into account.

In addition, when human translators are enlisted as post-editors, they must have a positive attitude toward the capabilities of MT, and, for true gains in productivity, they must be willing to use the keyboard and to become adept with the special editing features that have been developed for the word processor.

In dealing with the output, there must be flexibility in regard to quality. For example, if the *rapporteur* of a meeting has an hour in which to write up what her speakers said, and she can't understand the Spanish without a translation, there must be a "can-do" type of staff that will produce a document that can be worked from. *The need met* is the true criterion.

7 Discussion of the Approach Adopted

Macdonald (1979:130-145) pointed out that MT systems tend to polarize toward either an empirical or a theoretical approach. Development of the empirical system proceeds "on the basis of actual experience with appropriate texts" (1981:1), whereas the theoretical approach begins by postulating the adequacy of some particular model of language description which it is hoped will be able to cover all contingencies (1979:130, 1981:1).

Each position has its advantages and its disadvantages. In an empirical approach, a big advantage is that the system concentrates on only that which is of immediate usefulness for the task at hand. Yet as the system expands, "it becomes difficult to add in new operations without reworking some of what has already been done" (1981:1). The theoretical system, on the other hand, is able to proceed with less disruption, but the disadvantage is that "it is extremely difficult to predict as to which of all the complexities will actually arise; complexities may be foreseen and planned for in the system which do not actually appear in the type of texts to be translated" (1981:1).

Rather than advocating one extreme or the other, Macdonald believed that benefit was to be gained from both; ideally, he felt, the two positions should be combined in a *melded system* (1979:143):

> On the whole, the best approach is a compromise between the two extremes, a basically empirical approach in which, however, the researchers strive for an overall perspective (1981:1) ...
>
> The preliminary research on the empirical system will serve the purpose of establishing the nature and extent of the problem of machine translation clearly and definitively. When the nature of the problem has been recognized as fully as possible, a rigorous and elegant solution of the problem can be devised (1979:145).

This view, which came through strongly in the 1981 recommendations of Macdonald and Zarechnak, is what has guided the development of SPANAM/ ENGSPAN in the last four years. While SPANAM began as a purely empirical system, ENGSPAN is a melded system. The flexibility of the basic SPANAM/ENGSPAN architecture has made it possible to introduce a theoretical focus while still preserving that part of the working system which could be used both in the interim and as the safety net in the event of failed parses.

Rather than weighing the techniques of one MT system against those of another, it is felt that a more fruitful approach is to establish certain "positive criteria of relevance" (inspired by Halliday, 1979):

- Who are the system's users?
- In what environment is it being implemented?
- What purpose does it serve?
- On what basis is its use to be justified?

The strength of a system lies ultimately in its capacity to be relevant for its users, its environment, its purpose, its justification. Judgment from this standpoint is believed to be more effective in the long run than evaluation of the relative success or failure of a given theory.

By these standards, SPANAM and ENGSPAN have proven themselves over the years of ongoing production: through the accessibility of their programs, the user-friendliness of their dictionaries, their rapid throughput time, the broad range of texts for which they produce usable translations, and the savings they have effected in terms of both time and money.

Acknowledgments

The authors wish to express special acknowledgment to their coworker Lee Ann Schwartz. As the second computational linguist working on ENGSPAN, Lee has given unstinting support to the project and its objectives.

Growth of the dictionaries is attributable in great part to the contributions of Rebecca Naidis, who served as post-editor of SPANAM, and Susana Santangelo, who has worked on ENGSPAN. Other assistance on the dictionaries has been given by Catherine Howe, David

Landeck, José Luiz Meurer, Patricia Schmid, and Lucretia Vanderwende. The workflow is coordinated by Clara Inés Rubiano.

The occasional consultants to the project since 1981 have been R. Ross Macdonald, Michael Zarechnak, Leonard Shaefer, William Cressey, Mary Jane Ruhl, Naomi Sager, and Veronica Lawson.

Within PAHO, the project has had continuing support and encouragement over the years from Luis Larrea Alba, Jr., Chief of the Department of General Services.

Finally, both PAHO and the project are most appreciative of the financial support received from the U.S. Agency for International Development.

References

Ahlroth, E., and Armstrong-Lowe D. (1983), The WHO Terminology Information System: Interim Report. World Health Organization, Geneva. HBI/ISS-83.1. (offset)

Dostert, B. (1979), Users' Evaluation of Machine Translation: Georgetown MT system. Undated typewritten report later expanded into article of the same title in: Henisz-Dostert, *et al.*: 149-244.

Halliday, M. A. K. (1967), Notes on Transitivity and Theme in English, Part 2. *Journal of Linguistics* 3: 199-244.

Halliday, M. A. K. (1979), *Explorations in the Function of Language.* Elsevier North-Holland, Amsterdam, New York, Oxford.

Henisz-Dostert, B., Macdonald, R. R., and Zarechnak, M. (1979), *Machine Translation.* Mouton, The Hague.

Kaplan, R. M. (1973), A General Syntactic Parser. In: Rustin, R. (ed.): 193-241.

Kay, M. (1982), Machine Translation. *AJCM* 8(2): 74-77.

Lawson, V. (1982), Machine Translation and People. In: Lawson, V. (ed.): 3-9.

Lawson, V., ed. (1982), *Practical Experience of Machine Translation.* North-Holland, Amsterdam.

Lawson, V., ed. (1985), *Translating and the Computer 5: Tools for the Trade.* Aslib, London.

León, M., and Schwartz, L. A., Integrated Development of English-Spanish Machine Translation: From pilot to full operational capability. Technical Report, Grant DPE-5543-G-SS-3048-00, U.S. Agency for International Development, Washington, D.C. Pan American Health Organization, October 1986.

Leonard, I. (1985), How Many Words Does a Translator Produce in a Day? A report on statistics gathered at the 1984 convention of the American Translators Association. *Language Monthly*, no. 21, June 1985. Reprinted from the *ATA Chronicle*, April 1985.

Macdonald, R. R. (1979), The Problem of Machine Translation. In: Henisz-Dostert *et al.*: 89-145.

Macdonald, R. R. (1981), A Study of the PAHO Machine Translation System. Report of short-term consultant under Personal Services Contract APO-09435(WU1) [typescript, 13 pp]. Pan American Health Organization, Washington, D.C.

Rustin, R., ed. (1971), *Natural Language Processing.* Algorithmics Press, New York.

Sager, N. (1981), *Natural Language Information Processing: A computer grammar of English and its applications.* Addison-Wesley, Reading, Massachusetts.

Vasconcellos, M. (1984), Machine Translation at the Pan American Health Organization: A review of highlights and insights. *British Computer Society Natural Language Translation Specialist Group Newsletter* 14.

Vasconcellos, M. (1985a), Management of the Machine Translation Environment: Interaction of functions at the Pan American Health Organization. In: Lawson, V. (ed.): 115-129.

Vasconcellos, M. (1985b), Theme and focus: Cross-language comparison via translations from extended discourse. Ph.D. dissertation, Georgetown University, Washington, D. C.

Vasconcellos, M. (1986), Functional Considerations in the Post-editing of Machine-translated Output. *Computers and Translation* 1(1): 21-38.

Winograd, T. (1983), *Language as a Cognitive Process, volume 1: Syntax.* Addison-Wesley, Reading, Massachusetts.

Woods, W. A. (1969), Augmented Transition Networks for Natural Language Analysis. Report No. CS-1 to the National Science Foundation. BBN, Cambridge, Massachusetts.

Woods, W. A. (1971), An Experimental Parsing System for Transition Network Grammars. In: Rustin, R. (ed.): 111-154.

Appendix: Sample ENGSPAN translations

Sentences that were parsed completely are flagged with an "OK." Partial parses are indicated with a "PP," and those sentences that could not be parsed by the current version of the program are marked "NO." "TU" means that a transfer rule has been applied, and "SD" means that a word was not found in the source dictionary.

Sample Input		ENGSPAN Output
We request that each potential participant send biographical information and a 100-word abstract of the demostration or paper, so that we can select those who will make the greatest contribution to a useful exchange of information at the symposium.	OK TU	Solicitamos que cada participante potencial envíe información biográfica y un resumen analítico de 100 palabras de la demostración o documento, para que podamos seleccionar los que harán la contribución mayor a un intercambio útil de información en el simposio.
The task of hiring and assigning staff to perform the work is one which must be completed prior to training.	OK	La tarea de contratación y asignación de personal para realizar el trabajo es una que se debe completar anterior a adiestramiento.
Laboratory studies have shown marijuana to impair perceptual and perceptual-motor functions important to driving.	OK TU	Estudios de laboratorio han revelado que marihauna deteriora funciones de percepción y perceptomotrices importantes a conducción.

The mothers who lived within a 5-mile radius were asked to bring their children to the vaccination center.	OK TU TU	A las madres que vivían dentro de un radio de 5 millas se les pidió que trajeran a sus hijos al centro de vacunación.
Often the cold chain is thought to refer only to the refrigeration of vaccine.	OK	A menudo la cadena de frío se piensa que se refiere solamente a la refrigeración de vacuna.
The relationship between dietary fat and mamary carcinogenesis in experimental models will be presented and, finally, the possible relationship between dietary fat and hormones will be discussed.	OK	Se presentará la relación entre grasa en la alimentación y carcinogénesis mamaria en modelos experimentales y, finalmente, se tratará la relación posible entre grasa en la alimentación y hormonas.
A privately organized by publicly funded foundation is responsible for primary health care in the interior of the country where 10% of the population lives.	OK	Una fundación privadamente organizada pero públicamente financiada es responsable de atención primaria de salud en el interior del país donde vive un 10% de la población.
The National Program for Drinking Water Supply has the goal to expand to full coverage the already existing distribution system.	PP	El Programa Nacional para Abastecimiento de Agua Potable tiene la meta para ampliar a cobertura total el sistema de distribución ya existente.

Other analyses will test the epidemiologic association between 1) ethylene oxide exposure and leukemia and 2) *PAH exposure in the cola hydrogenation process and cancer of the respiratory system, urogenital system, and the skin.	SD NO	Otros análisis examinarán la asociación epidemiológica entre 1) la exposición de óxidos de etileno y leucemia y 2) la exposición de PAH en el proceso de hidrogenación de carbón y cáncer del aparato respiratorio, aparato urogenital, y la piel.

TAUM-AVIATION: its Technical Features and Some Experimental Results

Pierre Isabelle and Laurent Bourbeau
Département de Linguistique
Université de Montréal
C.P. 6128, Succ. A, Montréal, Qué., Canada H3C 3J7

Abstract

Upon the completion of its highly successful TAUM-METEO machine translation system, the TAUM group undertook the construction of TAUM-AVIATION, an experimental system for English-to-French translation in the sublanguage of technical maintenance manuals. A detailed description of the resulting prototype is offered. In particular, the paper includes: a) some figures on the size of the system; b) a description of the underlying translation model (indirect approach, analysis/transfer/synthesis scheme); c) a presentation of the basic computational techniques (use of a specialized high-level metalanguage for each linguistic component); and d)some results of the evaluation of the prototype.

1 Background

1.1 Historical Notes

In 1965, with funding from the National Research Council of Canada, the CETADOL research center in computational linguistics was created at l'Université de Montréal. Around 1970, the center narrowed its focus to the problem of machine translation (MT), renaming itself TAUM (Traduction Automatique Université de Montréal). In the next few years, several MT prototypes were developed: TAUM-71, TAUM-73, and TAUM-76 (Colmerauer *et al.* 1971, Kittredge *et al.* 1973, Kittredge *et al.* 1976).

Starting in 1973, the Canadian Secretary of State Department (Translation Bureau) assumed responsibility for funding the project, in the hope that tangible results would soon emerge. Between 1974 and 1976, TAUM produced its first practical application: the TAUM-METEO system, for the translation of weather forecasts (Chevalier *et al.* 1978). Since 1977, this system has been used on a daily basis for the Canadian Environment Department (Chandioux and Guéraud 1981). Its current workload represents an annual volume of 8.5 million words (Bourbeau 1984). In spite of its very narrow scope, TAUM-METEO represents an important breakthrough in MT since it is the only system that currently produces high quality translation without the need for human revision (although approximately 20% of the input is rejected).

The AVIATION project was undertaken in 1976, even before the on-site implementation of TAUM-METEO was completed. The aim was to develop a system capable of translating aircraft maintenance manuals. Obviously, this was a more difficult challenge than translating weather forecasts. The magnitude of the task necessitated a massive infusion of new personnel and the development of a set of new metalanguages (*e.g.* LEXTRA, SISIF). A prototype of the TAUM-AVIATION system, restricted to hydraulic system maintenance manuals, was demonstrated in 1979.

The following year, an independent evaluation (Gervais 1980) concluded that it was not possible to envisage immediate cost-effective production using TAUM-AVIATION. This evaluation led the Translation Bureau to stop funding the TAUM-AVIATION project, and to look for a broader funding base for MT research and development in Canada. In the meantime, the TAUM Group had to be disbanded.

1.2 Languages Translated

TAUM-AVIATION is designed in such a way that a core portion of the system is independent of particular language pairs: linguistic descriptions constitute *data* for the system. However, from a linguistic perspective, the project was exclusively focused on English-to-French translation.

In addition, the linguistic descriptions incorporated into the system are addressed not to general language but to the particular sublanguage of maintenance manuals (Lehrberger 1982). The notion of

Table 1: Sizes of compiled files and memory requirements.

Component	Compiled code (6-bit chars) (a)	(b)	Runtime req's (60-bit words)
Pre-processing	60K	15K	34K
Morphological analysis	77K	48K	40K
Source language dictionary	1958K	72K	40K
Syntactic/semantic analysis	205K	56K	120K
Bilingual dictionary	1919K	107K	40K
Syntactic transfer/synthesis	113K	63K	56K
Morphological synthesis	99K	64K	24K
Post-processing	43K	15K	34K

(a) - compiled linguistic data; (b) - compiled interpreter for (a).

sublanguage is presented in Kittredge and Lehrberger (1982).

1.3 Project Size

The initial staff of seven researchers in 1976 was rapidly increased to a peak of 20 people during 1979, and then slowly decreased until the project was terminated.

1.4 System Size

TAUM-AVIATION was implemented on a CYBER 173 computer, with the NOS/BE 1.4 operating system, but was designed so as to be practically machine-independent. Most components of the system are based on the following scheme: certain linguistic data (dictionaries, grammars) are compiled into an object code interpreted at run time against the input text. Table 1 gives an idea of the size of the runtime code, together with typical memory requirements for execution. Table 2 gives the size of the programs used to compile the linguistic data.

Table 2: Metalanguage compiler sizes.

Metalanguage	Used for	Size (x 6 bits)
SISIF	pre- and post-processing	43K
REZO	syntactic/semantic analysis	155K
LEXTRA	lexical transfer	130K
SYSTEMES-Q	structural transfer; syntactic synthesis	28K

NB. Size is expressed in terms of 6-bit bytes

1.5 Size of Dictionaries

The dictionaries list only the base form of a word (roughly speaking, the entry form in a conventional dictionary). In March 1981, the source language (English) dictionary included 4054 entries; these entries represented the core vocabulary of maintenance manuals, plus a portion of the specialized vocabulary of hydraulics. Of these, 3280 had a corresponding entry in the bilingual English-French dictionary.

2 Application Environment

TAUM-AVIATION remains an experimental system. It is designed to take as input a text that is in a photocomposition-ready format; a pre-processing program stores the formatting codes, which will be reinserted in the translated text. No use is made of manual pre-editing.

The translation process is fully automatic. If desired, it can be interrupted after dictionary lookup to obtain a list of unidentified words, and enter any such words in the dictionary.

Revision of the machine output is normally necessary: the domain is too complex for results comparable to those of TAUM-METEO. The designers of the system decided not to rely heavily on "fail-soft" strategies such as constraint relaxation or partial parses; these strategies make the quality of the output totally unpredictable. Thus, the material passing through the system is translated relatively well (very well by MT standards), and the reviser is less likely to feel overwhelmed by linguistic garbage. The price to be paid is a failure to produce any output for a relatively high proportion of the input sentences (somewhere between 20 and 40 per cent, at the stage of development reached in 1981). For a sample of translations produced by TAUM-AVIATION, see the Appendix.

The development of TAUM-AVIATION has not been taken far enough for a definitive assessment to be made of the linguistic and computational strategies that it embodied: the total system throughput was approximately 100,000 words.

3 General Translation Approach

The TAUM-AVIATION system is based on a typical second generation design (Isabelle *et al.* 1978, Bourbeau 1981). The translation is produced *indirectly*, by means of an analysis/transfer/synthesis scheme. The internal organization of the major components of the system is based on the notion of linguistic level. Finally, the linguistic data are generally separated from the algorithmic specifications.

3.1 Transfer Model

The overall design of the system is based on the assumption that translation rules should not be applied directly to the input string, but rather to a formal object that represents a structural description of the content of this input. Thus, the source language (SL) text (or successive fragments of it) is mapped onto the representations of an **intermediate language**, (also called **normalized structure**) prior to the application of any target language-dependent rules.

No one knows how to construct a universal, language-independent semantic interlingua. The intermediate language used in the TAUM-AVIATION system is largely language dependent: it consists of semantically annotated deep structures for SL and TL sentences. A certain degree of language independence is attained by the use of a common "base component" (a context-free grammar that enumerates the admissible deep structures) for both SL and TL. But the lexical items are left intact, and a transfer module is used in order to map the lexical items of SL onto those of TL.

3.2 Linguistic Organization

The arrangement of the system into three major modules (analysis, transfer, synthesis) reflects a theoretical model of translation operations: it is claimed that these operations take place at a "deep" level, between language-dependent meaning representations. Moreover, each one of the three modules is arranged internally along the lines of a linguistic theory: the components of these modules correspond to the standard levels of linguistic description (lexicon, morphology, syntax, semantics). This contrasts with older systems, the structure of which frequently had no direct relationship to any definite theory of language and translation. Figure 1 shows the internal structure of the TAUM-AVIATION system.

4 Linguistic Techniques

4.1 Processing Units

It is well known that some translation problems can only be solved through textual, as opposed to sentential, processing. However, we still know too little about discourse analysis techniques to use them effectively in large-scale systems. Thus, the processing unit in TAUM-AVIATION is the sentence.

Fortunately, anaphoric pronouns are quite rare in technical manuals. A more frequent problem is the use of anaphoric definite noun phrases. Consider for example the text fragment in (1):

(1) Remove hydraulic filter bypass valve. This valve is located below accumulator No. 1.

A word like *valve* cannot be translated correctly in isolation. Depending on the type of valve, French will use *clapet, robinet, soupape,* etc. In the second sentence of (1), the word *valve* is used anaphorically. To translate it correctly, one has to refer to its antecedent: the modifier *bypass* determines a specific French equivalent.

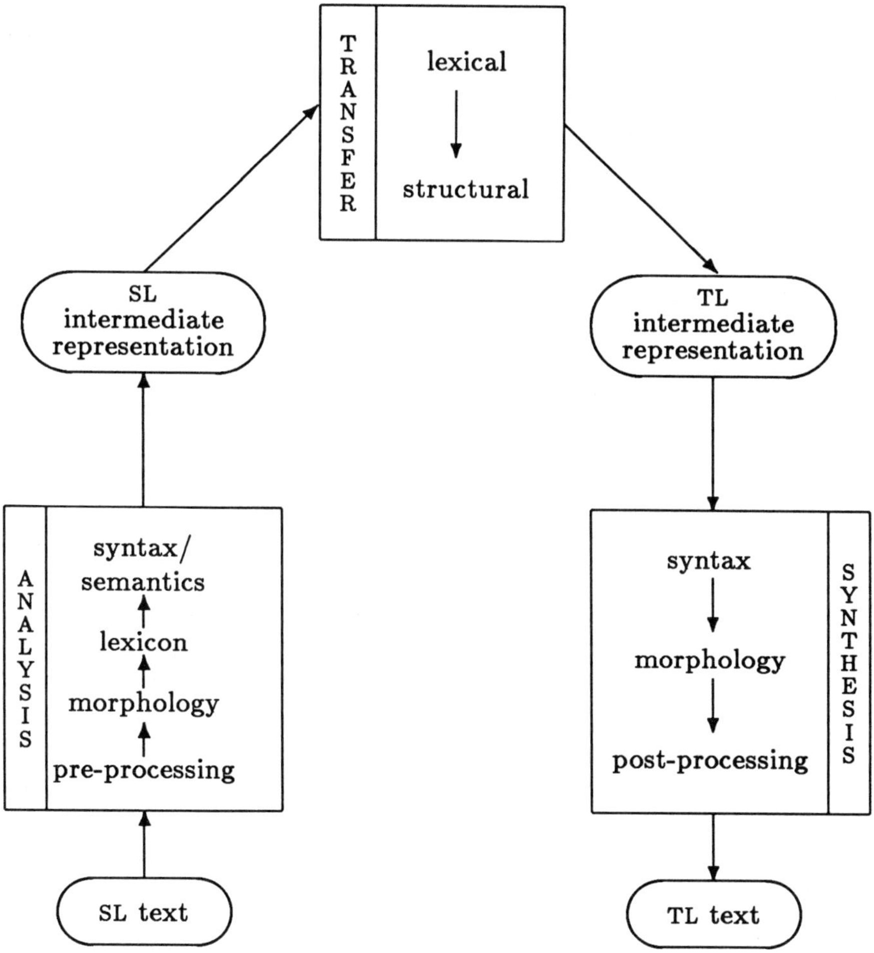

Figure 1. Overall structure of the TAUM-AVIATION system

TAUM-AVIATION cannot solve problems of this type. The designers of the system preferred to concentrate their efforts on the best possible sentential analysis. And in fact, in spite of a relatively advanced sentence analyzer, translation failures due to weaknesses in sentential processing (*e.g.*, scoping problems for conjunctions, nominal compounds, etc.) turned out to be *much more frequent* than failures due to anaphora problems, as evidenced by the error compilations of Lehrberger (1981).

4.2 The Analysis Module: Ambiguity Problems

Ambiguity is a language-internal phenomenon and it is the responsibility of the analysis module to resolve it. Sometimes, it is possible to ignore certain ambiguities, in the hope that the same ambiguities will carry over in translation. This is particularly true in systems like TAUM-AVIATION that deal with only one pair of closely related languages. The difficult problem of prepositional phrase attachment, for example, is frequently bypassed in this way. Generally speaking, however, analysis is aimed at producing an unambiguous intermediate representation.

The analysis module comprises four components: preprocessing, morphology, lexicon and syntactic/semantic analysis (see Figure 1). The pre-processing component segments the input text into successive words and into processing units. In this latter function, it can be seen as a degenerate text grammar. Because this is carried out deterministically, without interaction from the other components, segmentation problems occasionally arise.

Morphological analysis includes complete rules and exception lists for English inflectional morphology, category assignment rules for numbers and rules for dealing with unknown words. No rules are provided for derivational morphology. The system handles some types of compositional morphology, but this is done in the syntactic component, since compounds frequently exhibit properties that are otherwise thought of as syntactic; for example, internal conjunction is possible (*e.g. four- and six-cell batteries*).

Syntactic and semantic analysis are very tightly integrated in the

TAUM-AVIATION system. First, both of them are implemented using the same metalanguage, a particular version of Wood's ATNs (see section 5 below). Second, both components interact freely during analysis. It is nevertheless convenient to describe them separately.

4.2.1 Syntax

The TAUM-AVIATION system includes a large-scale grammar of English capable of handling most constructions that occur with some frequency in the sublanguage of maintenance manuals (Lehrberger 1982). The rules are based on an extensive lexical subcategorization scheme: 12 standard categories are further subclassified using more than 75 features (excluding morpho-syntactic features). This is in addition to the use of lexical "strict subcategorization" frames comparable to those of transformational grammar.

Since the intermediate representation used for transfer is a type of semantically annotated "deep structure," and since maintenance manuals make use of a very complex syntax, it was necessary to provide the parser with a rich transformational component. Thus, the inverses of several transformations from standard transformational theory are used: passive, extraposition, raising, etc.

In dealing with texts as complex as technical manuals, the parser is faced with difficult ambiguity problems. Ambiguities are already present in the input to the parser, at the lexical level. These ambiguities may concern the syntactic properties of the lexical element (*e.g.*, *light* is a noun, a verb, or an adjective); or they may concern primarily its semantic properties: pure homographs like the two nouns *lead* or polysemous items like the noun *line*.

The parser will as a side effect eliminate some lexical ambiguities; for example, if *Check valve* is to be taken as a sentence, syntax tells us that *check* must be a verb. However, the parser will itself introduce *structural* ambiguities, owing to the existence of syntactically undetermined choice points in the application of grammar rules. Two examples of structural ambiguity are adjective scope, as in (2), and conjunction scope, as in (3).

(2)	a)		(liquid oxygen) tanks
	a′)	??	liquid (oxygen tanks)
	b)		correct (oil level)
	b′)	??	(correct oil) level
(3)	a)		(pressure and return) lines
	a′)	??	pressure and (return lines)
	b)		jack and (jacking adapter)
	b′)	??	(jack and jacking) adapter

These examples show that with ADJ NOUN NOUN sequences and NOUN CONJ NOUN NOUN sequences two different syntactic groupings are possible. But only one of them is semantically acceptable and results in a correct translation.

Moreover, some lexical ambiguities, instead of being eliminated in the parsing process, will constitute a further source of structural ambiguity, each reading of the relevant lexical item being compatible with a different syntactic structure. In example (4), *drain* can be taken either as a noun or as a verb, when appropriate adjustments are made to the surrounding syntactic structure.

(4) Remove dust cap and drain plug.

Thus by itself, a syntactic parser produces a highly ambiguous output, and further constraints are needed in a practical MT system.

4.2.2 Semantics

Semantic processing in the TAUM-AVIATION system performs two related tasks: a) it filters the syntactic structures, eliminating as many ambiguities as possible; and b) it associates with each node of the tree a set of semantic features which will be used by transfer rules.

Most semantic features originate in the dictionary, where lexical items are described in terms of some 35 features that form a **tangled hierarchy**. Predicative lexical items (verbs, adjectives, certain prepositions) are assigned selectional restrictions on their possible arguments in terms of these semantic features.

Selectional restrictions constitute the main semantic mechanism used by the system to eliminate ambiguities of two types:

a. structural ambiguities introduced by syntactic rules; thus the spurious structure proposed by the parser for (4) is eliminated because the verb *drain* does not accept as direct object something in the semantic category of *plug,*

b. lexical ambiguity in the semantic properties of certain lexical items; polysemous words like the noun *line* (which can denote either an abstract geometrical object, or physical objects such as conductors) are frequently disambiguated by selectional restrictions; for example, in *Flush the line,* the concrete sense is selected.

In order for selectional restrictions to work properly and for trees to be correctly annotated, it is necessary to apply **semantic projection rules** which assign sets of features to tree nodes. In TAUM-AVIATION, the semantic rules work in a compositional fashion, raising selectively certain features from daughter nodes to their mothers (Isabelle 1987). Rules such as the following are used:

- all of the semantic features of a head noun are raised onto the dominating NP node;
- the intersection of the features of two conjoined NP nodes is raised onto the dominating NP node; and
- when the head noun is a partitive noun (*e.g. portion),* and the NP has an *of NP* complement, the features of this complement are raised onto the dominating NP node.

The system also makes use of standard control rules for subjectless infinitives and gerundives, and of some pronoun/antecedent rules, in order to enforce semantic constraints wherever possible.

Semantic ambiguity, whether real homography (*e.g.,* the two nouns *lead)* or polysemy (*e.g.,* the various senses of the noun *line)*, is not handled by creating multiple entries in the source language dictionary. Rather, in its single entry, the word is assigned a number of *semantically incompatible* features. The semantic rules seek to filter out some of these features, so that no incompatibility remains. This strategy prevents the redundant syntactic search that results from a multiple-entry strategy.

4.3 The Transfer Module

In principle, transfer rules state correspondences between two sets of unambiguous structural descriptions. Their most obvious task is to relate the lexical items of SL to those of TL. Even if the rules are applied to unambiguous lexical elements, the correspondences are by no means one-to-one: the lexical system of each natural language reflects a specific way of breaking down the conceptual universe. For this reason, equivalences have to be stated in terms of structural patterns rather than in terms of words or strings of words.

To take an example, there is no language-internal evidence that *hard* is ambiguous in English; however, depending on the context, it is translated into French as *difficile, dur,* etc. The French equivalents have more restricted collocations. In all those cases, transfer rules are needed to select the contextually appropriate equivalent.

Moreover, very frequently, these **lexical transfer rules** cannot simply substitute lexical items, leaving the tree structure unaffected. Since SL and TL lexical items frequently have different contextual requirements (*i.e.*, subcategorization frames), translation rules have to establish correspondences between a source and a target structural pattern, as illustrated by the examples in (5).

(5) a. check x against y → comparer x à y
  b. supply x with y → fournir y à x
  c. cantilever x → monter x en porte-à-faux
  d. bond x electrostatically → métalliser x
  e. service x → faire l'entretien de x

It is clear that lexical transfer rules must include powerful transformational mechanisms. This basic fact has not so far received the attention it deserves in the MT community. The TAUM-AVIATION system provides for full transformational power at the level of lexical transfer (Chevalier *et al.* 1981).

The transfer component also involves rules for **structural transfer**, that is, rules that deal with linguistic contrasts not tied to any specific lexical item. Since the same base rules are used for SL and TL, this sub-component is kept to a minimum. Nevertheless, a number of structural differences between SL and TL have to be accounted for by means of contrastive rules. For example, because the intermediate language does not provide for "universal semantic tenses," the tense systems of SL and TL have to be explicitly contrasted by a set of rules.

Another task left to structural transfer is to deal with observable contrasts concerning the use of **optional movement transformations**. In all likelihood, the use of these transformations is governed by discourse phenomena that the system does not attempt to analyze. The strategy used in TAUM-AVIATION is to take advantage of the frequent parallels between SL and TL regarding these aspects of surface structure organization. Thus, the intermediate representation retains "traces" from SL surface structure used by the synthesis component to maintain a certain parallel with the SL. However, in some cases we know that the two languages exhibit systematic differences in their use of certain movement transformations. The structural transfer grammar describes these facts. For instance, TAUM-AVIATION includes complex rules for translating English passives with various French constructions, as illustrated in the following examples:

(6) Quick-disconnect fittings should not be removed.
→ Ne pas enlever les raccords à démontage rapide.

(7) Ensure that pump and lines are bled.
→ S'assurer qu'on a purgé la pompe et les canalisations.

(8) The flaps are operated by hydraulic system no. 1.
→ Le circuit hydraulique no. 1 actionne les volets.

4.4 The Synthesis Module

Synthesis of the TL text involves three steps: syntactic synthesis, morphological synthesis, and post-processing.

Syntactic synthesis is carried out on the basis of a large-scale transformational grammar of French. Since the input to the synthesis component is normally a well-formed unambiguous sentential deep structure, synthesis here is much simpler than analysis. This is not to say that synthesis of natural language texts is generally easy. Generating a coherent text from an abstract discourse representation is certainly a very difficult problem. But in TAUM-AVIATION, synthesis can only be achieved on a sentential basis. Therefore, no attempt can be made to describe the complex discourse factors that influence sentence generation (*e.g.*, application of "optional" movement transformations). As mentioned in the previous section, the strategy adopted is to try to preserve a certain parallel with the SL sentences, since both languages have relatively similar means of expressing discourse cohesion.

Syntactic synthesis produces a string of lexical items annotated with all the information required to inflect them correctly. The morphological synthesis component then determines the final form of each word. This is done on the basis of an exhaustive description of the rules of French inflection (together with their exceptions). Post-processing reformats the TL text, making use, wherever possible, of the formatting codes of the SL text.

5 Computational Techniques

From the computational point of view, the TAUM-AVIATION system is more complex than TAUM-METEO, which is entirely written in the Q-SYS- TEMS metalanguage (Colmerauer 1971). One of the ideas underlying TAUM-AVIATION is to make use of specialized tools for different tasks in the interests of increased efficiency, though somewhat at the expense of overall simplicity.

In the implementation, the actual modules closely match the components of the linguistic model presented in Figure 1. They are applied sequentially and communication between components is achieved by means of a chart structure (a type of loop-free graph). The arcs of these charts are labelled with tree structures whose nodes are labelled with complex symbols: a categorical label plus a set of features.

Most components are based on the following scheme. Certain linguistic data are described with a high-level metalanguage; in this metalanguage, the linguist expresses facts about tree structures. These descriptions are compiled into an abstract formal structure interpreted at run time against the material to be translated. Most of these compilers and interpreters are written in PASCAL.

5.1 Pre- and Post-Processing

These relatively simple components, which map character strings onto sequences of chart structures and vice-versa, are implemented as sets of rules in a metalanguage called SISIF; a set of SISIF rules amounts to a deterministic finite-state automaton. These rules are compiled into list structures, which are interpreted against the input text at run time.

5.2 Inflectional Morphology

Since it was possible to exhaustively describe the inflectional morphology of both French and English, there was no compelling reason to use a very high-level formalism. Consequently, in the interests of efficiency, two PASCAL programs were written for morphological analysis of English and morphological synthesis of French.

5.3 Dictionaries

5.3.1 Source Language Dictionary

A dictionary system called SYDICAN enables the linguist to write lexical rules that associate a complex of lexical information with a string of base forms, forming a path in an input chart. Two types of rules are provided: a) rules that simply add a new path (labelled with the complex of lexical information) to the chart; and b) rules that, in addition, have the effect of taking precedence over shorter matches in the chart (the "longest-match" strategy).

The rules are compiled into list structures. At run time they are retrieved from an arbitrarily large lexical data base and applied to the chart. The lexical database system includes some maintenance facilities, such as integrity constraints on its contents, and facilities for retrieving entries through arbitrarily complex requests on their contents.

5.3.2 Bilingual Dictionary

We saw in 4.3 that lexical transfer involves rules that perform complex transformations on tree structures. The LEXTRA metalanguage makes it possible to associate with any lexical item an arbitrarily complex set of tree transformations. These transformations describe a pattern (anchored in the relevant lexical item), which is to be matched against the tree structure at run time. When a match is found, a series of associated actions specifying structural changes is performed.

An important idea embodied in LEXTRA is that a transfer component should have an explicit description of the intermediate language. In the TAUM approach this intermediate language is partially defined by a set of context-free rules that describe a common base component for SL and TL. LEXTRA takes as *data* this context-free grammar and guarantees that any manipulated tree structure corresponds to a permissible derivation in terms of that context-free grammar. This notion is to be related to computational formulations of transformational grammar such as Petrick (1973), where the deep structures produced by the inverse transformations are checked against the rules of the base component. No equivalent check is performed with parsing systems like ATNs.

LEXTRA rules are compiled into list structures. It was found that some of the constraints on admissible tree structures could be enforced at compile time (Gérin-Lajoie 1980). This mechanism is very useful in the complex task of dictionary development. It helps validate the work of the lexicographer. At run time, the LEXTRA interpreter searches the tree structure for SL lexical items, retrieves the associated lexical rules and applies them to the tree.

5.4 Syntax and Semantics

5.4.1 Analysis

The English grammar for syntactic analysis is written in REZO (Stewart 1975, 1978), TAUM's version of augmented transition networks (ATNs). The REZO metalanguage is different from Woods' ATNs (Woods 1970) in several respects. Some of the differences are:

- REZO does not support morphological analysis, which is performed in a separate component;
- tree nodes are complex symbols that include sets of features on which boolean operations can be performed;
- REZO includes a number of primitives to perform pattern matching over tree structures;
- in addition to regular ATN states where all transitions are tried, REZO includes "deterministic" states where only the first transition whose test is met is followed;
- REZO accords special status to the states to which a recursive call can be made, so that the resulting grammar is a collection of sub-networks.

The REZO grammar is compiled into a set of instructions for a virtual machine, which is simulated by the runtime interpreter. Parsing is done in the usual top-down, depth-first, left-to-right manner. The interpreter can either work in an all-paths or in a first-path mode. One important difference from Woods' ATN interpreter is that REZO takes as input a chart structure in which lexical ambiguities are encoded and applies the grammar in parallel to all the paths of this chart. The result is also a chart structure: REZO is thus a chart-to-chart transducer.

In 4.2, it was mentioned that syntactic rules create structural ambiguities, and that semantic processing can eliminate some of these. Serial parsing provides another means of selecting a particular reading. Since the transitions of the REZO networks are followed in a fixed order, the grammar can be made to produce the most likely reading first. In TAUM-AVIATION's analysis grammar, the ordering of the transitions reflects:

- general parsing principles such as those discussed in human performance studies (*e.g.*, Kimball 1973); and
- sublanguage-specific statistical tendencies.

5.4.2 Structural Transfer and Synthesis

Structural transfer and syntactic synthesis are implemented in the well-known Q-SYSTEMS, which we will not describe here. This introduces some heterogeneity into TAUM-AVIATION, since: a) unlike the other metalanguages, Q-SYSTEMS do not support trees with complex symbols as node labels; and b) the compiler and the interpreter are written in FORTRAN while PASCAL is used for the other metalanguages.

In fact, the original design of the system included provisions for a new metalanguage well suited to synthesis; but time constraints precluded its development.

6 Experimental Results

6.1 Cost-Benefit Evaluation

In 1981, the sponsor submitted TAUM-AVIATION to a cost-benefit evaluation, in order to determine if the system was usable in a production environment. This evaluation, made by an independent consultant, is reported in Gervais (1980), and we will only summarize the main conclusions.

Raw machine output was deemed to have a degree of intelligibility, fidelity, and style that reaches 80% of unrevised human translations (HT). Revised MT and revised HT have a comparable degree of quality, but revision costs are twice as high for MT; thus, globally, revised MT turns out to be more expensive than revised HT as shown in Table 3. However, it is noted in the evaluator's report that MT reduces by half the human time required in the translation/revision process.

Table 3: MT/HT – compared costs per word ($CDN).

Tasks	MT		HT	
Preparation/input	$0.014	(8%)	—	
Translation	$0.079	(43%)	$0.100	(69%)
Human Revision	$0.068	(37%)	$0.030	(21%)
Transcription/Proofreading	$0.022	(12%)	$0.015	(10%)
TOTAL	$0.183		$0.145	

The direct costs of MT could probably be reduced to an acceptable level, for example by interfacing the system with a suitable word-processing environment and by reducing the percentage of sentences for which no translation is produced (Isabelle 1981).

Cost-effective production would require the system to be applicable to at least 6 million words per year. In order to reach that target, the system would have to be extended to translate domains other than hydraulics. But the indirect costs involved in these extensions (*e.g.*, dictionary development) are very high. Gervais concludes that it is impossible to assert that translation using TAUM-AVIATION would be globally cheaper than human translation.

6.2 Technical Evaluation of Performance

Cost-benefit evaluations are certainly necessary, but a single evaluation of this type tells one very little about how the system can be expected to perform on different texts, or after further investment. TAUM developed a methodology for analyzing the performance of an MT system through a systematic examination of its translation errors.

The first step is to collect *all* the errors in the translation of the sample text; translators/revisors then have the responsibility of deciding what is to be counted as an error. A classification scheme for translation errors will include headings such as the following: incorrect TL equivalent for a word, incorrect word order, lack of an article, etc.

In itself, an absolute number of such errors for a given text is not very revealing; but a comparison of the ratio of errors to word tokens in different texts, or at various stages of development of the system, is an initial source of useful information.

Still, from the point of view of system development, these "surface" translation problems are merely symptoms for problems in some component of the system. To provide an answer to questions such as:

- how many of these problems have a known solution?
- how long would it take to correct them?
- how much better would the performance of the system be after n person/months of work?
- what should the priorities be?

it is necessary to identify, for each surface problem, one or several causes in the functioning of the system. For example, the fact that, in the translation of a given sentence, a French adjective is incorrectly inflected could be caused by one or more of the following factors:

- incorrect marking in a dictionary entry;
- mistake in TL syntactic rules for agreement;
- incorrect scoping in SL analysis (*e.g.*, the wrong bracketing in an ADJ NOUN NOUN sequence); or
- absence of relevant marking in SL (*e.g.*, when translating *federal and provincial governments* into French, should one pluralize the adjectives?).

A sophisticated error classification grid was developed, so that the sources of translation errors could be investigated in a coherent and meaningful way. Basically, this error grid reflects the internal organization of the system, so that translation errors can be assigned a precise cause in the operation of the system.

Once a coherent scheme is available, one can proceed with the classification of the translation errors found in the sample text. This classification process is difficult and tedious, but it is crucial that it be done with accuracy and consistency. Frequently, one has to follow "execution traces" to discover the exact source of a given error.

The final step is to look at the possible remedies for the problems that have been identified. A careful examination of each problem source will reveal whether or not there is a known way of eliminating it, and if so, what amount of effort is needed.

If this type of technical evaluation can be carried out at successive stages of development (with both old and new texts), one gets a clear picture of the evolution of the system. The figures obtained will reveal whether or not:

- there has been substantial progress compared to previous stages;
- an asymptote has been reached in the investment/improvement curve.

The same figures will also help determine development and research priorities.

This sort of technical evaluation was applied twice to TAUM-AVIATION in the final year of the project; only a few person-months of development had been invested in the system between the two tests. The main goal was to see how well a system developed on the basis of corpora from the domain of hydraulics would fare in the domain of electronics. Some results were as follows:

- In both tests, more than 70% of the failures were classified as having a known solution; the vast majority of these could be corrected in 12 person/months of work.
- From a syntactic point of view, there is no notable difference between hydraulics and electronics. In fact, as a result of a minimal effort in correcting some problems discovered in the test on hydraulics, the overall performance of the parser turned out to be better in the electronics test.

- As expected, there was a major dictionary problem in going from one domain to the other. Selectional restrictions as assigned for hydraulics worked so poorly for electronics that they did more harm than good to the final result.

A definitive assessment of the linguistic and computational techniques on which TAUM-AVIATION is based would have required a few more applications of this evaluation/correction cycle.

7 Future Directions

Before TAUM was disbanded, Isabelle (1981) voiced the views of the group on a possible course for short- and long-term machine translation R&D activities.

The difficulties encountered in the AVIATION project convinced the Translation Bureau that a more permanent and broader R&D base would be required for MT to be viable in Canada. In 1983 the Translation Bureau, in conjunction with the Canadian Department of Communications, funded a large-scale study to review natural language processing technologies and examine opportunities for Canada in this field.

The consultants have submitted their report and the two Departments involved now have to determine the best way to implement the recommendations that are made therein. In the area of MT, there would appear to be three fronts on which R&D could be pursued:

- the development and integration of various computer aids to human translation within a translator's workstation;
- the application of second-generation MT technology to promising sublanguages (Kittredge 1983);
- research on third-generation MT technology.

References

Bourbeau, Laurent (1981), Linguistic Documentation of the TAUM-AVIATION Translation System, Groupe TAUM, Université de Montréal, Montréal, Canada.

Bourbeau, Laurent (1984), Transfert du système METEO sur micro-ordinateur: étude de faisabilité, Bureau des traductions, Secrétariat d'Etat, Ottawa.

Chandioux, John and Guéraud, Marie-France (1981), METEO: un système l'épreuve du temps, *META* 26(1): 18-22.

Chevalier, Monique; Dansereau, Jules; and Poulin, Guy (1978), TAUM-METEO: description du système, Groupe TAUM, Université de Montréal, Montréal, Canada.

Chevalier, Monique; Isabelle, Pierre; Labelle, François; and Lainé, Claude (1981), La traductologie appliquée à la traduction automatique, *META* 26(1): 35-47.

Colmerauer, Alain (1971), Les SYSTEMES-Q: un formalisme pour analyser et synthétiser des phrases sur ordinateur, Groupe TAUM, Université de Montréal, Montréal, Canada.

Colmerauer, Alain, *et al.* (1971), TAUM-71, Groupe TAUM, Université de Montréal, Montréal, Canada.

Gérin-Lajoie, Robert (1980), Vérification des manipulations d'arbres en LEXTRA, M.Sc. thesis, Université de Montréal, Montréal, Canada.

Gervais, Antoni (1980), Evaluation of the TAUM-AVIATION Machine Translation Pilot System, Translation Bureau, Secretary of State, Ottawa, Canada.

Isabelle, Pierre (1981), Some Views on the Future of the TAUM Group and the TAUM-AVIATION System, Groupe TAUM, Université de Montréal, Canada.

Isabelle, Pierre (1987), Machine Translation at the TAUM Group. In: King, M. (ed.), *Machine Translation Today: The State of the Art*, Edinburgh University Press, Edinburgh: 247-277.

Isabelle, Pierre; Bourbeau, Laurent; Chevalier, Monique; and Lepage, Suzanne (1978), TAUM-AVIATION: description d'un système de traduction automatisée de manuels d'entretien en aéronautique, *COLING-78*, Bergen, Norway.

Kimball, John (1973), Six or Seven Principles of Surface Structure Parsing in Natural Language, Indiana University Linguistics Club, Bloomington.

Kittredge, Richard (1983), Sublanguage-Specific Computer Aids to Translation: A Survey of the Most Promising Application Areas. Translation Bureau, Secretary of State, Ottawa, Canada.

Kittredge, Richard *et al.* (1973), TAUM-73, Groupe TAUM, Université de Montréal, Montréal, Canada.

Kittredge, Richard; Bourbeau, Laurent; and Isabelle, Pierre (1976), Design and Implementation of a French Transfer Grammar, *COLING-76*, Ottawa, Canada.

Kittredge, Richard and Lehrberger, John (1982), *Sublanguage: Studies of Language in Restricted Semantic Domains*, Walter de Gruyter, New York.

Lehrberger, John (1981), Possibilités d'extension du système TAUM-AVIATION, Groupe TAUM, Université de Montréal, Montréal, Canada.

Lehrberger, John (1982), Automatic Translation and the Concept of Sublanguage. In: Kittredge and Lehrberger (1982): 81-106.

Petrick, Stanley (1973), Transformational Analysis. In: Rustin, R. (ed.), *Natural Language Processing*, Algorithmic Press: 27-41.

Stewart, Gilles (1975), Le langage de programmation REZO, M.Sc.

thesis, Université de Montréal, Montréal, Canada.

Stewart, Gilles (1978), Spécialisation et compilation des ATN: REZO, *COLING-78*, Bergen, Norway.

Woods, William A. (1970), Transition Network Grammars for Natural Language Analysis, *Communications of the ACM* 3(10): 591-606.

Appendix: Sample TAUM-AVIATION Translation

Input Text:

HYDRAULIC PRESSURE IN-LINE RELIEF VALVE

(See figures 2-4 and 2-5.)

30 Identical interchangeable hydraulic pressure in-line relief valves (in-line relief valve) are provided for each ac hydraulic pump and for the dc hydraulic pump. The in-line relief Valves are located in the hydraulic service center. Those for the No. 1, No. 1A, and No. 1B ac and dc hydraulic pumps are on the left side next to the No. 1 service centre assembly. The in-line relief valve for the No. 2 ac hydraulic pump is incorporated in the No. 2 service centre assembly.

31 The in-line relief valves are poppet-type, spring-loaded to the closed position. A pressure of 3450 psi impinging on the poppet is sufficient to overcome the opposing spring force, and the poppet will move from its knife-edge seat.

Raw Machine Output:

CLAPET DE DECHARGE INCORPORE DE PRESSION HYDRAULIQUE

(Voir les figures 2-4 et 2-5.)

30 Les clapets de décharge incorporés interchangeables identiques de pression hydraulique (clapets de décharge incorporés) sont prévus pour chaque pompe hydraulique ca et pour la pompe hydraulique cc. Les clapets de décharge incorporés sont situés dans le compartiment hydraulique. Ceux pour les pompes hydrauliques ca et cc no 1, no 1A et no 1B sont du côté gauche à côté du bloc collecteur no 1. Le clapet de décharge incorporé pour la pompe hydraulique ca no 2 est intégré au bloc collecteur no 2.

31 Les clapets de décharge incorporés sont champignon, sont rappelés par ressort à la position fermée. Une pression de 3450 psi s'exerçant sur le clapet-champignon est suffisante pour vaincre la force de rappel du ressort et le clapet-champignon se déplacera de son siège en couteau.

Human Revision:

CLAPET DE DECHARGE INCORPORE DE PRESSION HYDRAULIQUE

(Voir les figures 2-4 et 2-5.)

30 *Des* clapets de décharge incorporés interchangeables identiques de pression hydraulique (clapets de décharge incorporés) sont prévus pour chaque pompe hydraulique ca et pour la pompe hydraulique cc. Les clapets de décharge incorporés sont situés dans le compartiment hydraulique. Ceux *des* pompes hydrauliques ca et cc no 1, no 1A et no 1B sont du côté gauche à côté du bloc collecteur no 1. Le clapet de décharge incorporé pour la pompe hydraulique ca no 2 est intégré au bloc collecteur no 2.

31 Les clapets de décharge incorporés, *du type* champignon, sont rappelés par ressort à la position fermée. Une pression de 3450 psi s'exerçant sur le clapet-champignon est suffisante pour vaincre la force de rappel du ressort et le clapet-champignon *s'écartera* de son siège en couteau.

A Machine(-Aided) Translation Bibliography

generally restricted to currently accessible documents
written in English, French, or German
during the years 1973-1986

Compiled by Jonathan Slocum
Microelectronics and Computer
Technology Corporation (MCC)

Titles and Acronyms in Bibliography

ACL	Association for Computational Linguistics
ACM	Association for Computing Machinery, New York
AJCL	American Journal of Computational Linguistics
ALLC	Association for Literary and Linguistic Computing
ARIST	Annual Review of Information Science and Technology
ASIS	American Society for Information Science
ATA	American Translators Association, Ossining, New York, USA
Babel	International Journal of Translation
BCS	British Computer Society, London, England
CACM	Communications of the ACM
CAIS	Canadian Association for Information Science, Ottawa, Ontario, Canada
CaT	Computers and Translation
Daedalus	Journal of the American Academy of Arts and Sciences
ECAI	European Conference on Artificial Intelligence
EDRS	ERIC Document Reproduction Service, Arlington, Virginia, USA

FBIS	Foreign Broadcast Information Service, Washington D.C.
FTD	Foreign Technology Division, U.S. Air Force, Wright Patterson Air Force Base, Ohio, USA
GETA	Groupe d'Études pour la Traduction Automatique, Grenoble, France
ICCL	International Conference on Computational Linguistics [COLING]
IEEE	Institute of Electronics and Electrical Engineers
IJCAI	International Joint Conference on Artificial Intelligence
ISSCO	Institute for the Study of Semantics and Cognition, Geneva, Switzerland
ITL	Review of the Institute of Applied Linguistics, Louvain, Belgium
JPRS	Joint Publications Research Service, Washington, D.C.
LRC	Linguistics Research Center, University of Texas, Austin, Texas, USA
MCC	Microelectronics and Computer Technology Corporation, Austin, Texas, USA
Meta	Journal des traducteurs (Translators' Journal)
NTIS	National Technical Information Service, Springfield, Virginia, USA
RADC	Rome Air Development Center, Griffiss Air Force Base, New York, USA
UMIST	University of Manchester Institute of Science and Technology, U.K.

AAT. Fujitsu has 2-way Translator System. AAT Report 66, Advanced American Technology, Inc., Los Angeles, 1 October 1984, p. 8.

AAT. Hitachi develops English-to-Japanese Translating Machine. AAT Report 66, Advanced American Technology, Inc., Los Angeles, 1 October 1984, p. 8.

Ablett, S., "Demolishing the Language Barrier," *Infomatics* 6, 5, (May) 1985, pp. 22-24.

ACM, "Natural Language Translation by Computer Emerges from Government Research Stage," *CACM* 16, 3, 1973, p. 196.

Addis, T. R., "Machine Understanding of Natural Language," *International Journal for Man-Machine Studies* 9, 2, 1977, pp. 207-222.

Adorni, G., and L. Massone, "Production of Sentences: A General Algorithm and Case Studies," presented at the International Conference on the Methodology and Techniques of Machine Translation, Cranfield Institute of Technology, England, 13-15 February 1984.

ALPAC. Languages and Machines: Computers in Translation and Linguistics. Report of the Automatic Language Processing Advisory Committee, Division of Behavioral Sciences, National Academy of Sciences, National Research Council Publication 1416, Washington, D.C., 1966.

Amano, S. Machine Translation Project at Toshiba Corporation. Technical note, R&D Center, Information Systems Laboratory, Toshiba Corporation, Kawasaki, Japan, November 1982.

Ambrosi, A., R. Ayotte, I. Bellert, J. Dansereau, R. Kittredge, G. Poulin, and G. Stewart, "Le système de traduction automatique de l'Université de Montréal (T.A.U.M.)," *Meta* 18, 1-2, 1973, pp. 277-289.

Ammon, R. von, and R. Wessoly, "Das Evaluationskonzept des automatischen Übersetzungsprojekts SUSY-DJT (Deutsch-Japanische Titelübersetzung)," *Multilingua* 3, 4, 1984, pp. 189-195 & 4, 1, 1985, pp. 27-33.

Ananiadou, S., "A Brief Survey of some Current Operational Systems," in M. King (ed.), *Machine Translation Today: the State of the Art* [proceedings of the Third Lugano Tutorial, Lugano, Switzerland, 2-7 April 1984]. Edinburgh University Press, 1987, pp.171-191.

Ananiadou, S., and S. Warwick, "An Overview of Post-ALPAC Developments," presented at the ISSCO Tutorial on Machine Translation, Lugano, Switzerland, 2-6 April 1984.

Andreyewski, A., "Whither Automation and the Translator," *ATA Chronicle* 9, 2, (April-May) 1980, pp. 3-4.

Andreyewski, A., "Translation: Aids, Robots, and Automation," *Meta* 26, 1, (March) 1981, pp. 57-66.

Appelo, L., "A Compositional Approach to the Translation of Temporal Expression in the Rosetta System," *Proceedings of the 11th ICCL* [COLING 86], Bonn, West Germany, 25-29 August 1986, pp. 313-318.

Appelo, L., and A. Schenk, "Linguistic Problems in the Machine Translation Project Rosetta," in G. Dehaan and W. Zonnevel (eds.), *Formal Parameters of Generative Grammar I: Yearbook 1985*, Dordrecht (ICG Printing), 1985, pp. 11-16.

Arnold, D., and R. L. Johnson, "Robust Processing in Machine Translation," presented at the International Conference on the Methodology and Techniques of Machine Translation, Cranfield Institute of Technology, England, 13-15 February 1984.

Arnold, D., and R. L. Johnson, "Robust Processing in Machine Translation," *Proceedings of the 10th ICCL* [COLING 84] *and the 22nd Annual Meeting of the ACL*, Stanford University, California,

2-6 July 1984, pp. 472-475.

Arnold, D., L. Jaspaert and L. des Tombe, "EUROTRA Linguistic Specifications," 134p., 1984.

Arnold, D. J., S. Krauwer, M. Rosner, L. des Tombe and G. B. Varile, "The <C,A>,T Framework in EUROTRA: A Theoretically Committed Notation for MT," *Proceedings of the 11th ICCL* [COLING '86], Bonn, West Germany, 25-29 August 1986, pp. 297-303.

Arnold, D. J., L. Jaspaert, R. Johnson, S. Krauwer, M. Rosner, L. des Tombe, G. B. Varile, and S. Warwick, "A MU1 View of the <C,A>,T Framework in EUROTRA," in S. Nirenburg (ed.), *Proceedings of the Conference on Theoretical and Methodological Issues in Machine Translation of Natural Languages*, 1985, pp. 1-14.

Arthern, P. J., "Aids Unlimited: The Scope for Machine Aids in a Large Organization," *ASLIB Proceedings* 33, 7-8, (July-August) 1981, pp. 309-319.

Arthern, P. J., "Machine Translation and Computerized Terminology Systems: A Translator's Viewpoint," in B. M. Snell (ed.), *Translating and the Computer*, North-Holland, Amsterdam, 1979.

Ashman, B. D. Production Systems and Their Application to Machine Translation: Transfer Report. Report no. 82-9, Centre for Computational Linguistics, UMIST, 1982.

Austin, W. M. (ed.). *Papers in Linguistics in Honor of Leon Dostert.* Mouton, The Hague, 1967.

Bachut, D., and N. Verastegui, "Software Tools for the Environment of a Computer Aided Translation System," *Proceedings of the 10th ICCL* [COLING 84] *and the 22nd Annual Meeting of the ACL*, Stanford University, California, 2-6 July 1984, pp. 330-333.

Bar-Hillel, Y., "The Present Status of Automatic Translation of Languages," in F. L. Alt (ed.), *Advances in Computers, vol. 1.*

Academic Press, New York, 1960, pp. 91-163.

Bar-Hillel, Y., "Some Reflections on the Present Outlook for High-Quality Machine Translation," in W. P. Lehmann and R. Stachowitz (eds.), Feasibility Study on Fully Automatic High Quality Translation. Final technical report RADC-TR-71-295. Linguistics Research Center, University of Texas at Austin, December 1971.

Barnes, A. M. N. An Investigation into the Syntactic Structures of Abstracts, and the Definition of an 'Interlingua' for Their Translation by Machine. MSc. thesis, Centre for Computational Linguistics, UMIST, 1983.

Baron, N. S., "Language, Sublanguage, and the Promise of Machine Translation," *Computers and Translation* 1, 1, (January-March) 1986, pp. 3-19.

Bateman, R., "Introduction to Interactive Translation," in V. Lawson (ed.), *Tools for the Trade.* [Proceedings of a conference held in London, 10-11 November 1983.] Aslib, London, 1985, pp. 193-198.

Bátori, I., "Die Paradigmen der Maschinellen Sprachübersetzung," in I. Bátori and H. J. Weber (eds.), *Neue Ansätze in Maschineller Sprachübersetzung: Wissensrepräsentation und Textbezug.* Niemeyer, Tübingen, 1986, pp. 3-27.

Bátori, I., and H. J. Weber (eds.). *Neue Ansätze in Maschineller Sprachübersetzung: Wissensrepräsentation und Textbezug.* Niemeyer, Tübingen, 1986.

Baudot, Jean, *et al.*, "Un modèle de mini-banque de terminologie bilingue," *Meta* 26, 4, 1981, pp. 315-331.

Baudot, J., *et al.*, "Projet Aviation," Rapport d'étape mai 1977, Montréal: TAUM, 1977.

Beesley, K. R., "Machine-assisted Translation with a Human Face," *Data Processing* 28, 5, (June) 1986, pp. 251-257.

Bektaev, K. B., S. K. Kenesbaev, and R. G. Piotrovskii. Discussion of Engineering Linguistics. JPRS, 1973.

Bennett, W. S. The Linguistic Component of METAL. Working Paper LRC-82-2, Linguistics Research Center, University of Texas, Austin, July 1982.

Bennett, W. S., and J. Slocum, "The LRC Machine Translation System," *Computational Linguistics* 11, 2-3, 1985, pp. 111-121.

Berg, H.-H., "Übersicht zur maschinellen Verarbeitung von Texten des 'neueren Deutsch'," in H.-H. Berg and W. Lenders (eds.), Bericht über die Arbeiten der Clearingstellen zum älteren und neueren Deutsch. Institut für deutsche Sprache, Abteilung Linguistische Datenverarbeitung, Mannheim, October 1973, pp. 8-69.

Bertsch, E., "Automatische Lexikographie, Analyse und Übersetzung: Resume einer Fachtagung," *Sprache und Datenverarbeitung* 1, 1, 1977, pp. 74-75.

Bevan, N. Human Factors in the Use of Eurodicautom and Systran. Report on the CETIL workshop for the Commission of European Communities, Luxembourg, 1980.

Bevan, N., "Psychological and Ergonomic Factors in Machine Translation," in V. Lawson (ed.), *Practical Experience of Machine Translation*, North-Holland, Amsterdam, 1982, pp. 75-78.

Biewer, A., C. Feneyrol, J. Ritzke, and E. Stegentritt, "ASCOF - A Modular Multilevel System for French-German Translation," *Computational Linguistics* 11, 2-3, 1985, pp. 137-154.

Billmeier, R., "Zu den linguistischen Grundlagen von SYSTRAN," *Multilingua* 1, 2, 1982, pp. 83-96.

Blatt, A., "Nominalanalyse des Englischen im Übersetzungssystem SUSY," Dokumentation K7, Sonderforschungsbereich 100-K, Saarbrücken, 1983.

Boitet, C. Un essai de réponse à quelques questions théoriques et pratiques liées à la traduction automatique: Définition d'un système prototype. Doctoral thesis. Université de Grenoble, France, 1976.

Boitet, C., "Méthodes sémantiques en traduction automatique," *T.A. Informations* 17, 1, 1976, pp. 3-42.

Boitet, C., "Problèmes actuels en traduction automatique: un essai de réponse," *Proceedings of the 6th ICCL* [COLING 76], Ottawa, Canada, 1976. Also in *AJCL* 13, 2, 1976, microfiche 48, p. 68.

Boitet, C., "Towards an Adaptive and Interactive System in Automatic Translation," in A. Zampolli (ed.), *Computational and Mathematical Linguistics: Proceedings of the ICCL, Pisa, 27 August - 1 September 1973.* Florence, 1976.

Boitet, C., "Où en est le GETA début 1977?" *T.A. Informations* 18, 1977, pp. 3-20.

Boitet, C., "Wo steht die GETA Anfang 1977?" Dritter Europäischer Kongress über Dokumentationssysteme und -netze, Luxembourg, 3-6 Mai 1977. Verlag Dokumentation, Munich, 1977.

Boitet, C. Mechanical Translation and the Problem of Understanding Natural Languages. Table-Ronde IFIP, Toronto, August 1977, and Colloque Franco-Sovietique sur la TA, Moscow, December 1977.

Boitet, C., "Where Does GETA Stand at the Beginning of 1977?" in Commission of the European Communities, *Overcoming the Language Barrier: Proceedings of the Third European Congress on Information Systems and Networks, Luxembourg, 3-6 May 1977.* Verlag Dokumentation, Munich, 1977-1978, pp. 88-120.

Boitet, C., "Automatic Production of CF and CS Analyzers using a General Tree-Transducer," presented at the Second International Colloquium on Machine Translation, Lexicography, and Analysis, Saarbrücken, West Germany, 16-17 November 1979.

Boitet, C., "Research and Development on MT and Related Techniques at Grenoble University (GETA)," in M. King (ed.), *Machine Translation Today: the State of the Art* [proceedings of the Third Lugano Tutorial, Lugano, Switzerland, 2-7 April 1984]. Edinburgh University Press, 1987, pp. 133-153.

Boitet, C., and R. Gerber, "Expert Systems and Other New Techniques in MT," *Proceedings of the 10th ICCL* [COLING 84] *and the 22nd Annual Meeting of the ACL*, Stanford University, California, 2-6 July 1984, pp. 468-471.

Boitet, C., and R. Gerber, "Expert Systems and Other New Techniques in M(A)T," in I. Bátori and H. J. Weber (eds.), *Neue Ansätze in Maschineller Sprachübersetzung: Wissensrepräsentation und Textbezug*. Niemeyer, Tübingen, 1986, pp. 103-119.

Boitet, C., and N. Nedobejkine, "Russian-French at GETA: Outline of the Method and Detailed Example," *Proceedings of the 8th ICCL* [COLING 80], Tokyo, 30 September - 4 October 1980.

Boitet, C., and N. Nedobejkine, "Recent Developments in Russian-French Machine Translation at Grenoble," *Linguistics* 19, 3/4, 1981, pp. 199-271.

Boitet, C., and N. Nedobejkine, "Russian-French Machine Translation at Grenoble: A General Software Used for Implementing a Particular Linguistic Strategy," *Linguistics* 20, 1982.

Boitet, C., and N. Nedobejkine, "Toward Integrated Dictionaries for M(A)T: Motivations and Linguistic Organization," *Proceedings of the 11th ICCL* [COLING 86], Bonn, West Germany, 25-29 August 1986, pp. 423-428.

Boitet, C., P. Chatelin, and P. Daun Fraga, "Present and Future Paradigms in the Automatized Translation of Natural Languages," *Proceedings of the 8th ICCL* [COLING 80], Tokyo, 30 September - 4 October 1980, pp. 430-436.

Boitet, C., P. Guillaume, and M. Quezel-Ambrunaz, "Manipulations d'arborescences et parallelisme: le système ROBRA," *Proceedings of the 7th ICCL* [COLING 78], Bergen, Norway, 1978.

Boitet, C., P. Guillaume, and M. Quezel-Ambrunaz, "Implementation and Conversational Environment of ARIANE-78.4, An Integrated System for Automated Translation and Human Revision," *Proceedings of the 9th ICCL* [COLING 82], Prague, 5-10 July 1982, pp. 19-27.

Boitet, C., P. Guillaume, and M. Quezel-Ambrunaz, "A Case Study in Software Evolution: from ARIANE-78.4 to ARIANE-85," in S. Nirenburg (ed.), *Proceedings of the Conference on Theoretical and Methodological Issues in Machine Translation of Natural Languages*, 1985, pp. 27-58.

Bonner, M., "Report of the Saarbrücken Colloquium, 2. Internationales Kolloquium 'Maschinelle Übersetzung, Lexikographie und Analyse', Saarbrücken 16-17 November 1979," *ALLC Bulletin* 9, 3, 1981, pp. 11-12.

Booth, A. D. (ed.). *Machine Translation.* North Holland, Amsterdam, 1967.

Bostad, D. A., "Quality Control Procedures in Modification of the Air Force Russian-English MT System," in V. Lawson (ed.), *Practical Experience of Machine Translation.* North-Holland, Amsterdam, 1982, pp. 129-133.

Bostad, D. A., "Soviet Patent Bulletin Processing: A Particular Application of Machine Translation," *Calico* 2, 4, (June) 1985, pp. 27-30.

Bourbeau, L. La nominalisation. Groupe TAUM, Université de Montréal, 1974.

Bourbeau, L. (ed.) Linguistic Documentation of the Computerised Translation Chain of the TAUM-AVIATION Translation System. TAUM, University of Montreal, 1981.

Brinkmann, K.-H., "On the Development and Operation of Terminology Data Banks as a Requirement for Machine-Aided Translation," *Nachrichten für Dokumentation* 25, 3, (June) 1974, pp. 99-104.

Brinkmann, K.-H., "Terminologists, Lexicographers, and Computers," *Philips Terminology Bulletin* 3, 3/4, 1974, pp. 8-9.

Brinkmann, K.-H., "Überlegungen zum Aufbau und Betrieb von Terminologiedatenbanken als Voraussetzung der maschinenunterstützten Übersetzung," *Nachrichten für Dokumentation* 25, 1974, pp. 99-105.

Brinkmann, K.-H., "The TEAM Program System," *Philips Terminology Bulletin* 4, 2/3, 1975, pp. 20-37.

Brinkmann, K.-H., "Perspectives of Machine Translation," *Nachrichten für Dokumentation* 29, 3, (June) 1978, pp. 104-108.

Brinkmann, K.-H., "Perspectives d'avenir de la traduction automatique (Future Prospects for Machine Translation)," *Meta* 24, 3, (September) 1979, pp. 315-325.

Brinkmann, K.-H., "Terminology Data Banks as a Basis for High-Quality Translation," *Proceedings of the 8th ICCL* [COLING 80], Tokyo, 30 September - 4 October 1980.

Brinkmann, K.-H., and E. Tanke, "The TEAM Program System and International Co-operation in Terminology/Le système des programmes TEAM et la coopération internationale dans le domaine de la terminologie," presented at the First Infoterm Symposium on International Co-operation in Terminology, Vienna, 9-11 April 1975. Infoterm Series, vol. 3, Munich, 1976, pp. 180-192.

Brockhaus, K., "Zum formalen Aufbau einer Grammatik für automatische Übersetzungsverfahren (unter Berücksichtigung der Programmierung)," Vorabdrucke des Internationalen Kolloquiums 'Automatische Lexikographie, Analyse und Übersetzung', Saarbrücken, 23-25 September 1976.

Brown, G. P. Some Problems in German to English Machine Translation. Master's thesis, Massachusetts Institute of Technology, 1974.

Bruderer, H. E., "Maschinelle Sprachübersetzung für den Apollo-Sojus-Flug," *Neue Züricher Zeitung* 156, 9 July 1975, p. 42.

Bruderer, H. E., "The Present State of Machine Translation and Machine-Aided Translation," *ALLC Bulletin* 3, 3, 1975, pp. 258-261.

Bruderer, H. E., "Vorführung eines automatischen Übersetzungsverfahrens im Rechenzentrum der Universität Zürich," *ALLC Bulletin* 3, 3, 1975, pp. 197-200.

Bruderer, H. E., "A Register of Machine Translation and Machine-Aided Translation Projects," *Computers and the Humanities* 10, 1, 1976, p. 45.

Bruderer, H. E. *Handbook of Machine Translation and Machine-Aided Translation: Automatic Translation of Natural Languages and Multilingual Terminology Data Banks.* North-Holland, Amsterdam, 1977.

Bruderer, H. E., "Automatic Language Processing in Switzerland: A State of the Art Report (Nov. 1976)," *Sprache und Datenverarbeitung* 1, 1, 1977, pp. 76-77.

Bruderer, H. E., "The Present State of Machine and Machine-Assisted Translation," in Commission of the European Communities, *Overcoming the Language Barrier: Proceedings of the Third European Congress on Information Systems and Networks, Luxembourg, 3-6 May 1977*, vol. 1. Verlag Dokumentation, Munich, 1977, pp. 529-556.

Bruderer, H. E. *Handbuch der maschinellen und maschinenunterstützten Sprachübersetzung: Automatische Übersetzung natürlicher Sprachen und mehrsprachige Terminologiedatenbanken.* Verlag Dokumentation, Munich, 1978.

Bruderer, H. E., and D. G. Hays, "LATSEC Shows MT in Zürich," *AJCL* 12, 4, 1975, microfiche 29, p. 9.

Buchmann, B., "Early History of Machine Translation," in M. King (ed.), *Machine Translation Today: the State of the Art* [proceedings of the Third Lugano Tutorial, Lugano, Switzerland, 2-7 April 1984]. Edinburgh University Press, 1987, pp. 3-21.

Buchmann, B., S. Warwick, and P. Shann, "Design of a Machine Translation System for a Sublanguage," *Proceedings of the 10th ICCL* [COLING 84] *and the 22nd Annual Meeting of the ACL*, Stanford University, California, 2-6 July 1984, pp. 334-337.

Burden, D., "Natural Human Languages Automatically Translated by Computer: The SYSTRAN II System," *Computers and People* 30, 5-6, (May-June) 1981, pp. 12-15, 24.

Burge, J., "The TARGET Project's Interactive Computerized Multilingual Dictionary," *AJCL*, June 1978.

Bush, C. Structural Passives and the "Massive Passive" Transfer. M.A. thesis, Brigham Young University, Provo, Utah, 1974.

Carbonell, J. G., and M. Tomita, "New Approaches to Machine Translation," in S. Nirenburg (ed.), *Proceedings of the Conference on Theoretical and Methodological Issues in Machine Translation of Natural Languages*, 1985, pp. 59-74.

Carbonell, J. G., R. E. Cullingford, and A. V. Gershman, "Towards Knowledge-Based Machine Translation," *Abstracts, 7th ICCL* [COLING 78], Bergen, Norway, 1978. Also available as NTIS Report RR-146.

Carbonell, J. G., R. E. Cullingford, and A. V. Gershman, "Steps Toward Knowledge-Based Machine Translation," *IEEE Transactions on Pattern Analysis and Machine Intelligence* 3, 4, (July) 1981, pp. 376-392.

Case, R., and L. Berglund. FTD Edit System. Final technical

report, January 1974-June 1976, Operating Systems, Inc., Woodland, California, 1976.

Chafe, W. L. An Approach to Verbalization and Translation by Machine. Final report RADC-TR-74-271, Department of Linguistics, University of California at Berkeley, October 1974. Also in *AJCL* 11, 3, 1974, microfiche 10, p. 10.

Chafe, W. L., "Foundations of Machine Translation Linguistics," *AJCL* 13, 2, 1976, microfiche 46, pp. 8-9.

Chaloupka, B., "[excerpt from presentation on] Xonics MT System" *AJCL* 13, 2, 1976, microfiche 46, pp. 37-39.

Chandioux, J., "Leibniz, A Multilingual System," *AJCL* 13, 2, 1976, microfiche 46, p. 25.

Chandioux, J., "METEO: An Operational System for the Translation of Public Weather Forecasts," *AJCL* 13, 2, 1976, microfiche 46, pp. 27-36.

Chandioux, J., "METEO: un système opérationnel pour la traduction automatique des bulletins météorologiques destinés au grand public," *Meta* 21, 2, (June) 1976, pp. 127-133.

Chandioux, J., "Histoire de la traduction automatique au Canada," *Meta* 22, 1977, pp. 54-56.

Chandioux, J., and M. Gueraud, "METEO: un système à l'épreuve du temps," *Meta* 26, 1, (March) 1981, pp. 18-22.

Chauche, J. Transducteurs et arborescences: Étude et réalisation de systèmes appliqués aux grammaires transformationnelles. Thèse Docteur Ès-Sciences Mathématiques, Université de Grenoble, France, 1974.

Chauche, J., "Les systèmes ATEF et CETA," *T.A. Informations* 16, 2, 1975, pp. 27-38.

Chauche, J., "The ATEF and CETA Systems," *AJCL*, 2, 1975,

microfiche 17, pp. 21-40.

Chauche, J., "Vers un modèle algorithmique pour le traitement automatique des langues naturelles," *AJCL* 13, 2, 1976, microfiche 48, p. 25.

Chauche, J., P. Guillaume, and M. Quezel-Ambrunaz. Le système ATEF. GETA report G-2600-A, Université de Grenoble, France, 1973.

Chaumier, J., M. C. Mallen, and G. Van Slype. Évaluation du système de traduction automatique SYSTRAN. Commission des Communautés Européenes, Luxembourg, 1977.

Chevalier, M., J. Dansereau, and G. Poulin. TAUM-METEO: déscription du système. Groupe TAUM, Université de Montréal, January 1978.

Chevalier, M., P. Isabelle, F. Labelle, and C. Laine, "La traductologie appliquée à la traduction automatique," *Meta* 26, 1, (March) 1981, pp. 35-47.

Chung, H. S. and T. L. Kunii, "NARA: A Two-way Simultaneous Interpretation System Between Korean and Japanese - A Methodological Study," *Proceedings of the 11th ICCL* [COLING 86], Bonn, West Germany, 25-29 August 1986, pp. 325-328.

Clark, R., "Machine Aids: A Small User's Reaction," *ASLIB Proceedings* 33, 7-8, (July-August) 1981, pp. 278-289.

Cochard, J.-L, "Software Background for Machine Translation, Part I," presented at the ISSCO Tutorial on Machine Translation, Lugano, Switzerland, 2-6 April 1984.

Cochard, J.-L., "A Brief Look at a Typical Software Architecture," in M. King (ed.), *Machine Translation Today: the State of the Art* [proceedings of the Third Lugano Tutorial, Lugano, Switzerland, 2-7 April 1984]. Edinburgh University Press, 1987, pp. 117-123.

Commission of the European Communities. Plan of Action for the

Improvement of the Transfer of Information between European Languages. Brussels, 1976.

Commission of the European Communities. *Overcoming the Language Barrier: Proceedings of the 3rd European Congress on Information Systems and Networks, Luxembourg, 3-6 May 1977.* Verlag Dokumentation, Munich, 1977 (vol. 1) - 1978 (vol. 2).

Commission of the European Communities. The EUROTRA Council Decision. Official Journal of the European Communities, no. L 317/21, 13 November 1982.

Cordier, M. O., and C. Moghrabi, "An Experiment towards More Efficient Automatic Translation," *Proceedings of ECAI-82*, Orsay, France, 1982, pp. 228-231.

Couture, B., "La Banque de terminologie au service de l'entreprise," *Meta* 21, 1, (March) 1976, pp. 100-109.

Crawford, T. D., "A Review of the Cardiff Machine Translation Project," in A. Zampolli (ed.), *Computational and Mathematical Linguistics: Proceedings of the Third Symposium on the Use of Computers in Literary and Linguistic Research.* Cardiff, 1974.

Crawford, T. D., "Machine Translation: The Development of BABEL Program," *Lettera* 8, 1974, pp. 54-60.

Crawford, T. D., "Project BABEL: Machine Translation with English as the Target Language," in A. Zampolli (ed.), *Computational and Mathematical Linguistics: Proceedings of the Third Symposium on the Use of Computers in Literary and Linguistic Research.* Cardiff, 1974.

Culhane, P. T., "Semantics via Machine Translation," *Russian Language Journal* 31, 108, (Winter) 1977, pp. 35-42.

Cullingford, R. E., and B. A. Onyshkevych, "Lexicon-driven Machine Translation," in S. Nirenburg (ed.), *Proceedings of the Conference on Theoretical and Methodological Issues in Machine*

Translation of Natural Languages, 1985, pp. 75-115.

Daley, D. H., and R. F. Vachino, "The West German Federal Bureau of Languages and Machine-Aided Translation in Germany," *Federal Linguist* 5, 3-4, (Winter) 1973, pp. 14-18.

Danik, A., "The ALPS Computer Assisted Translation System," *BCS Natural Language Translation Specialist Group Newsletter* 14, 1984, pp. 5-14.

Dansereau, J., "Traduction automatique et terminologie automatique," *Meta* 23, 2, (June) 1978, pp. 132-140.

Darke, D., "Arabic Translations By Computer?," *Middle East Computing* 13, (May) 1984, pp. 16-18.

de Roeck, A., "Linguistic Theory and Early Machine Translation," in M. King (ed.), *Machine Translation Today: the State of the Art* [proceedings of the Third Lugano Tutorial, Lugano, Switzerland, 2-7 April 1984]. Edinburgh University Press, 1987, pp. 38-57.

Desroches, S., and L. Bourbeau. TAUM-BESCH. Groupe TAUM, Université de Montréal, 1980.

des Tombe, L., D. J. Arnold, L. Jaspaert, R. Johnson, S. Krauwer, M. Rosner, G. B. Varile, and S. Warwick, "A Preliminary Linguistic Framework for EUROTRA (June 1985)," in S. Nirenburg (ed.), *Proceedings of the Conference on Theoretical and Methodological Issues in Machine Translation of Natural Languages*, 1985, pp. 283-288.

Dostert, L. E. (ed.) *Research in Machine Translation.* Georgetown University Press, Washington, D.C., 1957.

Dubuc, R., and J.-F. Gregoire, "Banque de terminologie et traduction," *Babel* 20, 4, 1974, pp. 180-184.

Duckitt, P., "Translating and Online," *ASLIB Proceedings* 33, 7-8, (July-August) 1981, pp. 290-296.

Ducrot, J.-M., "Perspectives et avantages offerts par la traduction automatique des analyses de documents selon la méthode 'TITUS'," in *1er Congrès national français sur l'information et la documentation.* Communications, Paris, 1974, pp. 321-333.

Ducrot, J.-M., "TITUS IV System: système de traduction automatique et simultanée en quatre langues," in P. J. Taylor and B. Cronin (eds.), *Information Management Research in Europe: Proceedings of the EURIM 5 Conference, Versailles, 12-14 May 1982.* Aslib, London, 1984.

Du Feu, V. M., "Acta Mathematica Sinica (review)," *ALLC Bulletin* 3, 3, 1975, p. 277.

Earp, R., and J. Cherinka, "Getting Started in a Natural Language Translation Project," *Journal of Educational Data Processing* 15, 2, 1978, pp. 25-34.

Edmonds, E., "A Software Tool for Implementing Machine Translation," presented at the International Conference on the Methodology and Techniques of Machine Translation, Cranfield Institute of Technology, England, 13-15 February 1984.

Edmundson, H. P. (ed.) *Proceedings of the National Symposium on Machine Translation.* Prentice-Hall, Englewood Cliffs, New Jersey, 1961.

Eggers, H., "Probleme der Identifikationsgrammatik und ihrer Anwendung," Vorabdrucke des Internationalen Kolloquiums 'Automatische Lexikographie, Analyse und Übersetzung', Saarbrücken, 23-25 September 1976, pp. 24-29.

Eggers, H. *Maschinelle Übersetzung, Lexikographie und Analyse.* 2 vols. Saarland University, Saarbrücken, 1980.

Eggers, H., "Das Lemmatisierungssystem SALEM des Sonderforschungsbereichs 90 'Elektronische Sprachforschung' in Saarbrücken," *ALLC Bulletin* 9, 2, 1981, pp. 9-15.

Elliston, J. S. G., "Computer Aided Translation: A Business Viewpoint," in B. M. Snell (ed.), *Translating and the Computer.* North-Holland, Amsterdam, 1979, pp. 149-158.

Eman, H., and D. Clarke, "Machine Translation of English into Persian," presented at the International Conference on the Methodology and Techniques of Machine Translation, Cranfield Institute of Technology, England, 13-15 February 1984.

Euvrard, A., and J. Lecomte. Élaboration d'une chaine de traduction automatique d'anglais en français: bilan d'une expérience. Report no. 36, Centre de Recherches et d'Applications Linguistiques, Nancy, France, 1979.

Faiss, K., "Übersetzung und Sprachwissenschaft – eine Orientierung," *Babel* 19, 2, 1973, pp. 75-86.

Farrington, B., "A Microcomputer Program for Checking English/French Translation at Sentence Level," presented at the International Conference on the Methodology and Techniques of Machine Translation, Cranfield Institute of Technology, England, 13-15 February 1984.

Feng, Z. W., "Mémoire pour une tentative de traduction multilingue du Chinois en Français, Anglais, Japonais, Russe et Allemand," presented at the 9th ICCL [COLING 82], Prague, 5-10 July 1982.

Figge, U. L., "Gedächtnis und Maschinelle Übersetzung," in I. Bátori and H. J. Weber (eds.), *Neue Ansätze in Maschineller Sprachübersetzung: Wissensrepräsentation und Textbezug.* Niemeyer, Tübingen, 1986, pp. 29-44.

François, P., "La banque de données terminologiques EURODICAUTOM de la Commission des Communautés Européennes: Le résultat d'un travail pluri-disciplinaire," Comptes rendus du Colloque international de terminologie, Terminologies 76, Paris-La Défense, 15-18 June 1976. Association française de terminologie, Paris, 1977.

Freigang, K.-H., "Erfahrungen bei der Anpassung eines Mü-Systems an eine neue Sprache bzw. einen neuen Texttyp," *Sprache und Datenverarbeitung* 5, 1-2, 1981, pp. 29-32.

Freigang, K.-H., and K.-D Schmitz. Wörterbucherstellung, Wörterbuchsuche und Flexionsanalyse im Übersetzungssystem Englisch-Deutsch. Dokumentation KI2, SFB-100-K, Universität des Saarlandes, Saarbrücken, 1982.

Fukushima, M., and H. Arita, "A MAHA Machine Translation System from Japanese to English," presented at the EUROTRA Joint Japanese-European Workshop, Brussels, November 1983.

Ganeshsundaram, P. C. Automatic Translation from English into Hindi Using the PCG-Theory and a Scheme of Pre-Editing. Series: AILA 1978 0124, Foreign Languages Section, Indian Institute of Science, Bangalore, 1978.

Garside, R. G., "The Grammatical Tagging of Unrestricted English Text," presented at the International Conference on the Methodology and Techniques of Machine Translation, Cranfield Institute of Technology, England, 13-15 February 1984.

Garvin, P. L., "The Fulcrum Approach – Twelve Years Later," *International Forum on Information and Documentation* 5, 2, 1980, pp. 27-29.

Garvin, P. L., "Grammar in the Light of Machine Translation," *International Forum on Information and Documentation* 9, 2, (April) 1984, pp. 28-30.

Geens, D., "Machine Translation: Evaluation of the EUROTRA Interface Mechanism," Université Libre de Bruxelles Rapport d'Activités de l'Institut de Phonétique, 15, 1981, pp. 67-108.

Gerber, R., and C. Boitet, "On the Design of Expert Systems Grafted on MT Systems," in S. Nirenburg (ed.), *Proceedings of the Conference on Theoretical and Methodological Issues in Machine Translation of Natural Languages*, 1985, pp. 116-134.

Gerrard, M., "Regular Use of Machine Translation of Russian at Oak Ridge National Laboratory," *AJCL* 13, 2, 1976, microfiche 46, pp. 53-56.

Gervais A. Evaluation of the TAUM-AVIATION Machine Translation Pilot System. Translation Bureau, Secretary of State, Ottawa, Ontario, Canada, June 1980.

Gibb, D. K., "Interactive Analysis: A Synergistic Approach," *AJCL* 13, 2, 1976, microfiche 48, p. 45.

Gobeil, F., "La traduction automatique au Canada," *L'Actualité terminologique* 14, 5, (May) 1981.

Gobeil, F. Machine Translation Feasibility Study. Translation Bureau, Ottawa, Canada, 1981.

Godden, K. S. Montague Grammar and Machine Translation between Thai and English. Ph.D. dissertation, University of Kansas, January 1982.

Goetschalckx, J., "Eurodicautom," in B. Snell (ed.), *Translating and the Computer.* North Holland, Amsterdam, 1979, pp. 71-76.

Goetschalckx, J., "Translation, Terminology, and Documentation in International Organizations," *Babel* 20, 4, 1974, pp. 185-187.

Green, R., "The MT Errors Which Cause Most Trouble to Posteditors," in V. Lawson (ed.), *Practical Experience of Machine Translation.* North-Holland, Amsterdam, 1982, pp. 101-104.

Greenfield, C. C., and D. Serain. Machine-Aided Translation: From Terminology Banks to Interactive Translation Systems. Department of Computer Science, Carnegie-Mellon University, Pittsburgh, Pennsylvania, and Institut de Recherche en Informatique et Automatique, Paris, France, 1977. Available from EDRS.

Gross, M. Notes on the Feasibility of High Quality Mechanical Translation. Final scientific report, Laboratoire D'Automatique

Documentaire et Linguistique, University of Paris, France, 1973.

Guilbaud, J.-P. Analyse morphologique de l'allemand en vue de la traduction par ordinateur de textes techniques specialisés. Thèse de Troisième Cycle, l'Université de la Sorbonne nouvelle, Paris, 1980.

Guilbaud, J.-P., "Principles and Results of a German to French MT System at Grenoble University (GETA)," in M. King (ed.), *Machine Translation Today: the State of the Art* [proceedings of the Third Lugano Tutorial, Lugano, Switzerland, 2-7 April 1984]. Edinburgh University Press, 1987, pp. 278-318.

Habermaan, F. W. A., "Application of SYSTRAN for Translation of Nuclear Technology Texts at the Nuclear Centre of Karlsruhe," presented at the International Seminar on Machine Translation, Cranfield Institute of Technology, England, February 1984.

Hajičova, E., and Z. Kirschner, "Automatic Translation from English to Czech," *Prague Bulletin of Mathematical Linguistics* 35, 1981, pp. 55-65.

Halliday, T. C., and E. A. Briss. The Evaluation and Systems Analysis of the SYSTRAN Machine Translation System. Final technical report RADC-TR-76-399, November 1974-August 1976. Battelle Columbus Laboratories, Ohio, 1977. Available as NTIS report AD-A036 070/1GA, January 1977.

Hanakata, K., A. Lesniewski, and S. Yokoyama, "Semantic Based Generation of Japanese German Translation System," *Proceedings of the 11th ICCL* [COLING 86], Bonn, West Germany, 25-29 August 1986, pp. 560-562.

Hardt, S. L., "Automated Text Translation and the Organization of Conceptual and Lexical Information," *Proceedings of Trends and Applications 1983: Automating Intelligent Behavior – Applications and Frontiers.* IEEE, New York, 1983, pp. 261-262.

Hauenschild, C., "KIT/NASEV oder die Problematik des Transfers bei der Maschinellen Übersetzung," in I. Bátori and H. J. Weber (eds.), *Neue Ansätze in Maschineller Sprachübersetzung: Wissensrepräsentation und Textbezug.* Niemeyer, Tübingen, 1986, pp. 167-195.

Hauenschild, C., E. Huckert, and R. Maier, "SALAT: Machine Translation via Semantic Representation," in R. Baeuerle, U. Egli, and A. von Stechow (eds.), *Semantics From Different Points of View.* Springer Verlag, Berlin, 1979, pp. 324-352.

Hawes, R. E., "Logos: The Intelligent Translation System," in V. Lawson (ed.), *Tools for the Trade.* [Proceedings of a conference held in London, 10-11 November 1983.] Aslib, London, 1985, pp. 131-140.

Hays, D. G., and J. Mathias (eds.), "Summary Proceedings of the FBIS Seminar on Machine Translation, Rosslyn, Virginia, 8-9 March 1976," *AJCL* 13, 2, 1976, microfiche 46, pp. 1-96.

Henisz-Dostert, B. A Review of the State of Machine Translation. 1979. Available from EDRS.

Henisz-Dostert, B., R. R. Macdonald, and M. Zarechnak. *Machine Translation.* Mouton, The Hague, 1979.

Heriard Dubreuil, S., "Automatic Translation and Computer-Assisted Translation," *Inf. and Gestion* 107, June-July 1979, pp. 49-54.

Hidano, Y., Y. Nitta, and K. Ishiwara, "A Brief Sketch of the Evaluation Techniques for Machine Translation Systems," presented at the EUROTRA Joint Japanese-European Workshop, Brussels, November 1983.

Hitachi. Research on Machine Translation in Hitachi Ltd. Technical note, Systems Development Laboratory, Hitachi Ltd., Tama-ku, Kawasaki, October 1981.

Hoffman, T., "Semantics in Aid of Automatic Translation," *Proceedings of the 6th ICCL* [COLING 76], Ottawa, Ontario, Canada, 1976. Also in *AJCL* 13, 2, 1976, microfiche 48, p. 27.

Huang, X.-M., "Dealing with Conjunctions in a Machine Translation Environment," *Proceedings of the ACL European Chapter Meeting*, Pisa, Italy, 1983.

Huang, X.-M., "Dealing with Conjunctions in a Machine Translation Environment," *Proceedings of the 10th ICCL* [COLING 84] *and the 22nd Annual Meeting of the ACL*, Stanford University, California, 2-6 July 1984, pp. 243-246.

Huang, X.-M., "The Generation of Chinese Sentences from the Semantic Representation of the Input English Text," presented at the International Conference on the Methodology and Techniques of Machine Translation, Cranfield Institute of Technology, England, 13-15 February 1984.

Huang, X.-M., "Machine Translation in the Semantic Definite Clause Grammar Formalism," in S. Nirenburg (ed.), *Proceedings of the Conference on Theoretical and Methodological Issues in Machine Translation of Natural Languages*, 1985, pp. 135-144. Also available as Tech. Report MCCS-85-7, Computing Research Laboratory, New Mexico State University, Las Cruces, New Mexico, 1985.

Huang, X.-M., "A Bidirectional Chinese Grammar in a Machine Translational System," Tech. Report MCCS-86-52, Computing Research Laboratory, New Mexico State University, Las Cruces, New Mexico, 1986.

Hubert, J., J. Ibuki, M. Kume, and M. Nagao, "A System of Japanese-French Automatic Translation for Paper Titles," presented at the 26th Annual Convention of the Information Processing Society of Japan, 1983.

Hundt, M. G., "Working with the Weidner Machine-Aided Translation System," in V. Lawson (ed.), *Practical Experience of Machine Translation*. North-Holland, Amsterdam, 1982, pp. 45-51.

Hutchins, W. J., "Progress in Documentation: Machine Translation and Machine-Aided Translation," *Journal of Documentation* 34, 2,

(June) 1978, pp. 119-159.

Hutchins, W. J., "Linguistic Models in Machine Translation," *University of East Anglia Papers in Linguistics* 9, 1979, pp. 29-52.

Hutchins, W. J., "The Evolution of Machine Translation Systems," in V. Lawson (ed.), *Practical Experience of Machine Translation.* North-Holland, Amsterdam, 1982, pp. 21-37.

Hutchins, W. J., "Elements of Linguistic Methods of Analysis," presented at the International Conference on the Methodology and Techniques of Machine Translation, Cranfield Institute of Technology, England, 13-15 February 1984.

Hutchins, W. J. *Machine Translation: Past, Present, Future.* Ellis Horwood, Ltd., Chichester, West Sussex, England, 1986.

Hutton, F. C., "Georgetown University MT System Usage," *AJCL* 13, 2, 1976, microfiche 46, p. 57.

Ibrahim, M., "A Generalized Computer-assisted Language Translation Model: English to Arabic - Problems and Solutions," presented at the International Conference on the Methodology and Techniques of Machine Translation, Cranfield Institute of Technology, England, 13-15 February 1984.

Iida, H., K. Ogura, and H. Nomura, "A Case Analysis Method Cooperating with ATNG and its Application to Machine Translation," *Proceedings of the 10th ICCL* [COLING 84] *and the 22nd Annual Meeting of the ACL*, Stanford University, California, 2-6 July 1984, pp. 154-158.

Isabelle, P. A Linguistic Description of the TAUM-AVIATION Computerized Translation System. Groupe TAUM, Université de Montréal, 1981.

Isabelle, P. Some Views on the Future of the TAUM Group and the TAUM-AVIATION System. TAUM Group, University of Montreal, 1981.

Isabelle, P., "Machine Translation at the TAUM Group," in M. King (ed.), *Machine Translation Today: the State of the Art* [proceedings of the Third Lugano Tutorial, Lugano, Switzerland, 2-7 April 1984]. Edinburgh University Press, 1987, pp. 247-277.

Isabelle, P., and L. Bourbeau, "TAUM-AVIATION: Its Technical Features and some Experimental Results," *Computational Linguistics* 11, 1, 1985, pp. 18-27.

Isabelle, P., and E. Macklovitch, "Transfer and MT Modularity," *Proceedings of the 11th ICCL* [COLING 86], Bonn, West Germany, 25-29 August 1986, pp. 115-117.

Isabelle, P., L. Bourbeau, M. Chevalier, and S. Lepage, "TAUM-AVIATION: description d'un système de traduction automatisée des manuels d'entretien en aeronautique," *Proceedings of the 7th ICCL* [COLING 78], Bergen, Norway, 1978.

Jaspaert, L., "Linguistic Developments in EUROTRA since 1983," *Proceedings of the 11th* ICCL [COLING 86], Bonn, West Germany, 25-29 August 1986, pp. 294-296.

Jelinek, J., and J. Hawgood, "The Automatic Integrated Dictionary Systems," presented at the International Conference on the Methodology and Techniques of Machine Translation, Cranfield Institute of Technology, England, 13-15 February 1984.

Johnson, R. L., "Contemporary Perspectives in Machine Translation," in S. Hanon and V. H. Pedersen (eds.), *Human Translation Machine Translation (Noter og Kommentarer 39).* Romansk Institut, Odense Universitet, 1980, pp. 133-147.

Johnson, R. L., "Parsing - an MT Perspective," in K. S. Jones and Y. Wilks (eds.), *Automatic Natural Language Parsing.* Ellis Horwood, Ltd., Chichester, West Sussex, England, 1983.

Johnson, R. L., and M. A. Rosner, "Machine Translation and Software Tools," in M. King (ed.), *Machine Translation Today: the State of the Art* [proceedings of the Third Lugano Tutorial, Lugano,

Switzerland, 2-7 April 1984]. Edinburgh University Press, 1987, pp. 154-167.

Johnson, R. L., and P. J. Whitelock, "Machine Translation as an Expert Task," in S. Nirenburg (ed.), *Proceedings of the Conference on Theoretical and Methodological Issues in Machine Translation of Natural Languages*, 1985, pp. 145-153.

Johnson, R. L., M. King, and L. des Tombe, "EUROTRA: A Multilingual System Under Development," *Computational Linguistics* 11, 2-3, 1985, pp. 155-169.

Johnson, R. L., S. Krauwer, M. A. Rosner, and G. B. Varile, "The Design of the Kernal Architecture for the EUROTRA Software," *Proceedings of the 10th ICCL* [COLING 84] *and the 22nd Annual Meeting of the ACL*, Stanford University, California, 2-6 July 1984, pp. 226-235.

Jordan, S. R., A. F. R. Brown,, and F. C. Hutton, "Computerized Russian Translation at ORNL," *Proceedings of the ASIS Annual Meeting*, San Francisco, 1976, p. 163. Also in *ASIS Journal* 28, 1, 1977, pp. 26-33.

Jordan, S. R., A. F. R. Brown, and F. C. Hutton. SLC Primer for Russian Translation Users. Computer Sciences Division, Oak Ridge National Laboratory, Oak Ridge, Tennessee, 1977.

JPRS. Machine-Assisted Translation in West Germany [Translations of articles in German by various authors]. NTIS document JPRS-68726, 1977.

Kanchanawan, N., "Automatic Translation of English to Thai," presented at the 31st International Congress of Human Sciences in Asia and North Africa, Tokyo-Kyoto, 31 August - 7 September 1983.

Kay, M., "Automatic Translation of Natural Languages," *Daedalus* 102, 3, (Summer) 1973, pp. 217-230. Reprinted in E. Haugen and M. Bloomfield (eds.), *Language as a Human Problem.* Lutterworth, Guildford, 1975, pp. 219-232.

Kay, M., "The Proper Place of Man and Machines in Translation," *AJCL* 13, 2, 1976, microfiche 46.

Kay, M. The Proper Place of Men and Machines in Language Translation. Technical report CSL-80-11. Xerox Palo Alto Research Center, California, October 1980.

Kay, M., "Machine Translation," *AJCL* 8, 2, (April-June) 1982, pp. 74-78.

Kay, M., "Functional Unification Grammar: A Formalism for Machine Translation," *Proceedings of the 10th ICCL* [COLING 84] *and the 22nd Annual Meeting of the ACL*, Stanford University, California, 2-6 July 1984, pp. 75-78.

Kay, M., "Machine Translation will not Work," *Proceedings of the 24th Annual Meeting of the ACL*, Columbia University, New York, July 1986, p. 268.

Keil, G. C., "Machine Translation Software," presented at BCS 79, London, 4-6 January 1979.

Kertesz, F., "How to Cope with the Foreign-Language Problems: Experience Gained at a Multidisciplinary Laboratory," *ASIS Journal* 25, 2, 1974, pp. 86-104.

King, M., "Design Characteristics of a Machine Translation System," *Proceedings of the 7th IJCAI*, Vancouver, B.C., Canada, Aug. 1981, pp. 43-46.

King, M., "EUROTRA - A European System for Machine Translation," *Lebende Sprachen* 26, 1981, pp. 12-14.

King, M., "Semantics and Artificial Intelligence in Machine Translation," in *Sprache und Datenverarbeitung*, 1981, pp. 5-8.

King, M., "EUROTRA: An Attempt to Achieve Multilingual MT," in V. Lawson (ed.), *Practical Experience of Machine Translation*. North-Holland, Amsterdam, 1982, pp. 139-147.

King, M., "Machine Translation already does Work," *Proceedings of the 24th Annual Meeting of the ACL*, Columbia University, New York, July 1986, pp. 269-270.

King, M. (ed.). *Machine Translation Today: the State of the Art* [proceedings of the Third Lugano Tutorial, Lugano, Switzerland, 2-7 April 1984]. Edinburgh University Press, 1987.

King, M., and S. Perschke, "EUROTRA and its Objectives," *Multilingua* 1, 1, 1982, pp. 27-32.

King, M., and S. Perschke, "EUROTRA," in M. King (ed.), *Machine Translation Today: the State of the Art* [proceedings of the Third Lugano Tutorial, Lugano, Switzerland, 2-7 April 1984]. Edinburgh University Press, 1987, pp. 373-391.

Kinoshita, T., T. Miyazaki, and H. Yasuhara, "A Japanese Language Analysis Aimed at a Japanese to English Machine Translation," presented at the EUROTRA Joint Japanese-European Workshop, Brussels, November 1983.

Kirschner, Z., "On a Device in Dictionary Operations in Machine Translation," *Proceedings of the 9th ICCL* [COLING 82], Prague, 5-10 July 1982, pp. 157-160.

Kirschner, Z., "On a Dependency Analysis of English for Automatic Translation," in P. Sgall (ed.), *Contributions to Functional Syntax, Semantics and Language Comprehension*, Benjamins, Amsterdam, 1984, pp. 335-358.

Kittredge, R. I., "The Development of Automated Translation Systems in Canada," *Lebende Sprachen* 26, 3, 1981, pp. 100-103.

Kittredge, R., L. Bourbeau, and P. Isabelle, "Design and Implementation of an English-French Transfer Grammar," *Proceedings of the 6th ICCL* [COLING 76], Ottawa, Canada, 1976. Also in *AJCL* 13, 2, 1976, microfiche 48, p. 69.

Kittredge, R., R. Ayotte, G. Stewart, J. Dansereau, G. Poulin, A.

Ambrosi, and I. Bellert. TAUM 73. Projet de Traduction Automatique de l'Université de Montréal, publications internes, Jan. 1973, pp. 1-262.

Knowles, F. E., "Error Analysis of SYSTRAN Output: A Suggested Criterion for the 'Internal' Evaluation of Translation Quality and a Possible Corrective for System Design," in B. M. Snell (ed.), *Translating and the Computer.* North-Holland, Amsterdam, 1979, pp. 109-133.

Knowles, F. E., "Re-emergence of Interest in Machine Translation (MT)," presented at BCS 79, London, 4-6 January 1979.

Knowles, F. E., "The Pivotal Role of the Various Dictionaries in an MT System," in V. Lawson (ed.), *Practical Experience of Machine Translation.* North-Holland, Amsterdam, 1982, pp. 149-162.

Knowles, F. E., "Machine-aided Translation and Lexical Strategies," presented at the International Conference on the Methodology and Techniques of Machine Translation, Cranfield Institute of Technology, England, 13-15 February 1984.

Korovina, T. I., "Multilingual Word-for-Word Translation Using a Display," *Cybernetics* 14, 2, (March-April) 1978, pp. 282-283.

Kotov, R. G., "Language in Real Communication as an Object of Applied Linguistics," *International Forum on Information and Documentation* 9, 4, (Oct.) 1984, pp. 17-21.

Kraass, K.-H., "Computer sind Dolmetscher der Zukunft," *Zeitschrift für Phonetik, Sprachwissenschaft und Kommunikationsforschung* 27, 4, 1974, pp. 334-335.

Krauwer, S., and L. des Tombe, "Reflections on Transfer in Machine Translation," *Contrastes* A4, January 1984, pp. 69-80.

Krauwer, S., and L. des Tombe, "Transfer in a Multilingual MT System," *Proceedings of the 10th ICCL* [COLING 84] *and the 22nd Annual Meeting of the ACL*, Stanford University, California, 2-6

July 1984, pp. 464-467.

Krollmann, F., "Data Processing at the Translator's Service," *Babel* 20, 3, 1974, pp. 121-129.

Krollmann, F., "Translation Aids," *AJCL* 13, 2, 1976, microfiche 48, p. 58.

Krollmann, F., "Benutzeraspekte beim Umgang mit einer maschinellen Übersetzungshilfe aus der Sicht eines grossen Sprachendienstes," *Dritter Europäischer Kongress über Dokumentationssysteme und -netze, Luxembourg, 3-6 May 1977*, vol. 1. Munich, 1977, pp. 201-214.

Krollmann, F., "User Aspects of an Automatic Aid to Translation as Employed in a Large Translation Service," in Commission of the European Communities, *Overcoming the Language Barrier: Proceedings of the Third European Congress on Information Systems and Networks, Luxembourg, 3-6 May 1977.* Verlag Dokumentation, Munich, 1977.

Krollmann, F., "Computer Aids to Translation," *Meta* 26, 1, (March) 1981, pp. 85-94.

Kudo, I., and H. Nomura. Lexical-Functional Transfer: A Transfer Framework in a Machine Translation System Based on LFG," *Proceedings of the 11th ICCL* [COLING 86], Bonn, West Germany, 25-29 August 1986, pp. 112-114.

Kulagina, O. S., "History and Present State of Machine Translation," *Cybernetics*, November-December 1976, pp. 937-944.

Lamb, J., "Systems for Breaking Language Barriers," *Computing* 17, (Aug.) 1984.

Lamb, S. M., "Stratificational Linguistics as a Basis for Machine Translation," in A. Makkai and W. B. Lockwood (eds.), *Readings in Stratificational Linguistics*, Univ. Alabama Press, 1973, pp. 34-59.

Landsbergen, J., "Machine Translation Based on Logically Isomorphic Montague Grammars," *Proceedings of the 9th ICCL* [COLING 82], Prague, 1982, pp. 175-181.

Landsbergen, J., "Isomorphic Grammars and their Use in the ROSETTA Translation System," in M. King (ed.), *Machine Translation Today: the State of the Art* [proceedings of the Third Lugano Tutorial, Lugano, Switzerland, 2-7 April 1984]. Edinburgh University Press, 1987, pp. 351-372.

LATSEC. Technical Proposal for Further Development of the SYSTRAN English-French Machine Translation System and Initial Development of the SYSTRAN French-English Translation System. Latsec Incorporated, La Jolla, California, June 1975.

Laubsch, J., D. Roesner, K. Hanakata, and A. Lesniewski, "Language Generation from Conceptual Structure: Synthesis of German in a Japanese/German MT Project," *Proceedings of the 10th ICCL* [COLING 84] *and the 22nd Annual Meeting of the ACL*, Stanford University, California, 2-6 July 1984, pp. 491-494.

Laurian, A.-M., "Machine Translation: What Type of Post-Editing on What Type of Documents for What Type of Users," *Proceedings of the 10th ICCL* [COLING 84] *and the 22nd Annual Meeting of the ACL*, Stanford University, California, 2-6 July 1984, pp. 236-238.

Laurian, J. M., "SYSTRAN et EUROTRA: la traduction automatique à la Commission des Communautés Européennes," *Contrastes*, Hors serie A4, 1984, pp. 11-42.

Lavorel, B., "Experience in English-French Post-Editing," in V. Lawson (ed.), *Practical Experience of Machine Translation*. North-Holland, Amsterdam, 1982, pp. 105-109.

Lawson, V., "Tigers and Polar Bears, Or: Translating and the Computer," *The Incorporated Linguist* 18, 1979, pp. 81-85.

Lawson, V. Final Report on EEC Study Contract TH-21 (Feasibility Study on the Applicability of the Systran system of Computer-Aided

Translation to Patent Texts). Commission of the European Communities, Luxembourg, 1980.

Lawson, V., "Introduction: Help from the Computer," *ASLIB Proceedings* 33, 7-8, (July-August) 1981, pp. 265-267.

Lawson, V. (ed.). *Practical Experience of Machine Translation.* [Proceedings of a conference held in London, 5-6 November 1981.] North-Holland, Amsterdam, 1982.

Lawson, V., "Machine Translation and People," in V. Lawson (ed.), *Practical Experience of Machine Translation.* North-Holland, Amsterdam, 1982, pp. 3-9.

Lawson, V., "Machine Translation," in C. Picken (ed.), *The Translator's Handbook.* Aslib, London, 1983, pp. 81-88

Lawson, V., "A Basic Survey of Practical MT," presented at the International Conference on the Methodology and Techniques of Machine Translation, Cranfield Institute of Technology, England, 13-15 February 1984.

Lawson, V., "Users of Machine Translation System Report Increased Output," *Language Monthly* 11, 1984, pp. 6-10.

Lawson, V. (ed.). *Tools for the Trade.* [Proceedings of a conference held in London, 10-11 November 1983.] Aslib, London, 1985.

Lawson, V., "The Background to Practical Machine Translation," *Computers and Translation* 1, 2, (April-June) 1986, pp. 109-112.

Lee, K.-F., review of "Machine Translation" by S.-C. Loh *et al.*, *ALLC Bulletin* 4, 3, 1976, pp. 267-268.

Lehmann, W. P., "Machine Translation," *Encyclopedia of Computer Science and Technology.* Dekker, New York, 1978, vol. 10, pp. 151-164.

Lehmann, W. P., and R. A. Stachowitz. Development of German-English Machine Translation System. Final report

RADC-TR-73-309, Linguistics Research Center, University of Texas at Austin, 1973. Available as NTIS report AD-774-564.

Lehmann, W. P., and R. A. Stachowitz. Development of German-English Machine Translation System. Final report RADC-TR-75-2, Linguistics Research Center, University of Texas at Austin, 1974. Available as NTIS report AD-A008-525.

Lehmann, W. P., W. S. Bennett, J. Slocum, H. Smith, S. M. V. Pfluger, and S. A. Eveland. The METAL System. Final technical report RADC-TR-80-374, Linguistics Research Center, University of Texas at Austin, January 1981. Available as NTIS report AO-97896.

Lehrberger, J. (ed.). Possibilités d'extension du système TAUM-AVIATION. Groupe TAUM, Université de Montréal, 1981.

Lehrberger, J., "Automatic Translation and the Concept of Sublanguage," in R. Kittredge and J. Lehrberger (eds.), *Sublanguage: Studies of Language in Restricted Semantic Domains.* De Gruyter, Berlin, 1982, pp. 81-106.

Lenders, W., "Das Problem des Verstehens in der maschinellen Übersetzung," Abstracts of the Fourth International Congress on Applied Linguistics, Stuttgart, 25-30 August 1975, p. 22.

León, M., "Development of English-Spanish Machine Translation," presented at the International Conference on the Methodology and Techniques of Machine Translation, Cranfield Institute of Technology, England, 13-15 February 1984.

Lippmann, E. O., "On Computational Linguistics and Computer-Aided Translation," *ATA Chronicle* 3, 5, 1974, pp. 7-8.

Lippmann, E. O., "On-Line Generation of Terminological Digests in Language Translation: An Aid in Terminology Processing," *IEEE Transactions on Professional Communications* 18, 4, 1975, pp. 309-319.

Lippmann, E. O., "Experimental On-Line Computer Aids for the

Human Translator," *AJCL* 13, 2, 1976, microfiche 46, pp. 11-13.

Lippmann, E. O., "Computer Aids for the Human Translator," presented at the Eighth World Congress of FIT, Montreal, 1977.

Lippmann, E. O., "Human Factors in the Design of Computer Aids for Translators," *ATA Chronicle* 9, 6, 1980, p. 5.

Liu, S. S., "Translation of English into Chinese on a Microcomputer," presented at the International Conference on the Methodology and Techniques of Machine Translation, Cranfield Institute of Technology, England, 13-15 February 1984.

Liu, Y.-Q., "Machine Translation in China – A Report," *ALLC Journal* 1, 2, 1980, pp. 60-66.

Liu, Y.-Q., "The System of Intermediate Constituents in Machine Translation from Foreign Languages into Chinese," presented at the Conference on Chinese Language Use, The Australian National University, 29-30 Aug. 1981.

Liu, Y.-Q., "Aspects of Chinese Information Processing," presented at the Conference on International Cooperation in Chinese Bibliographical Automation, Canberra, Australia, 29 Aug. - 1 Sept. 1982.

Ljudskanov, A. *Mensch und Maschine als Übersetzer.* Niemeyer, Halle, 1975.

Locke, W. N., "Machine Translation," *Encyclopedia of Library and Information Science.* Marcel Dekker, New York, 1975, vol. 16, pp. 414-444.

Locke, W. N., and A. D. Booth (eds.) *Machine Translation of Languages.* Wiley, New York, 1955.

Loffler-Laurian, A.-M., "Rapid Post-editing and Conventional Post-editing. I. Two Models of a Specific Acitivity," *Multilingua* 5, 2, 1986, pp. 81-88.

Loh, S.-C. Final Report on Machine Translation Project. Department of Computer Science, Chinese University of Hong Kong, 1975.

Loh, S.-C., "Computer Translation of Chinese Journals," *AJCL* 12, 3, 1975, microfiche 22, p. 43.

Loh, S.-C., "Computer Translation of Chinese Scientific Journals," *ALLC Bulletin* 3, 3, 1975, p. 258.

Loh, S.-C., "CULT: Chinese University Language Translator," in FBIS Seminar on Machine Translation, *AJCL* 13, 2, 1976, microfiche 46, pp. 46-50.

Loh, S.-C., "Machine Translation: Past, Present, and Future," *ALLC Bulletin* 4, 2, (March) 1976, pp. 105-114.

Loh, S.-C., "Translation of Three Chinese Scientific Texts into English by Computer," *ALLC Bulletin* 4, 2, (March) 1976, pp. 104-105.

Loh, S.-C., and L. Kong, "Automatische Übersetzung chinesischer wissenschaftlicher Zeitschriften," Dritter Europäischer Kongress über Dokumentationssysteme und Dokumentationsnetze, Luxembourg, 3-6 May 1977, vol. 1. Munich, 1977, pp. 563-578.

Loh, S.-C., and L. Kong, "Computer Translation of Chinese Scientific Journals," in Commission of the European Communities, *Overcoming the Language Barrier: Proceedings of the Third European Congress on Information Systems and Networks, Luxembourg, 3-6 May 1977.* Verlag Dokumentation, Munich, 1977, pp. 631-646.

Loh, S.-C., and L. Kong, "An Interactive On-Line Machine Translation System (Chinese into English)," in B. M. Snell (ed.), *Translating and the Computer.* North-Holland, Amsterdam, 1979, pp. 135-148.

Loh, S.-C., and L. Kong, "A New Dictionary Structure for

Bi-directional MT System," presented at the International Conference on the Methodology and Techniques of Machine Translation, Cranfield Institute of Technology, England, 13-15 February 1984.

Loh, S.-C., H.-S. Hung, and L. Kong, "A Dual Language Translator," in D. E. Ager *et al.* (eds.), *Advances in Computer-Aided Literary and Linguistic Research*, Aston Univ. Press, Birmingham, 1979, pp. 107-115.

Loh, S.-C., L. Kong, and H.-S. Hung, "Machine Translation of Chinese Mathematical Articles," *ALLC Bulletin* 6, 2, 1978, pp. 111-120.

Loh, S.-C., L. Kong, and H.-S. Hung, "A New Dictionary Structure for Bi-directional MT System," presented at the International Conference on the Methodology and Techniques of Machine Translation, Cranfield Institute of Technology, England, 13-15 February 1984.

Lonsdale, D., "Notes on Interactive Translation," presented at the International Conference on the Methodology and Techniques of Machine Translation, Cranfield Institute of Technology, England, 13-15 February 1984.

Luckhardt, H.-D., "Weshalb SUSY mehrsprachig ist," LA Neue Folga, Heft 3.2, Saarbrücken, 1980.

Luckhardt, H.-D., "SUSY - Capabilities and Range of Application," *Multilingua* 1-4, 1982.

Luckhardt, H.-D., "Erste Überlegungen zur Verwendung des Sublanguage-Konzepts in SUSY," *Multilingua*, 1984.

Luckhardt, H.-D. Valenz und Tiefenkasus in der Maschinellen Übersetzung. Ms., SFB 100/A2, Universität des Saarlandes, Saarbrücken, 1984.

Luctkens, E., and P. Fermont, "A Prototype Machine Translation

Based on Extracts from Data Processing Manuals," *Proceedings of the 11th ICCL* [COLING 86], Bonn, West Germany, 25-29 August 1986, pp. 643-645.

Luther, D. A., C. Montgomery, and R. M. Case, "An Interactive Text-Editing System in Support of Russian Translation by Machine," *IFIPS National Computer Conference Proceedings.* AFIPS Press, Montvale, New Jersey, 1977, vol. 46, pp. 789-790.

Lytinen, S. L., and R. C. Schank, "Representation and Translation," *Text* 2(1/3), 1982, pp. 83-111.

Lytinen, S. L., "Integrating Syntax and Semantics," in S. Nirenburg (ed.), *Proceedings of the Conference on Theoretical and Methodological Issues in Machine Translation of Natural Languages,* 1985, pp. 167-178.

Lytle, E. G., "Automatic Language Processing Project," *AJCL* 13, 2, 1976, microfiche 46, pp. 14-23.

Lytle, E. G., and D. Packard, "Junction Grammar as a Base for Automatic Language Processing," Preprints of the 12th Annual Meeting of the ACL, Amherst, Massachusetts, 26-27 July 1974.

Lytle, E. G., D. Packard, D. Gibb, A. K. Melby, and F. H. Billings, "Junction Grammar as a Base for Natural Language Processing," *AJCL* 12, 3, 1975, microfiche 26, pp. 1-77.

Maas, H.-D., "Die Synthese deutscher Sätze im Rahmen der automatischen Übersetzung," Vorabdrucke des Internationalen Kolloquiums 'Automatische Lexikographie, Analyse und Übersetzung', Saarbrücken, 23-25 September 1976, pp. 30-35.

Maas, H.-D., "Das Saarbrücker automatische Übersetzungssystem SUSY," *Dritter Europäischer Kongress über Dokumentationssysteme und -netze, Luxembourg, 3-6 May 1977*, vol. 1. Munich, 1977, pp. 527-535.

Maas, H.-D., "Die transformationelle Synthese deutscher Sätze im

Saarbrücker Verfahren der Maschinellen Uebersetzung," LA 25, Saarbrücken, 1977.

Maas, H.-D., "Maschinelle Übersetzung mit dem Saarbrücker System SUSY," *Sprache und Datenverarbeitung* 1, 2, 1977.

Maas, H.-D., "The Saarbrücken Automatic Translation System (SUSY)," in Commission of the European Communities, *Overcoming the Language Barrier: Proceedings of the Third European Congress on Information Systems and Networks, Luxembourg, 3-6 May 1977.* Verlag Dokumentation, Munich, 1977-1978, pp. 585-592.

Maas, H.-D., "Das Saarbrücker Übersetzungssystem SUSY," *Sprache und Datenverarbeitung* 1, 4, 1978, pp. 43-62.

Maas, H.-D., "Zum Stand der automatischen Übersetzung im Sonderforschungsbereich (SFB) 100. Das Übersetzungssystem SUSY," in D. Krallmann (ed.), *Kolloquium zur Lage der linguistischen Datenverarbeitung.* Essen, 1978.

Maas, H.-D., "Zur Entwicklung des Übersetzungssystems SUSY und seiner Einzelen Komponentan," LA Neue Folge, Heft 3.1, Saarbrücken, 1980.

Maas, H.-D., "SUSY I and SUSY II - verschiedene Analysestrategien in der Maschinellen Übersetzung," *Sprache und Datenverarbeitung,* Heft 1981, 1983.

Maas, H.-D., "Repräsentation und Strategie bei der Automatischen Analyse mit SUSY," *Sprache und Information,* Band 4, 1982.

Maas, H.-D., "Anforderungen an Datenstrukturen in einem maschinellen Übersetzungssystem," *Zeitschrift fur Phonetik, Sprachwissenschaft und Kommunikationsforschung* 36, 1983.

Maas, H.-D., "Control and Data Structures in the MT System SUSY-E," presented at the International Conference on the Methodology and Techniques of Machine Translation, Cranfield Institute of Technology, England, 13-15 February 1984.

Maas, H.-D., "The MT System SUSY," in M. King (ed.), *Machine Translation Today: the State of the Art* [proceedings of the Third Lugano Tutorial, Lugano, Switzerland, 2-7 April 1984]. Edinburgh University Press, 1987, pp. 209-246.

Macdonald, R. R., "The Problem of Machine Translation," in B. Henisz-Dostert, R. R. Macdonald, and M. Zarechnak (eds.), *Machine Translation.* Mouton, The Hague, 1979, pp. 89-145.

Macdonald, R. R. A Study of the PAHO Machine Translation System, report of short-term consultant under Personal Services Contract APO-09435(WU1). Pan American Health Organization, Washington, D.C., 1981.

Macklovitch, E., "Recent Canadian Experience in MT," presented at the International Conference on the Methodology and Techniques of Machine Translation, Cranfield Institute of Technology, England, 13-15 February 1984.

Maegaard, B., "The Recognition of Finite Verbs in French Texts," *ALLC Bulletin* 4, 1, 1976, pp. 49-52.

Magnusson-Murray, U., "Operational Experience of a Machine Translation Service," in V. Lawson, (ed.), *Tools for the Trade.* [Proceedings of a conference held in London, 10-11 November 1983.] Aslib, London, 1985, pp. 171-180.

Mankin, R., "How to Boldly Split Infinitives," presented at the International Conference on the Methodology and Techniques of Machine Translation, Cranfield Institute of Technology, England, 13-15 February 1984.

Marchuk, Y. N., "Machine Translation in the U.S.S.R.," presented at the International Conference on the Methodology and Techniques of Machine Translation, Cranfield Institute of Technology, England, 13-15 February 1984.

Marcus, R. S., and J. F. Reintjes, "A Translating Computer Interface for End-User Operation of Heterogeneous Retrieval

Systems, I: Design," *ASIS* 32, 4, (July) 1981, pp. 287-303.

Marcus, R. S., and J. F. Reintjes, "A Translating Computer Interface for End-User Operation of Heterogeneous Retrieval Systems, II: Evaluations," *ASIS* 32, 4, (July) 1981, pp. 304-317.

Masterman, M., "Essential Mechanism of Machine Translation," presented at BCS 79, London, 4-6 January 1979.

Masterman, M., "The Essential Skills to Be Acquired for Machine Translation," in B. M. Snell (ed.), *Translating and the Computer.* North-Holland, Amsterdam, 1979, pp. 159-180.

Masterman, M., "The Limits of Innovation in Machine Translation," in V. Lawson (ed.), *Practical Experience of Machine Translation.* North-Holland, Amsterdam, 1982, pp. 163-186.

Masterman, M., and R. J. Smith. The Automatic Annotation of SYSTRAN. Final Report TH-29, Cambridge Language Research Unit, Cambridge, 1980.

Masterman, M., and B. Williams, "The Nature of Proof in Machine Translation," presented at the International Conference on the Methodology and Techniques of Machine Translation, Cranfield Institute of Technology, England, 13-15 February 1984.

Mathias, J., "Some Computer Functions for Machine-Aided Translation," in S. Gould (ed.), *Proceedings of the First International Symposium on Computers and the Chinese Input/Output Systems, Taipei, Taiwan, 14-16 August 1973.* Academia Sinica, vol. 13, pp. 589-592.

Mathias, J., "The Chinese-English Translation Assistance Group and Its Computerized Glossary Project," *Federal Linguist* 5, 3-4, (Winter) 1973, pp. 7-13.

Mbaeyi, P. N. O., "What is the Language of Memory?" presented at the International Conference on the Methodology and Techniques of Machine Translation, Cranfield Institute of Technology, England,

13-15 February 1984.

McCord, M. C., "LMT: A PROLOG-based Machine Translation System," in S. Nirenburg (ed.), *Proceedings of the Conference on Theoretical and Methodological Issues in Machine Translation of Natural Languages*, 1985, pp. 179-182.

McDonald, D. D., "Recovering the Speaker's Decisions During Mechanical Translation," in S. Nirenburg (ed.), *Proceedings of the Conference on Theoretical and Methodological Issues in Machine Translation of Natural Languages*, 1985, pp. 183-199.

McNaught, J., "Terminological Data Banks: A Model for a British Linguistic Data Bank (LDB)," *ASLIB Proceedings* 33, 7-8, (July-August) 1981, pp. 297-308.

Melby, A. K. Forming and Testing Syntactic Transfers. M. A. thesis, Brigham Young University, Provo, Utah, 1974.

Melby, A. K., "Junction Grammar and Machine Assisted Translation," in A. Zampolli (ed.), *Computational and Mathematical Linguistics: Proceedings of the ICCL, Pisa, 27 August - 1 September 1973.* Florence, 1976.

Melby, A. K., "Design and Implementation of a Computer-Assisted Translation System," *BCS Natural Language Translation Specialist Group Newsletter* 9, 1980, pp. 7-19.

Melby, A. K., "A Suggestion Box Translator Aid," *Proceedings of the DLLS Symposium*, Brigham Young University, Provo, Utah, March 1981.

Melby, A. K., "Linguistics and Machine Translation," in J. Copeland and P. Davis (eds.), *The Seventh LACUS Forum 1980.* Hornbeam Press, Columbia, South Carolina, 1981.

Melby, A. K., "Translators and Machines – Can They Co-operate?" *Meta* 26, 1, (March) 1981, pp. 23-34.

Melby, A. K., "Multi-level Translation Aids in a Distributed System," *Proceedings of the 9th ICCL* [COLING 82], Prague, Czechoslovakia, July 1982, pp. 215-220.

Melby, A. K., "Computer-Assisted Translation Systems: The Standard Design and a Multi-Level Design," *Proceedings of the ACL-NRL Conference on Applied Natural Language Processing*, Santa Monica, California, 1-3 February 1983, pp. 174-177.

Melby, A. K., "Machine Translation with Post-editing vs. a Tri-level Integrated Translator Aid System," presented at the International Conference on the Methodology and Techniques of Machine Translation, Cranfield Institute of Technology, England, 13-15 February 1984.

Melby, A. K., "Recipe for a Translator Work Station," presented at the ISSCO Tutorial on Machine Translation, Lugano, Switzerland, 2-6 April 1984.

Melby, A. K., "Lexical Transfer: A Missing Element in Linguistic Theories," *Proceedings of the 11th ICCL* [COLING 86], Bonn, West Germany, 25-29 August 1986, pp. 104-106.

Melby, A. K., "Creating an Environemnt for the Translator," in M. King (ed.), *Machine Translation Today: the State of the Art* [proceedings of the Third Lugano Tutorial, Lugano, Switzerland, 2-7 April 1984]. Edinburgh University Press, 1987, pp. 124-132.

Melby, A. K., M. R. Smith, and J. Peterson, "ITS: Interactive Translation System," *Proceedings of the 8th ICCL* [COLING 80], Tokyo, 30 September - 4 October 1980, pp. 424-429.

Mel'cuk, I. A., "Grammatical Meanings in Interlinguas for Automatic Translation and the Concept of Grammatical Meaning," in V. J. Rozencvejg (ed.), *Machine Translation and Applied Linguistics*. Athenaion Verlag, Frankfurt am Main, 1974, vol. I, pp. 95-113.

Meyer, E., "The Storage and Retrieval of Alpha-Numeric

Information," *Rechentechnische Datenverarbeitung* 13, 5, 1976, pp. 43-47.

Mill, J., "Uniting a Divided Europe," *Infomatics* 5, 1, (Jan.) 1984, p. 14.

Morton, S. E., "Designing a Multilingual Terminology Bank for United States Translators," *ASIS* 29, 6, (November) 1978, pp. 297-303.

Morton, S. E., "Multilingual Terminology Banks Here and Abroad: Online Terminology Dissemination as an Aid to Translation," in E. H. Brenner, comp., *The Information Age in Perspective: Proceedings of the ASIS Annual Meeting*, 1978, vol. 15, pp. 242-244.

Muraki, K., "On a Semantic Model for Multi-Lingual Paraphrasing," *Proceedings of the 9th ICCL* [COLING 82], Prague, 5-10 July 1982, pp. 239-244.

Muraki, K., "Overview of VENUS Japanese-English Translation System," presented at the EUROTRA Joint Japanese-European Workshop, Brussels, November 1983.

Muraki, K., and S. Ichiyama. An Overview of Machine Translation Project at NEC Corporation. Technical note, NEC Corporation, C & C Systems Research Laboratories, 1982.

Nagao, M., "A Survey of Natural Language Processing and Machine Translation in Japan, 1980-1982," in T. Kitagawa (ed.), *Computer Science and Technologies.* North-Holland, Amsterdam, 1982, pp. 64-70.

Nagao, M., "La Traduction Automatique," *La Recherche* 150, 1983.

Nagao, M., "Machine Translation Project of the Japanese Government," presented at the EUROTRA Joint Japanese-European Workshop, Brussels, November 1983.

Nagao, M., "Natural Language Processing and Machine Translation in Japan," *Digest of Papers: Spring COMPCON 83, Intellectual Leverage for the Information Society.* IEEE, New York, 1983, pp. 306-307.

Nagao, M., "Outline of the Machine Translation Project of the Japanese Government," *International Forum on Information and Documentation* 9, 2, 1984, pp. 12-17.

Nagao, M., "Structural Transformation in the Generation Stage of Mu Japanese to English Machine Translation System," in S. Nirenburg (ed.), *Proceedings of the Conference on Theoretical and Methodological Issues in Machine Translation of Natural Languages*, 1985, pp. 200-223.

Nagao, M., and J. Tsujii, "A Machine Translation System from English into Japanese for Titles of Scientific Papers," presented at the Second International Seminar on Machine Translation, Moscow, 1979.

Nagao, M., and J. Tsujii, "PLATON (A Programming Language for Tree Operation)," presented at the Second International Seminar on Machine Translation, Moscow, 1979.

Nagao, M., and J. Tsujii, "Untersuchungen über Daten und Hilfsmittel zur Analyse der japanischen Sprache," *Sprache und Datenverarbeitung* 4, 2, 1980, pp. 129-138.

Nagao, M., and J. Tsujii, "Some Topics of Language Processing for Machine Translation," *International Forum on Information and Documentation* 5, 2, 1980.

Nagao, M., and J. Tsujii, "The Transfer Phase of the Mu Machine Translation System," *Proceedings of the 11th ICCL* [COLING 86], Bonn, West Germany, 25-29 August 1986, pp. 97-103.

Nagao, M., T. Nishida, and J. Tsujii, "Dealing with Incompleteness of Linguistic Knowledge in Language Translation: Transfer and Generation Stage of Mu Machine Translation Project," *Proceedings of the 10th ICCL* [COLING 84] *and the 22nd Annual Meeting of the*

ACL, Stanford University, California, 2-6 July 1984, pp. 420-427.

Nagao, M., J. Tsujii, and J. Nakamura, "The Japanese Government Project for Machine Translation," *Computational Linguistics* 11, 2-3, 1985, pp. 91-110.

Nagao, M., J. Tsujii, K. Yada, and T. Kakimoto, "An English Japanese Machine Translation System of the Titles of Scientific and Engineering Papers," *Proceedings of the 9th ICCL* [COLING 82], Prague, 5-10 July 1982, pp. 245-252.

Nagao, M., J. Tsujii, K. Mitamura, H. Hirakawa, and M. Kume, "A Machine Translation System from Japanese into English: Another Perspective of MT Systems," *Proceedings of the 8th ICCL* [COLING 80], Tokyo, 1980, pp. 414-423.

Naito, S., A. Shimazu, and H. Nomura, "Classification of Modality Function and Its Application to Japanese Language Analysis," *Proceedings of the 23rd Annual Meeting of the ACL*, Chicago, 8-12 July 1985, pp. 27-34.

Nakamura, J., and M. Nagao, "A Software System for Describing a Grammar of Machine Translation: GRADE," presented at the International Conference on the Methodology and Techniques of Machine Translation, Cranfield Institute of Technology, England, 13-15 February 1984.

Nakamura, J., J. Tsujii, and M. Nagao, "Grammar Writing System (GRADE) of Mu-Machine Translation Project and its Characteristics," *Proceedings of the 10th ICCL* [COLING 84] *and the 22nd Annual Meeting of the ACL*, Stanford University, California, 2-6 July 1984, pp. 338-343.

Nakamura, J., J. Tsujii, and M. Nagao, "Solutions for Problems of MT Parser. Methods Used in Mu-Machine Translation Project," *Proceedings of the 11th ICCL* [COLING 86], Bonn, West Germany, 25-29 August 1986, pp. 133-135.

Nancarrow, P. H., "The Chinese University Language Translator

(CULT) – A Report," *ALLC Bulletin* 6, 2, 1978, p. 121.

Nedobejkine, N., "Application du système A.T.E.F. à l'analyse morphologique de textes russes," in A. Zampolli (ed.), *Computational and Mathematical Linguistics: Proceedings of the ICCL, Pisa, 27 August - 1 September 1973*, vol. 2. Florence, 1976.

Nedobejkine, N., "Niveaux d'interprétation dans une traduction multilingue: Application à l'analyse du russe," *Proceedings of the 6th ICCL* [COLING 76], Ottawa, Ontario, Canada, 1976. Also in *AJCL* 13, 2, 1976, microfiche 48, p. 36.

Neijt, A., "Esperanto as the Focal Point of Machine Translation," *Multilingua* 5, 1, 1986, pp. 9-13.

Newmark, P. *Approaches to Translation.* Pergamon, Oxford, 1981.

Nikolova, B., and I. Nenova, "Termservice – An Automated System for Terminology Services," *Proceedings of the 9th ICCL* [COLING 82], Prague, 5-10 July 1982, pp. 265-269.

Nirenburg, S. (ed.) *Proceedings of the Conference on Theoretical and Methodological Issues in Machine Translation of Natural Languages*, Colgate University, Colgate, New York, 14-16 August, 1985.

Nirenburg, S., V. Raskin, and A. Tucker, "Interlingua Design for TRANSLATOR," in S. Nirenburg (ed.), *Proceedings of the Conference on Theoretical and Methodological Issues in Machine Translation of Natural Languages*, 1985, pp. 224-244.

Nirenburg, S., V. Raskin, and A. Tucker, "On Knowledge-Based Machine Translation," *Proceedings of the 11th ICCL* [COLING 86], Bonn, West Germany, 25-29 August 1986, pp. 627-632.

Nishida, F., and S. Takamatsu, "Japanese-English Translation Through Internal Expressions," *Proceedings of the 9th ICCL* [COLING 82], Prague, 5-10 July 1982, pp. 271-276.

Nishida, F., Y. Fujita, and S. Takamatsu, "Construction of a Modular and Portable Translation," *Proceedings of the 11th ICCL* [COLING 86], Bonn, West Germany, 25-29 August 1986, pp. 649-651.

Nishida, F., S. Takamatsu, and H. Kuroki, "English-Japanese Translation through Case-Structure Conversion," *Proceedings of the 8th ICCL* [COLING 80], Tokyo, Sept. 30 - Oct. 4, 1980, pp. 447-454.

Nishida, T., M. Kiyono, and S. Doshita. An English-Japanese Machine Translation System Based on Formal Semantics of Natural Languages. Technical Report, Tokyo University, 1981.

Nishida, T. Studies on the Application of Formal Semantics to English-Japanese Machine Translation. Ph.D. Dissertation, Department of Information Science, Faculty of Engineering, Kyoto University, Japan, 1983.

Nishida, T., "Machine Translation: Japanese Perspectives," presented at Translating and the Computer, 7th International Conference on Translating, London, (November) 1985.

Nishida, T., and S. Doshita, "An English-Japanese Machine Translation System Based on Formal Semantics of Natural Language," *Proceedings of the 9th ICCL* [COLING 82], Prague, 5-10 July 1982, pp. 277-282.

Nishida, T., and S. Doshita, "An Application of Montague Grammar to English-Japanese Machine Translation," *Proceedings of the ACL-NRL Conference on Applied Natural Language Processing*, Santa Monica, California, February 1983, pp. 156-165.

Nitta, Y., "Idiosyncratic Gap: A Tough Problem to Structure-bound Machine Translation," *Proceedings of the 11th ICCL* [COLING 86], Bonn, West Germany, 25-29 August 1986, pp. 107-111.

Nitta, Y., A. Okajima, F. Yamano, and K. Ishihara, "A Heuristic Approach to English-Into-Japanese Machine Translation," *Proceedings of the 9th ICCL* [COLING 82], Prague, 5-10 July 1982, pp. 283-288.

Nitta, Y., A. Okajima, H. Kaji, Y. Hidano, and K. Ishihara, "A Proper Treatment of Syntax and Semantics in Machine Translation," *Proceedings of the 10th ICCL* [COLING 84] *and the 22nd Annual Meeting of the ACL*, Stanford University, California, 2-6 July 1984, pp. 159-166.

Noel, J., "Document Analysis Algorithms and Machine Translation Research," *Revue des Langues Vivantes* 41, 3, 1975, pp. 237-260.

Nomura, H., "Towards the High Ability Machine Translation," presented at the EUROTRA Joint Japanese-European Workshop, Brussels, November 1983.

Nomura, H., and A. Shimazu. Machine Translation in Japan. Technical note, Musashino Electrical Communication Laboratory, Nippon Telegraph and Telephone Public Corporation, Tokyo, November 1982.

Nomura, H., H. Iida, and K. Ogura. Identification Method of Presupposed Items for References. Technical note, Musashino Electric Communication Laboratory, Nippon Telegraph and Telephone Public Corporation, Tokyo. November 1981.

Nomura, H., S. Naito, Y. Katagiri, and A. Shimazu, "Translation By Understanding: A Machine Translation System LUTE," *Proceedings of the 11th ICCL* [COLING 86], Bonn, West Germany, 25-29 August 1986, pp. 621-626.

Nomura, H., A. Shimazu, H. Iida, Y. Katagiri, Y. Saito, S. Naito, K. Ogura, A. Yokoo, and M. Mikami. Introduction to LUTE (Language Understander, Translator and Editor). Technical note, Musashino Electrical Communication Laboratory, Research Division, Nippon Telegraph and Telephone Public Corporation, Tokyo, November 1982.

Oh, Y.-O., "Maschinelle Übersetzung der Sprachen Koreanisch und Deutsch: syntaktische Basis für die kontrastive Linguistik," *Dhak*

Yonku (Language Research) 15, 1979, pp. 169-183.

Okajima, A., *et al.*, "Lexicon Structure for Machine Translation – An Example from English-into-Japanese Translation ATHENE," presented at ICTP 83, Tokyo, 1983.

Oubine, I. I., and B. D. Tikhomirov, "Machine Translation Systems and Computer Dictionaries in the Information Service: Ways of Their Development and Operation," *Proceedings of the 9th ICCL* [COLING 82], Prague, 5-10 July 1982, pp. 289-294.

Panevova, J., and P. Sgall, review of P. L. Garvin, *On Machine Translation: Selected Papers.* in *Prague Bulletin of Mathematical Linguistics*, 19, 1973, pp. 59-64.

Pankowicz, Z. L. Commentary on ALPAC Report. RADC, 1967.

Pankowicz, Z. L. Facts of Life in Assessment of Machine Translation. Report on CETIL Workshop on Evaluation Problems in Machine Translation, Luxembourg, 28 February 1978.

Papegaaij, B. C., V. Sadler, and A. P. M. Witkam, "Experiments with an MT-Directed Lexical Knowledge Bank," *Proceedings of the 11th ICCL* [COLING 86], Bonn, West Germany, 25-29 August 1986, pp. 432-434.

Papegaaij, B. C., V. Sadler, and A. P. M. Witkam (eds.) *Word Expert Semantics: an Interlingual Knowledge-Based Approach.* Foris Publications, Dordrecht, The Netherlands, 1986.

Pare, M., "La banque de terminologie de l'Université de Montréal," *Études françaises dans le monde* 2, 3, 1974, p. 9.

Pare, M., "Computerized Multilingual Word Banks Can Provide Terminological Assistance to International Standards Organization," presented at the Symposium on International Cooperation in Terminology, Vienna, 9-11 April 1975.

Pare, M., "Les banques automatisées de terminologies multilingues et les organismes de normalisation," presented at the First Infoterm Symposium on International Cooperation in Terminology, Vienna, 9-11 April 1975. Infoterm Series, Vol. 3. Munich, 1976, pp. 224-234.

Pare, M., "La banque de terminologie de l'Université de Montréal," Comptes rendus du Colloque international de terminologie, Terminologies 76, Paris-La Défense, 15-18 June 1976. Association française de terminologie, Paris, 1977.

Pare, M., "Y-a-t-il toujours une machine à traduire?" *Babel* 26, 2, 1980, pp. 77-82.

Pause, P. E., "Zur Modellierung des Übersetzungsprozesses," in I. Bátori and H. J. Weber (eds.), *Neue Ansätze in Maschineller Sprachübersetzung: Wissensrepräsentation und Textbezug*. Niemeyer, Tübingen, 1986, pp. 45-74.

Pericliev, V., "Handling Syntactical Ambiguity in Machine Translation," *Proceedings of the 10th ICCL* [COLING 84] *and the 22nd Annual Meeting of the ACL*, Stanford University, California, 2-6 July 1984, pp. 521-524.

Perschke, S. *et al.*, "Les travaux du CETIS dans le domaine de l'informatique documentaire," *Documentaliste* (numéro special), 1974, pp. 47-57.

Perschke, S., G. Fassone, C. Geoffrion, W. Kolar, and H. Fangmeyer. The SLC-II System Language Translator Package Concepts and Facilities. Bericht EUR 5116e, Joint Nuclear Research Centre, Scientific Data Processing Centre, CETIS, Ispra, Italy, 1974.

Perusse, D., "Machine Translation," *ATA Chronicle* 12, 8, 1983, pp. 6-8.

Petitpierre, D., "Software Background for Machine Translation: A Glossary," in M. King (ed.), *Machine Translation Today: the State of the Art* [proceedings of the Third Lugano Tutorial, Lugano, Switzerland, 2-7 April 1984]. Edinburgh University Press, 1987, pp. 111-116.

Petrick, S. R., "Summary: FBIS Seminar on Machine Translation," *AJCL* 13, 2, 1976, microfiche 46, pp. 72-76.

Pigott, I. M., "Theoretical Options and Practical Limitations of Using Semantics to Solve Problems of Natural Language Analysis and Machine Translation," in M. MacCafferty and K. Gray (eds.), *The Analysis of Meaning: Informatics 5.* Aslib, London, 1979, pp. 239-268.

Pigott, I. M., "How Does SYSTRAN Translate?" presented to the BCS Natural Language Translation Specialist Group, 23 April 1980.

Pigott, I. M., "The Importance of Feedback from Translators in the Development of High-Quality Machine Translation," in V. Lawson (ed.), *Practical Experience of Machine Translation.* North-Holland, Amsterdam, 1982, pp. 61-73.

Pigott, I. M., "The Difficulty of Developing Logical Algorithms for the Machine Translation of Natural Language," presented at the International Conference on the Methodology and Techniques of Machine Translation, Cranfield Institute of Technology, England, 13-15 February 1984.

Pigott, I. M., "Recent Developments in Practical MT," in V. Lawson (ed.), *Tools for the Trade.* [Proceedings of a conference held in London, 10-11 November 1983.] Aslib, London, 1985, pp. 97-104.

Pigott, I. M., "Essential Requirements for a Large-Scale Operational Machine-Translation System," *Computers and Translation* 1, 2, (April-June) 1986, pp. 67-72.

Piotrovsky, R. G., "The Semiotical Interpretation of Machine Translation," *International Forum on Information and Documentation* 9, 4, (Oct.) 1984, pp. 22-26.

Plum, T., "The State of Machine Translation," in *Translators and Translating: Selected Essays from the American Translators' Association.* State University of New York, Binghamton, New York, 1974, pp. 37-42.

Pons, H. B., "WCC's Translation Service Bureau," in V. Lawson (ed.), *Tools for the Trade.* [Proceedings of a conference held in London, 10-11 November 1983.] Aslib, London, 1985, pp. 165-170.

Quezel-Ambrunaz, M. ARIANE: Système interactif pour la traduction automatique multilingue, Version II. Report G.3400.A, Université de Grenoble, France, 1978.

Quezel-Ambrunaz, M. Transfert en ARIANE-78: Le modèle TRANSF. Université de Grenoble, France, November 1979.

Quezel-Ambrunaz, M., and P. Guillaume, "Analyse automatique de textes par un système d'états finis," in A. Zampolli (ed.), *Computational and Mathematical Linguistics: Proceedings of the ICCL, Pisa, 27 August - 1 September 1973*, vol. 2. Florence, 1976.

Raskin, V., "Linguistics and Natural Language Processing," in S. Nirenburg (ed.), *Proceedings of the Conference on Theoretical and Methodological Issues in Machine Translation of Natural Languages*, 1985, pp. 224-244.

Roberts, A. H., and M. Zarechnak, "Mechanical Translation," in T. A. Sebeok (ed.), *Current Trends in Linguistics, Vol. 12: Linguistics and Adjacent Arts and Sciences.* Mouton, The Hague, 1974, pt. 4, pp. 2825-2868.

Rohrer, C. (panel organizer), "Linguistic Bases for Machine Translation," *Proceedings of the 11th ICCL* [COLING 86], Bonn, West Germany, 25-29 August 1986, pp. 353-355.

Rohrer, C., "Maschinelle Übersetzung mit Unifikationsgrammatiken," in I. Bátori and H. J. Weber (eds.), *Neue Ansätze in Maschineller Sprachübersetzung: Wissensrepräsentation und Textbezug.* Niemeyer, Tübingen, 1986, pp. 75-99.

Rolling, L. N., "The Facts About Automatic Translation," *Proceedings of the 6th Annual CAIS Conference on Information Science*, Montreal, 10-13 May 1978, pp. 267-269.

Rolling, L. N., "Computer-aided Translation Today and Tomorrow," presented at the FID Congress, Edinburgh, September 1978.

Rolling, L. N., "The Second Birth of Machine Translation," presented at the Seventh Cranfield International Conference on Mechanised Information Storage and Retrieval Systems, Cranfield Institute of Technology, England, July 1979.

Rolling, L. N., "Automatic Translation Today and Tomorrow: The Computer Is Cheaper Than Human Translation," in P. J. Taylor (ed.), *New Trends in Documentation and Information. Proceedings of the 39th FID Congress*, 1980, pp. 333-338.

Rolling, L. N., "The Second Birth of Machine Translation: a timely event for database suppliers and operators," *Electronic Publishing Revue* 1, 3, 1981.

Rommel, B., "Language or Information: a New Role for the Translator?" presented at the International Conference on the Methodology and Techniques of Machine Translation, Cranfield Institute of Technology, England, 13-15 February 1984.

Root, R., "A Two-way Approach to Structural Transfer in MT," *Proceedings of the Second Conference of the European Chapter of the ACL,* University of Geneva, Switzerland, 28-29 March 1985, pp. 70-72.

Root, R., "Semantics, Translation, and Anaphora," *Computers and Translation* 1, 2, (April-June) 1986, pp. 93-108.

Rosenthal, J. Idiom Recognition for Machine Translation and Information Storage and Retrieval. Ph.D. dissertation, Georgetown University, February 1979.

Rösner, D., "When Mariko Talks to Siegfried – Experiences from a Japanese/German Machine Translation Project," *Proceedings of the 11th ICCL* [COLING 86], Bonn, West Germany, 25-29 August 1986, pp. 652-668.

Rösner, D., "SEMSYN – Wissensquellen und Strategien bei der Generierung von Deutsch aus einer semantischen Repräsentation," in I. Bátori and H. J. Weber (eds.), *Neue Ansätze in Maschineller Sprachübersetzung: Wissensrepräsentation und Textbezug.* Niemeyer, Tübingen, 1986, pp. 121-137.

Rossi, F., "The Impact of Posteditors' Feedback on the Quality of MT," in V. Lawson (ed.), *Practical Experience of Machine Translation.* North-Holland, Amsterdam, 1982, pp. 113-117.

Rothkegel, A., "Pragmatics in Machine Translation," *Proceedings of the 11th ICCL* [COLING 86], Bonn, West Germany, 25-29 August 1986, pp. 335-337.

Rothkegel, A., "Textverstehen und Transfer in der Maschinellen Übersetzung," in I. Bátori and H. J. Weber (eds.), *Neue Ansätze in Maschineller Sprachübersetzung: Wissensrepräsentation und Textbezug.* Niemeyer, Tübingen, 1986, pp. 197-227.

Rouvray, D., and G. Wilkinson, "Machines Break the Language Barrier," *New Scientist* 101, 1402, (March) 1984, pp. 19-21.

Rozencveig, V. J. (ed.). *Essays on Lexical Semantics.* Skriptor, Stockholm, 1974.

Rozencveig, V. J. (ed.). *Machine Translation and Applied Linguistics.* Athenäum, Frankfurt, 1974.

Ruffino, J. R., "Coping with Machine Translation," in V. Lawson (ed.), *Practical Experience of Machine Translation.* North-Holland, Amsterdam, 1982, pp. 57-60.

Sager, J. C., "Multilingual Communication: Chairman's Introductory Review of Translation and the Computer," in B. M. Snell (ed.), *Translating and the Computer.* North-Holland, Amsterdam, 1979, pp. 1-25.

Sager, J. C., "New Developments in Information Technology for Interlingual Communication," *ASLIB Proceedings* 33, 7-8,

(July-August) 1981, pp. 320-323.

Sager, J. C., "Types of Translation and Text Forms in the Environment of Machine Translation," in V. Lawson (ed.), *Practical Experience of Machine Translation.* North-Holland, Amsterdam, 1982, pp. 11-19.

Saito, Y., and H. Nomura, "JMACS: Screen Editor for Japanese and English and Programs – a Kernel for Unified Research Environment," presented at ICTP 83, Tokyo, 1983.

Sakamoto, Y., "Automatic Language Processing System – Natural Language Dictionary for Machine Translation," Res. Electrotech. Lab. no. 707, Tsukuba, Japan, March 1970, pp. 1-132.

Sakamoto, Y., M. Satoh, and T. Ishikawa, "Lexicon Features for Japanese Syntactic Analysis in Mu-Project-JE," *Proceedings of the 10th ICCL* [COLING 84] *and the 22nd Annual Meeting of the ACL*, Stanford University, California, 2-6 July 1984, pp. 42-46.

Sampson, G., "MT: A Nonconformist's View of the State of the Art," in M. King (ed.), *Machine Translation Today: the State of the Art* [proceedings of the Third Lugano Tutorial, Lugano, Switzerland, 2-7 April 1984]. Edinburgh University Press, 1987, pp. 91-108.

Samuelsdorf, P. O., "Relation of Machine Translation to Linguistics Exemplified by an English-German Translation Project," *Proceedings of the 3rd International Conference on Computers in the Humanities*, Waterloo, Ontario, Canada, 2-5 August 1977.

Sanamrad, M. A., and H. Matsumoto, "PERSIS: A Natural-language Analyzer for Persian," *Journal of Information Processing* 8, 4, 1985, pp. 271-279.

Sawai, S., H. Fukushima, M. Sugimoto, and N. Ukai, "Knowledge Representation and Machine Translation," *Proceedings of the 9th ICCL* [COLING 82], Prague, 5-10 July 1982, pp. 351-356.

Sawai, S., M. Sugimoto, and N. Ukai, "Knowledge Representaion and Machine Translation," *Fujitsu Science & Technology Journal* 18, 1, (March) 1982, pp. 117-134.

Schenk, A., "Idioms in the Rosetta Machine Translation System," *Proceedings of the 11th ICCL* [COLING 86], Bonn, West Germany, 25-29 August 1986, pp. 319-324.

Schmidt, P., "Valency Theory in Stratification MT-System," *Proceedings of the 11th ICCL* [COLING 86], Bonn, West Germany, 25-29 August 1986, pp. 307-312.

Schneider, T., "Maschinelle Übersetzungshilfen," *Terminologie Bulletin* 43, Luxembourg, 1983, pp. 15-21.

Schneider, T., "Some Notes on Machine Aids for Translators," *Meta* 28, 4, (December) 1983.

Schneider, T., "Maschinenübersetzung. Stand der Kunst 1983," *High Tech* 1, 1, 1984.

Schulz, J., "Der Computer hilft dem Übersetzer: Ein Verfahren zur Abfrage eines auf Magnetband gespeicherten mehrsprachigen Fachwörterbuchs," *Lebende Sprachen* 20, 4, 1975, pp. 99-103.

Schulz, J., "Automatische Abfrage einer Terminologie-Datenbank," *Nachrichten für Dokumentation* 27, 2, 1976, pp. 62-66.

Schulz, J., "Eine Terminologiedatenbank für Übersetzer: Abfragemöglichkeiten im System TEAM," Dritter Europäischer Kongress über Dokumentationssysteme und -netze, Luxembourg, 3-6 May 1977, vol. 1, pp. 97-140.

Schwanke, P. G., "On Machine Translation: A Difference in Postulates," *Eco-logos* 19, 70, 1973, pp. 3-7.

Seelbach, D., "Maschinelle Übersetzung von Key-Phrases," *Computerlinguistik und Dokumentation.* Munich, 1975, pp. 132-146.

Sereda, S. P., "Practical Experience of Machine Translation," in V. Lawson (ed.), *Practical Experience of Machine Translation.*

North-Holland, Amsterdam, 1982, pp. 119-123.

Shaak, B., "Machine Translation," *Comp. Bull.* 2, 16, (June) 1978, pp. 24-25.

Shalyapina, Z. M., "Automatic Translation as a Model of the Human Translation Activity," *International Forum on Information and Documentation* 5, 2, 1980, pp. 18-23.

Shalyapina, Z. M., "Problems of Formal Representation of Text Structure from the Point of View of Automatic Translation," *Proceedings of the 8th ICCL* [COLING 80], Tokyo, 30 Sept. - 4 Oct. 1980, pp. 174-182.

Shann, P., "AI Approaches to MT," presented at the ISSCO Tutorial on Machine Translation, Lugano, Switzerland, 2-6 April 1984.

Shann, P., "Machine Translation: A Problem of Linguistic Engineering or of Cognitive Modelling?" in M. King (ed.), *Machine Translation Today: the State of the Art* [proceedings of the Third Lugano Tutorial, Lugano, Switzerland, 2-7 April 1984]. Edinburgh University Press, 1987, pp. 71-90.

Sharp, R., "A Parametric NL Translator," *Proceedings of the 11th ICCL* [COLING 86], Bonn, West Germany, 25-29 August 1986, pp. 124-126.

Shudo, K., "On Machine Translation from Japanese into English for a Technical Field," *Information Processing in Japan* 14, 1974, pp. 44-50.

Sigurd, B., "Machine Translation: State of the Art," in *Theory and Practice of Translation.* Peter Lang, Stockholm, 1978, pp. 33-47.

Sinaiko, H. W., and R. W. Brislin, "Evaluating Langauge Translations: Experiments of Three Assessment Methods," *Journal of Applied Psychology* 57, 3, 1973, pp. 328-334.

Sinaiko, H. W., and G. R. Klare, "Further Experiments in Language

Translation: Readability of Computer Translations," *ITL* 15, 1972, pp. 1-29.

Sinaiko, H. W., and G. R. Klare, "Further Experiments in Language Translation: A Second Evaluation of the Readability of Computer Translations," *ITL* 19, 1973, pp. 29-52.

Slocum, J., "An Experiment in Machine Translation," *Proceedings of the 18th Annual Meeting of the ACL*, Philadelphia, 19-22 June 1980, pp. 163-167.

Slocum, J. A Practical Comparison of Parsing Strategies for Machine Translation and Other Natural Language Processing Purposes. Ph.D. dissertation, University of Texas, August 1981. Available from University Microfilms International, Ann Arbor, Michigan.

Slocum, J., "A Practical Comparison of Parsing Strategies," *Proceedings of the 19th Annual Meeting of the ACL*, Stanford University, 29 June - 1 July 1981, pp. 1-6.

Slocum, J. The METAL Parsing System. Working Paper LRC-81-2, Linguistics Research Center, University of Texas, Austin, February 1981.

Slocum, J., "The LRC Machine Translation System: An Application of State-of-the-Art Text and Natural Language Processing Techniques," presented at the 9th ICCL [COLING 82], Prague, Czechoslovakia, 5-10 July 1982.

Slocum, J., "A Status Report on the LRC Machine Translation System," *Proceedings of the ACL-NRL Conference on Applied Natural Language Processing*, Santa Monica, California, 1-3 February 1983, pp. 166-173.

Slocum, J., "Machine Translation: its History, Current Status, and Future Prospects," *Proceedings of the 10th ICCL* [COLING 84] *and the 22nd Annual Meeting of the ACL*, Stanford University, California, 2-6 July 1984, pp. 546-561. Also available as Working

Paper LRC-84-3, Linguistics Research Center, University of Texas, Austin, May 1984.

Slocum, J., "METAL: The LRC Machine Translation System," Working Paper LRC-84-2, Linguistics Research Center, University of Texas, Austin, April 1984.

Slocum, J., "Machine Translation," *Computers and the Humanities* 19, 2, (April-June) 1985, pp. 109-116.

Slocum, J., "A Survey of Machine Translation: Its History, Current Status, and Future Prospects," *Computational Linguistics* 11, 1, 1985, pp. 1-17.

Slocum, J., "Machine Translation: an American Perspective," *Proceedings of the IEEE* 74, 7, (July) 1986, pp. 969-978.

Slocum, J., and A. Aristar, "The Treatment of Grammatical Categories and Word Order in MT," presented at the International Workshop on CAT, Saudi Arabian National Center for Science and Technology, Riyadh, 16-19 March 1985. Available as Tech. Report AI-015-85, MCC, March 1985.

Slocum, J., and W. S. Bennett. The LRC Machine Translation System: An Application of State-of-the-Art Text and Natural Language Processing Techniques to the Translation of Technical Manuals. Working Paper LRC-82-1, Linguistics Research Center, University of Texas, Austin, July 1982.

Slocum, J., and M. G. Morgan, "The Role of Dictionaries and Machine-Readable Lexicons in Translation," presented at the Workshop on Automating the Lexicon, Grosseto, Italy, 19-23 May 1986.

Slocum, J., and L. Whiffin, "Machine Translation: Viewpoints from Both Sides," *AILA Bulletin* (last issue), 1984, pp. 27-58.

Slocum, J., W. S. Bennett, L. Whiffin, and E. Norcross, "An Evaluation of METAL: the LRC Machine Translation System,"

Proceedings of the Second Conference of the European Chapter of the ACL, University of Geneva, Switzerland, 28-29 March 1985.

Slocum, J., W. S. Bennett, J. Bear, M. Morgan, and R. Root, "METAL: The LRC Machine Translation System," in M. King (ed.), *Machine Translation Today: the State of the Art* [proceedings of the Third Lugano Tutorial, Lugano, Switzerland, 2-7 April 1984]. Edinburgh University Press, 1987, pp. 319-350.

Smith, J., "Searching Single-word and Multi-word Dictionaries," presented at the International Conference on the Methodology and Techniques of Machine Translation, Cranfield Institute of Technology, England, 13-15 February 1984.

Snell, B. M. (ed.). *Translating and the Computer.* [Proceedings of a seminar held in London, 14 November 1978.] North-Holland, Amsterdam, 1979.

Snell, B. M., "Electronic Translation?" *ASLIB Proceedings* 32, 4, (April) 1980, pp. 179-186.

Somers, H. L. Bede – The CCL/UMIST Machine Translation System: Rule-Writing Formalism (3rd revision). Report no. 81-5, Centre for Computational Linguistics, UMIST, 1981.

Somers, H. L., "Investigating the Possibility of a Microprocessor-Based Machine Translation System," *Proceedings of the Conference on Applied Natural Language Processing*, Santa Monica, California, February 1983, pp. 149-155.

Somers, H. L., "The Need for MT-oriented Versions of Case and Valency in MT," *Proceedings of the 11th ICCL* [COLING 86], Bonn, West Germany, 25-29 August 1986, pp. 118-123.

Somers, H. L., and J. McNaught, "The Translator as a Computer User," *The Incorporated Linguist* 19, 1980, pp. 49-53.

Stachowitz, R. A. *Voraussetzungen für maschinelle Übersetzung: Probleme, Lösungen, Aussichten.* Athenäum Skripten, Frankfurt am

Main, 1973.

Stachowitz, R. A., "Beyond the Feasibility Study: Lexicographic Progress," in A. Zampolli (ed.), *Computational and Mathematical Linguistics: Proceedings of the ICCL, Pisa, 27 August - 1 September 1973*, vol. 1. Florence, 1976.

Stachowitz, R. A., "Beyond the Feasibility Study: Syntax and Semantics," in A. Zampolli (ed.), *Computational and Mathematical Linguistics: Proceedings of the ICCL, Pisa, 27 August - 1 September 1973*, vol. 2. Florence, 1976.

Stegentritt, E., "Die Komplementanalyse im Saarbrücker Übersetzungssystem, dargestellt am Französischen," LA Neue Folge, Heft 3.2, 1980.

Steiff, S., "The Development of the 'Titus' Four-Language Automatic Translation Method," *International Forum on Information and Documentation* 4, (May) 1979, pp. 20-26.

Steiner, E., "Generating Semantic Structures in EUROTRA-D," *Proceedings of the 11th ICCL* [COLING 86], Bonn, West Germany, 25-29 August 1986, pp. 304-306.

Stessel, J. P. Une méthode pratique de décodage des messages météorologiques. Institut Royal Météorologique de Belgique, Brussels, 1973. Available from NTIS.

Stiegler, A. D., "Machine Aids for Translators: A Review," *ASLIB Proceedings* 33, 7-8, (July-August) 1981, pp. 268-277.

Straub, J. R., and C. A. Rogers, "Computer Analysis of Basic English as a First Step in Machine Translation," in R. Trappl, F. Hanika, and F. R. Pichler (eds.), *Progress in Cybernetics and Systems Research*, vol. 5, 1979, pp. 491-494.

Streiff, A. A., "New Developments in TITUS 4," in V. Lawson (ed.), *Tools for the Trade.* [Proceedings of a conference held in London, 10-11 November 1983.] Aslib, London, 1985, pp. 185-192.

Stutzman, W. J., "Organizing Knowledge for English-Chinese Translation," *Proceedings of the 6th ICCL* [COLING 76], Ottawa, Canada, 1976. Also in *AJCL* 13, 2, 1976, microfiche 48, p. 28.

Sugita, S., "Mechanical Translation Between English and Japanese," in S. Gould (ed.), *Proceedings of the First International Symposium on Computers and the Chinese Input/Output Systems, Taipei, Taiwan, 14-16 August 1973.* Academia Sinica, vol. 13, pp. 555-572.

Tanaka, H., H. Ishihara, and H. Yasukawa. An English-Japanese Machine Translation System using the Active Dictionary. Technical report, Electro-Technical Laboratory, Ibaraki, Japan, 1983.

Tanaka, H., H. Isahara, and H. Yasukawa, "An English-Japanese Machine Translation System using the Active Dictionary," presented at the EUROTRA Joint Japanese-European Workshop, Brussels, November 1983.

Tanke, E., "Electronic Data Processing in the Service of Translators, Terminologists, and Lexicographers," *Philips Terminology Bulletin* 4, 2/3, 1975, pp. 3-19.

Tanke, E., "Future Developments–Three Lectures Given at the Seminar on Computer Aids to Human Translation, Eindhoven, 25-26 September 1974," *Philips Terminology Bulletin* 4, 2/3, 1975, pp. 38-48.

Tanke, E., "Implementing Machine Aids to Translation," in B. M. Snell (ed.), *Translating and the Computer.* North Holland, Amsterdam, 1979, pp. 45-70.

Tenney, M. D., "Machine Translation, Machine-aided Translation and Machine-impeded Translation," in V. Lawson (ed.), *Tools for the Trade.* [Proceedings of a conference held in London, 10-11 November 1983.] Aslib, London, 1985, pp. 105-114.

Thiel, M., "Die Systemarchitektur von SUSY unter benutzerspezifischem Aspekt," *Sprache und Datenverarbeitung* 5, 1/2, 1983, pp. 20-25.

Thouin, B., "Système informatique pour la génération morphologique de langues naturelles en états finis," *Proceedings of the 6th ICCL* [COLING 76], Ottawa, 28 June - 2 July 1976. Also in *AJCL* 13, 2, 1976, microfiche 48, p. 56.

Thouin, B., "The Future of Computer Translation," *CIPS Revue* 3, 6, (December) 1979, pp. 18-19.

Thouin, B., "The METEO System," in V. Lawson (ed.), *Practical Experience of Machine Translation.* North-Holland, Amsterdam, 1982, pp. 39-44.

Thouin, B., "Machine Translation, from Designers to Users: Management Problems and Solutions," presented at the International Conference on the Methodology and Techniques of Machine Translation, Cranfield Institute of Technology, England, 13-15 February 1984.

Tikhomirov, B. D., "Some Specific Features of Software and Technology in the AMPAR and NERPA Systems of Machine Translation," *International Forum on Information and Documentation* 9, 2, 1984, pp. 9-11.

Toma, P., "Computer Translation: In Its Own Right," *Kommunikations- forschung und Phonetik: IKP-Forschungsberichte.* Buske, Hamburg, 1974, vol. 50, pp. 155-164.

Toma, P., "An Operational Machine Translation System," in R. W. Brislin (ed.), *Translation: Applications and Research.* Gardner Press, New York, 1976, pp. 247-259.

Toma, P., "SYSTRAN," in FBIS Seminar on Machine Translation, *AJCL* 13, 2, 1976, microfiche 46, pp. 40-45.

Toma, P., "SYSTRAN as a Multi-lingual Machine Translation System," in Commission of the European Communities, *Overcoming the Language Barrier: Proceedings of the Third European Congress on Information Systems and Networks, Luxembourg, 3-6 May 1977*, vol. 1. Verlag Dokumentation, Munich, 1977, pp. 569-581.

Toma, P., "SYSTRAN: A Third-Generation Machine Translation System," *Sprache und Datenverarbeitung* 1, 1, 1977, pp. 38-46.

Toma, P., "Generations of MT Systems: Historical Review and Perspectives for the Future," presented at the International Conference on the Methodology and Techniques of Machine Translation, Cranfield Institute of Technology, England, 13-15 February 1984.

Toma, P., and L. A. Kozlik. Rand Corporation Data in SYSTRAN. Final Report RADC-TR-73-262, LATSEC, Inc., La Jolla, California, 1973.

Toma, P., J. A. Carlson, D. R. Stoughton, and J. P. Ryan. Machine-Aided Editing. Final Report RADC-TR-73-368, LATSEC, Inc., La Jolla, California, 1973.

Toma, P., L. A. Kozlik, and D. G. Perwin. Optimization of SYSTRAN System. Final Technical Report RADC-TR-73-155-rev, LATSEC, Inc., La Jolla, California, 1974. Available as NTIS report AD-777-850.

Toma, P., L. Garrett, L. A. Kozlik, D. Perwin, and C. Starr. Some Semantic Considerations in Russian-English Machine Translation. Final Report RADC-TR-74-189, LATSEC Inc., La Jolla, California, 1974. Available as NTIS Report AD-787-671.

Tomita, M. The Design Philosophy of a Personal Machine Translation System. Technical Report CMU-CS-84-142, Department of Computer Science, Carnegie-Mellon University, Pittsburgh, Pennsylvania, 1984.

Tomita, M., "Disambiguating Grammatically Ambiguous Sentences by Asking," *Proceedings of the 10th ICCL* [COLING 84] *and the 22nd Annual Meeting of the ACL*, Stanford University, California, 2-6 July 1984, pp. 476-480.

Tomita, M., "Feasibility Study of Personal/Interactive Machine Translation Systems," in S. Nirenburg (ed.), *Proceedings of the*

Conference on Theoretical and Methodological Issues in Machine Translation of Natural Languages, 1985, pp. 289-297.

Tomita, M., "Sentence Disambiguation by Asking," *Computers and Translation* 1, 1, (January-March) 1986, pp. 39-52.

Tomita, M., and J. G. Carbonell, "Another Stride Towards Knowledge-Based Machine Translation," *Proceedings of the 11th ICCL* [COLING 86], Bonn, West Germany, 25-29 August 1986, pp. 633-638.

Tong, L.-C., "English-Malay Translation System: A Laboratory Prototype," *Proceedings of the 11th ICCL* [COLING 86], Bonn, West Germany, 25-29 August 1986, pp. 639-642.

Troike, R. C., "The Future of MT," *AJCL* 13, 3, 1976, microfiche 51, pp. 47-49.

Troike, R. C., "The View from the Center: The Future of MT," *The Linguistic Reporter* 18, 9, 1976, p. 2.

Tschira, K. E., "Looking Back at a Year of German-English MT with Logos," in V. Lawson (ed.), *Tools for the Trade.* [Proceedings of a conference held in London, 10-11 November 1983.] Aslib, London, 1985, pp. 215-236.

Tsujii, J., "The Transfer Phase in an English-Japanese Translation System," *Proceedings of the 9th ICCL* [COLING 82], Prague, 5-10 July 1982, pp. 383-390.

Tsuiji, J., "Technical Outlines of Japanese National MT Project," presented at the EUROTRA Joint Japanese-European Workshop, Brussels, November 1983.

Tsujii, J., "Future Directions of Machine Translation," *Proceedings of the 11th ICCL* [COLING 86], Bonn, West Germany, 25-29 August 1986, pp. 655-668.

Tsujii, J., J. Nakamura, and M. Nagao, "Analysis Grammar of

Japanese in the Mu-Project: a Procedural Approach to Analysis Grammar," *Proceedings of the 10th ICCL* [COLING 84] *and the 22nd Annual Meeting of the ACL*, Stanford University, California, 2-6 July 1984, pp. 267-274.

Tsutsumi, T., "A Prototype English-Japanese Machine Translation System for Translating IBM Computer Manuals," *Proceedings of the 11th ICCL* [COLING 86], Bonn, West Germany, 25-29 August 1986, pp. 646-648.

Tucker, A. B., "A Perspective on Machine Translation: theory and practice," *CACM* 27, 4, (April) 1984, pp. 322-329.

Tucker, A. B., and S. Nirenburg, "Machine Translation: A Contemporary View," *ARIST* 19, 1984, pp. 129-160.

Tucker, A. B. *et al.*, "Implementation Considerations for Machine Translation," *Proceedings of the* ACM *National Computer Conference*, 1979.

Tucker, A. B., M. Vasconcellos, and M. León. PAHO Machine Translation System: Introduction and Users' Manual. Pan American Health Organization, Washington, D.C., July 1980.

Uchida, H., "World Model-assisted Machine Translation," presented at the EUROTRA Joint Japanese-European Workshop, Brussels, November 1983.

Uchida, H., and K. Sugiyama, "A Machine Translation System from Japanese into English Based on Conceptual Structure," *Proceedings of the 8th ICCL* [COLING 80], 30 September - 4 October 1980, Tokyo, pp. 455-462.

Uchida, H., T. Hayashi, and H. Kushima, "ATLAS: Automatic Translations System," *Fujitsu Science & Technology Journal* 21, 3, (Summer) 1985, pp. 317-329.

Usui, T. An Experimental Grammar for Translating English to Japanese. Technical Report TR-201, Department of Computer

Sciences, University of Texas, Austin, May 1982.

van Eynde, F., "The Specification of Time Meaning for Machine Translation," *Proceedings of the Second Conference of the European Chapter of the ACL,* University of Geneva, Switzerland, 28-29 March 1985, pp. 35-40.

van Hoof, H., "Machine Translation," *International Bibliography of Translation*, Verlag Dokumentation, Munich, 1973, pp. 464-504.

van Slype, G. Second Evaluation of the SYSTRAN Automatic Translation System. Final report, Commission des Communautés Européenes, Luxembourg, 1978.

van Slype, G. Critical Study of Methods for Evaluating the Quality of Machine Translation. Final report, Commission des Communautés Européenes, Brussels/Luxembourg, 1979.

van Slype, G., "Evaluation by the EEC Commission of the 'SYSTRAN' Automatic Translation System, 1978 Version," *International Forum on Information and Documentation* 4, May 1979, pp. 27-35.

van Slype, G., "Évaluation du système de traduction automatique SYSTRAN anglais-français, version 1978, de la Commission des Communautés Européennes," *Babel* 25, 3, 1979, pp. 157-162.

van Slype, G., "Evaluation of the 1978 Version of the SYSTRAN English-French Automatic System of the Commission of the European Communities," *The Incorporated Linguist* 18, 3, 1979, pp. 86-89.

van Slype, G., "Conception d'une méthodologie générale d'évaluation de la traduction automatique, *Multilingua*, 18, 3, 1979, pp. 221-237.

van Slype, G., "Economic Aspects of Machine Translation," in V. Lawson (ed.), *Practical Experience of Machine Translation.* North-Holland, Amsterdam, 1982, pp. 79-93.

van Slype, G. *Better Translation for Better Communication: A Survey of the Translation Market, Present and Future.* Pergamon, Oxford, 1983.

van Slype, G., and I. Pigott, "Description du système de traduction automatique SYSTRAN de la Commission des Communautés Européennes," *Documentaliste* 16, 4, (July-August) 1979, pp. 150-159.

Vasconcellos, M. Management of the Machine Translation Environment: Interaction of Functions at the Pan American Health Organization. Pan American Health Organization, Washington, D.C., October 1983.

Vasconcellos, M., "Machine Translation at the Pan American Health Organization: A Review of Highlights and Insights," in *BCS Natural Language Translation Specialist Group Newsletter* 14, 1984, pp. 17-34.

Vasconcellos, M., "Management of the Machine Translation Environment," in V. Lawson (ed.), *Tools for the Trade.* Aslib, London, 1985, pp. 115-129.

Vasconcellos, M., "Functional Considerations in the Postediting of Machine-Translated Output," *Computers and Translation*, 1, 1, (January-March) 1986, pp. 21-38.

Vasconcellos, M., and M. León, "SPANAM and ENGSPAN: Machine Translation at the Pan American Health Organization," *Computational Linguistics* 11, 2-3, 1985, pp. 122-136.

Vauquois, B. *La traduction automatique à Grenoble.* Dunod, Paris, 1975.

Vauquois, B., "Automatic Translation – A Survey of Different Approaches," *Statistical Methods in Linguistics* 1, 1976, pp. 127-135.

Vauquois, B., "Les procédés formels de représentation des structures profondes," in Preprints of the International Colloquium

"Automatische Lexikographie, Analyse und Übersetzung," Saarbrücken, 23-25 September 1976, pp. 67-69.

Vauquois, B., "L'évolution des logiciels et des modèles linguistiques pour la traduction automatisée," *T.A. Informations* 19, 1978.

Vauquois, B., "Aspects of Mechanical Translation in 1979," presented at the Conference for Japan IBM Scientific Program, July 1979.

Vauquois, B., "L'informatique au service de la traduction," *Meta* 26, 1, 1981, pp. 8-17.

Vauquois, B., "Automatic Translation," Proceedings of the Summer School 'The Computer and the Arabic Language', Ch. 9, Rabat, October 1983.

Vauquois, B., and C. Boitet, "Automated Translation at Grenoble University," *Computational Linguistics* 11, 1, 1985, pp. 28-36.

Verastegui, N. Étude du parallelisme appliqué à la traduction automatisée par ordinateur. STAR-PALE: un système parallèle. Thèse de Doctéur-Ingénieur, USMG & INPG, Grenoble, May 1982.

Vernimb, C. O., "The European Network for Scientific, Technical, Economic, and Social Information," *Nachrichten für Dokumentation* 28, 1, (February) 1977, pp. 11-18.

Wagner, E., "Rapid Post-editing of SYSTRAN," in V. Lawson (ed.), *Tools for the Trade.* [Proceedings of a conference held in London, 10-11 November 1983.] Aslib, London, 1985, pp. 199-214.

Walker, P. A., "A Commission of the European Communities User Looks at Machine Translation," in V. Lawson (ed.), *Tools for the Trade.* [Proceedings of a conference held in London, 10-11 November 1983.] Aslib, London, 1985, pp. 145-164.

Wang, W. S. Y., "Chinese-English Machine Translation," *AJCL* 13, 2, 1976, microfiche 46, p. 24.

Wang, W. S. Y., and S. W. Chan. Development of Chinese-English Machine Translation System. Final Technical Report RADC-TR-74-22, University of California at Berkeley, 1974.

Wang, W. S. Y. *et al.* Chinese-English Machine Translation System. Final Technical Report RADC-TR-75-109, Department of Linguistics, University of California at Berkeley, 1975. Available as NTIS Report AD-A011-715.

Wang, W. S. Y., S. W. Chan, and P. Robyn. Chinese-English Machine Translation System. Final Technical Report RADC-TR-76-21, Department of Linguistics, University of California at Berkeley, 1976.

Wang, W. S. Y., S. W. Chan, and B. K. T'sou, "Chinese Linguistics and the Computer," *Linguistics* 118, 1973, pp. 89-117.

Warotamasikkhadit, U., "Computer Aided Translation Project, University Sains Malaysia, Penang, Malaysia," *Computers and Translation* 1, 2, (April-June) 1986, p. 113.

Warwick, S., "An Overview of Post-ALPAC Developments," in M. King (ed.), *Machine Translation Today: the State of the Art* [proceedings of the Third Lugano Tutorial, Lugano, Switzerland, 2-7 April 1984]. Edinburgh University Press, 1987, pp. 22-37.

Weaver, W., "Translation," reprinted in W. N. Locke and A. D. Booth (eds.), *Machine Translation of Languages.* Wiley, New York, 1955, pp. 15-23.

Weber, H.-J., "Semantische Merkmale zur Identifikation von Satz- und Textstrukturen," Vorabdrucke des Internationalen Kolloquiums 'Automatische Lexikographie, Analyse und Übersetzung', Saarbrücken, 23-25 September 1976, pp. 70-79.

Weber, H.-J., "Faktoren einer Textbezogenen Maschinellen Übersetzung: Satzstrukturen, Kohärenz- und Koreferenz-Relationen, Textorganisation," in I. Bátori and H. J. Weber (eds.), *Neue Ansätze in Maschineller Sprachübersetzung: Wissensrepräsentation und*

Textbezug. Niemeyer, Tübingen, 1986, pp. 229-261.

Wehrli, E., "Recent Developments in Theoretical Linguistics and Implications for Machine Translation," in M. King (ed.), *Machine Translation Today: the State of the Art* [proceedings of the Third Lugano Tutorial, Lugano, Switzerland, 2-7 April 1984]. Edinburgh University Press, 1987, pp. 58-70.

Weissenborn, J., "Zur Strategie der automatischen Analyse des Französischen im Hinblick auf die maschinelle Übersetzung," Vorabdrucke des Internationalen Kolloquiums 'Automatische Lexikographie, Analyse und Übersetzung', Saarbrücken, 23-25 September 1976, pp. 80-88.

Weissenborn, J., "The Role and Form of Analysis in Machine Translation: The Automatic Analysis of French at Saarbrücken," in *CEC*, 1977, pp. 593-611.

Wheeler, P. J., "The Errant Avocado (Approaches to Ambiguity in SYSTRAN Translation)," *BCS Natural Language Translation Specialist Group Newsletter* 13, February 1983.

Wheeler, P. J., "Changes and Improvements to the European Commission's SYSTRAN MT System 1976-1983," presented at the International Conference on the Methodology and Techniques of Machine Translation, Cranfield Institute of Technology, England, 13-15 February 1984.

Wheeler, P. J., "Changes and Improvements to the European Commission's SYSTRAN MT System 1976-1984," *Terminologie Bulletin* 45, 1984, pp. 25-37.

Wheeler, P. J., "SYSTRAN," in M. King (ed.), *Machine Translation Today: the State of the Art* [proceedings of the Third Lugano Tutorial, Lugano, Switzerland, 2-7 April 1984]. Edinburgh University Press, 1987, pp. 192-208.

White, J. S., "Characteristics of the METAL Machine Translation System at Production Stage," in S. Nirenburg (ed.), *Proceedings of the Conference on Theoretical and Methodological Issues in Machine Translation of Natural Languages*, 1985, pp. 359-369.

White, J. S., "What Should Machine Translation Be?" *Proceedings of the 24th Annual Meeting of the ACL*, Columbia University, New York, July 1986, p. 267.

Whitelock, P. J., and K. J. Kilby. An In-depth Study of Machine Translation Techniques. Interim Report submitted to Science and Engineering Research Council/Social Studies Research Council Joint Committee. Centre for Computational Linguistics, UMIST, 1982.

Whitelock, P. J., and K. J. Kilby. Linguistic and Computational Techniques in Machine Translation System Design. Final Report submitted to Science and Engineering Research Council/Social Studies Research Council Joint Committe, Contract No. GR/C 01276, Centre for Computational Linguistics, UMIST, December 1983.

Whitelock, P. J., M. McGee Wood, B. J. Chandler, N. Holden, and H. J. Horsfall, "Strategies for Interactive Machine Translation: The Experience and Implications of the UMIST Japanese Project," *Proceedings of the 11th ICCL* [COLING 86], Bonn, West Germany, 25-29 August 1986, pp. 329-334.

Widmann, R. L., "Trends in Computer Applications to Literature," *Computers and the Humanities* 9, 5, (September) 1975, pp. 231-235.

Wilks, Y., "An Artificial Intelligence Approach to Machine Translation," in R. C. Schank and K. M. Colby (eds.), *Computer Models of Thought and Language*. W. H. Freeman, San Francisco, 1973, pp. 114-151.

Wilks, Y., "The Stanford Machine Translation Project," in R. Rustin (ed.), *Natural Language Processing: Courant Computer Science Symposium, no. 8, 20-21 December 1971*. Algorithmics Press, New York, 1973, pp. 243-290.

Wilks, Y., "Semantic and World Knowledge in MT," *AJCL* 13, 2,

1976, microfiche 48, pp. 67-69.

Wilks, Y., "Four Generations of Machine Translation Research and Prospects for the Future," presented at the NATO Symposium, Venice, Italy, 25 September - 1 October, 1977.

Wilks, Y., "Frames for Machine Translation," *New Scientist* 76, 1977, pp. 802-803.

Wilks, Y., "Four Generations of Machine Translation Research and Prospects for the Future," in D. Gerver and H. W. Sinaiko (eds.), *Language, Interpretation and Communication.* Plenum, New York, 1978, pp. 171-184.

Wilks, Y., "Machine Translation and Artificial Intelligence," in B. M. Snell (ed.), *Translating and the Computer.* North-Holland, Amsterdam, 1979, pp. 27-43.

Wilks, Y., "Machine Translation and Artificial Intelligence," presented at BCS 79, London, 4-6 January 1979.

Wilks, Y. Machine Translation and Artificial Intelligence: issues and their histories. Tech. Report MCCS-85-29, Computing Research Laboratory, New Mexico State University, Las Cruces, New Mexico, 1985.

Wilks, Y., and LATSEC, Inc. Comparative Translation Quality Analysis. Final report on contract F 33657-77-C-0695, 1978.

Wilms, F. J. M., "Von SUSY zu SUSY-BSA: Forderungen an eine anwenderbezogenes Mü-Systems," *Sprache und Datenverarbeitung*, 5, 1/2, 1981, pp. 38-43.

Wilss, W. *Übersetzungswissenschaft: Probleme und Methoden.* Klett, Stuttgart, 1977.

Witkam, A. P. M. Distributed Language Translation: Feasibility Study of a Multilingual Facility for Videotex Information Networks. Buro voor Systeemontwickkeling, Utrecht, The Netherlands, 1983.

Witkam, A. P. M., "Distributed Language Translation, Another MT System," presented at the International Conference on the Methodology and Techniques of Machine Translation, Cranfield Institute of Technology, England, 13-15 February 1984.

Wyckoff, S. K., "Computer-Assisted Translation: Mainframe to Microprocessor," *Proceedings of COMPCON 79: Using Microprocessors - Extending Our Reach.* Washington, D.C., 4-7 September 1979, pp. 472-476.

Xyzyx Information Corporation. Computer Aided Language Translation System, English to French. Canoga Park, California, 25 November 1974.

Yang, C. J., "High Level Memory Structures and Text Coherence in Translation," *Proceedings of the 7th IJCAI*, Vancouver, B.C., Canada, August 1981, v. 1, pp. 47-49.

Yoshida, S., "A Consideration on the Concepts Structure and Language in Relation to Selections of Translation Equivalents of Verbs in Machine Translation Systems," *Proceedings of the 10th ICCL* [COLING 84] *and the 22nd Annual Meeting of the ACL*, Stanford University, California, 2-6 July 1984, pp. 167-169.

Young, M. E. Machine Translation (A Bibliography with Abstracts). NTIS report PS-78/0448/7GA, May 1978.

Young, M. E. Machine Translation 1964 - May 1981 (Citations from the NTIS Data Base). NTIS report PB81-806507, June 1981.

Yusoff, Z., "Strategies and Heuristics in the Analysis of a Natural Language in Machine Translation," *Proceedings of the 11th ICCL* [COLING 86], Bonn, West Germany, 25-29 August 1986, pp. 136-139.

Zachary, W. W., "Machine Aids to Translation: A Concise State of the Art Bibliography," *AJCL* 15, 4, 1978, microfiche 77, pp. 34-40.

Zachary, W. W., "A Survey of Approaches and Issues in

Machine-Aided Translation Systems," *Computers and the Humanities* 13, 1, (January-March) 1979, pp. 13-28.

Zachary, W. W., "Translation Databases: Their Content, Use, and Structure," in J. Raben and G. Marks (eds.), *Data Bases in the Humanities and Social Sciences.* North-Holland, Amsterdam, 1980, pp. 217-221.

Zarechnak, M., "Russian-English System, Georgetown University," in FBIS Seminar on Machine Translation, *AJCL* 13, 2, 1976, microfiche 46, pp. 51-52.

Zarechnak, M., "The History of Machine Translation," in B. Henisz-Dostert, R. R. Macdonald, and M. Zarechnak (eds.), *Machine Translation.* Mouton, The Hague, 1979, pp. 1-87.

Zarechnak, M., "Machine Translation: Past, Present, and Future," *ATA Chronicle* 6, 7, 1980, pp. 10-12.

Zarechnak, M., "The Intermediary Language for Multilanguage Translation," *Computers and Translation* 1, 2, (April-June) 1986, pp. 83-91.

Zhiwei, F., "Automatic Generation and Analysis of Chinese in Machine Translation," *Proceedings of the 1984 South East Asia Regional Computer Conference*, Hong Kong, 24-28 September 1984.

Zingel, H.-J., "Computer spricht vier Sprachen: Der Textildokumentation gelingt erstmals automatische Übersetzung wissenschaftlicher Texte," *VDI-Nachrichten* 16, 1974, pp. 2-6.

Zingel, H.-J., "TITUS, eine viersprachige Datenbank des VDI über Dokumentationen der Chemiefaser, Textil- und Bekleidungsindustrie," presented at the IBM-Seminar Dialogverarbeitung mit Bildschirmen in der Chemiefaser-, Textil- und Bekleidungsindustrie, Sindelfingen, 4-6 June 1975.

Zingel, H.-J. Das TITUS-System – die Fachdatenbank Textil – entstanden durch internationale Kooperation, internationales

Analysesystem und automatische Übersetzung. Bericht von der Tagung der Deutschen Gesellschaft für Dokumentation am 1. Oktober 1975, München.

Zingel, H.-J., "TITUS, Internationale Dokumentation der Textilindustrie und Bekleidungsindustrie," *Nachrichten für Dokumentation* 26, 2, 1975, pp. 77-78.

Zingel, H.-J., "Experiences with TITUS II," *Int. Classif.* 5, 1, (March) 1978, pp. 33-37.

Zubov, A. V., "Machine Translation Viewed as Generation of Text with a Pre-defined Content," *International Forum on Information and Documentation* 9, 2, (April) 1984, pp. 36-38.

